Chinese Activism of a Different Kind

Social Sciences in Asia

Edited by

Vineeta Sinha
Syed Farid Alatas
Kelvin Low

VOLUME 37

The titles published in this series are listed at brill.com/ssa

Chinese Activism of a Different Kind

The Chinese Students' Campaign to Stay in Australia

By

Jia Gao

BRILL

LEIDEN • BOSTON
2013

Cover illustration: "Doorways: Looking through open doors in the Forbidden City, Beijing"; iStockphoto File No. 4015808; Contributor: Paul Merrett.

Library of Congress Cataloging-in-Publication Data

Gao, Jia.
Chinese activism of a different kind : the Chinese students' campaign to stay in Australia / by Jia Gao.
pages cm — (Social sciences in Asia, ISSN 1567-2794 ; volume 37)
Includes bibliographical references and index.
ISBN 978-90-04-25861-7 (hardback : alk. paper) — ISBN 978-90-04-26059-7 (e-book : alk. paper)
1. Chinese students—Political activity—Australia. 2. Chinese students—Legals status, laws, etc.—Australia. 3. China—History—Tiananmen Square Incident, 1989—Influence. I. Title.

LC3089.A8G36 2013
378.1'9820994—dc23

2013033234

This publication has been typeset in the multilingual "Brill" typeface. With over 5,100 characters covering Latin, IPA, Greek, and Cyrillic, this typeface is especially suitable for use in the humanities. For more information, please see www.brill.com/brill-typeface.

ISSN 1567-2794
ISBN 978-90-04-25861-7 (paperback)
ISBN 978-90-04-26059-7 (e-book)

This book is printed on acid-free paper.

This book is dedicated to all the Chinese students who were living in Australia in the late 1980s and early 1990s

CONTENTS

LIST OF TABLES

LIST OF ABBREVIATIONS

AAT	Administrative Appeal Tribunal
AATA	Administrative Appeals Tribunal of Australia
ABC	Australian Broadcasting Corporation
ABS	Australian Bureau of Statistics
ACCI	Australian Chamber of Commerce and Industry
ACD	*Australian Chinese Daily* (*Xinbao*)
ACT	Australian Capital Territory
ACTU	Australian Council of Trade Unions
AFCS	Australia Federation of Chinese Students
AGPS	Australian Government Publishing Service
AIDAB	Australian International Development Assistance Bureau
ALD	Administrative Law Decisions
ALP	Australian Labor Party
ANU	Australian National University
ARC	Administrative Review Council
CAD	Chinese Alliance for Democracy
CASHR	Chinese Association for Safeguarding Human Rights
CCP	Chinese Communist Party
CCYL	Chinese Communist Youth League
CND	*China News Digest*
COSHG	Collective of Self Help Groups
CSSCD	Chinese Students Solidarity Campaign for Democracy
CSWC	Chinese Student Welfare Committee
DIAC	Department of Immigration and Citizenship (2006–now)
DIEA	Department of Immigration and Ethnic Affairs (1976–1987) (1993–1996)
DILGEA	Department of Immigration, Local Government and Ethnic Affairs (1987–1993)
DIMA	Department of Immigration and Multicultural Affairs (1996–2001)
DIMIA	Department of Immigration and Multicultural and Indigenous Affairs (2001–2006)
DORS	Determination of Refugee Status (Committee)
ELICOS	English Language Incentive Course for Overseas Students
FACSS	Friendship Association of Chinese Students and Scholars
FCA	Federal Court of Australia

FCFFPS	Federation of Chinese Full-Fee Paying Students
FCR	Federal Court Reports
FDC	Federation for Democratic China
GMD	Guomindang (Chinese Nationalist Party)
GRE	Graduate Record Examination
HCA	High Court of Australia
HIA	Housing Industry Association
IFCSS	Independent Federation of Chinese Students and Scholars
IFCSSA	Independent Federation of Chinese Students and Scholars in Australia
ISO	International Socialist Organization
JP	Justice of the Peace
KMT	Kuomintang (see GMD)
MFN	Most favored nation (in international trade)
MP	Member of the Federal Parliament of Australia
MRC	Migrant Resource Centre
NCA	National Crime Authority
NED	National Endowment for Democracy
OSO	Overseas Students Office
OSS	Overseas Students Section
PLA	People's Liberation Army (of China)
PRC	People's Republic of China
RACS	Refugee Advice and Casework Service
RSRC	Refugee Status Review Committee
SAT	Security Appeals Tribunal
SMH	*Sydney Morning Herald*
STN	*Sing Tao Newspaper*
TEP	Temporary Entry Permit
TOEFL	Test of English as a Foreign Language
UN	United Nations
UNHCR	United Nations High Commissioner for Refugees
USIP	US Institute for Peace
VOA	Voice of America
WLFD	World League for Freedom and Democracy

PREFACE AND ACKNOWLEDGMENTS

This book looks at the social behavior and pattern of actions of 45,000 or so Chinese students as they strategized and fought to obtain their right and their chance to stay permanently in Australia after the Tiananmen incident of 1989. At the time there were about 20,000 Chinese nationals, mostly students of English, living in Australia, and they were later joined by approximately 25,000 students who left China shortly after June 4. The 'June 4 incident' (as it came to be called in the Chinese community) and its impact on the Chinese students living in Australia provide the setting of this study. In November 1993, all the students were granted permanent residency in Australia. Over a period of four years from mid 1989 to late 1993, these students campaigned for the right to stay permanently in Australia. This is a unique example of Chinese activism which is relevant not only to the history of Chinese migration to Australia, but also to our knowledge of Chinese activism and this book is aimed at conveying a picture of how the students harnessed the available resources and campaigned for their right and chance to stay in Australia in the aftermath of the June 4 incident.

The 'June 4 incident' was a controversial event that has been debated from various perspectives. While some have regarded it as a democratic movement or a political disaster in the contemporary history of China, more and more people consider it the occasion that enabled China to focus on its economic development and to achieve the rapid and record growth it recorded in the 1990s and 2000s. On the other hand, as a significant event, the June 4 incident created a set of extraordinary circumstances in which a large number of Chinese nationals living overseas at the time could seek asylum in their host countries. One group of such students was those living in Australia at the time and this study specifically focuses on the active and strategic approach adopted by the 45,000 or so Chinese students to obtain residency in Australia over a period of four years from June 1989 to November 1993.

During this particular period, the Australian government introduced the most significant changes to its immigration administration since the end of World War II (Jupp, 1995; Gao and Kee, 2013), especially with regard to its humanitarian and refugee immigration policies, aimed at controlling the increased numbers of illegal entrants and onshore asylum seekers, and this included the Chinese students. In this culture of immigration control (Cronin, 1993; Crock, 1998b), the *Migration Act 1958* of Australia was amended 11 times between late 1989 and 1992, and the regulations governing different immigration programs saw 58 amendments during the same period. More than six major changes to the humanitarian and refugee programs were also introduced during the period, abandoning the onshore humanitarian program while toughening the residency terms for all asylum seekers who would only get four-year protection visas rather than immediate permanent residency.

This study is concerned with the type of activism that the Chinese nationals demonstrated in their efforts to negotiate the changing stance of the Australian government toward asylum seekers and to adopt a series of strategic approaches to campaign for their right and their chance to stay permanently in Australia. It was a type of activism that was strategic rather than primarily ideological or radical. By their success the students became the largest intake of onshore asylum seekers in the history of Australian immigration. The student issue had a significant impact on Australia's onshore humanitarian and refugee immigration policies in the late 1980s and 1990s, and reactivated direct immigration from China to Australia.

The significance of this particular case of Chinese activism is that the Chinese students living in Australia in the late 1980s and early 1990s provide an example and a case study, demonstrating the ways in which a new generation of Chinese must take actions to achieve what they would like to achieve. In this particular case, their desire was to stay in the country they would like to call home. This kind of activism provides a valuable insight into current Chinese sociopolitical life, and is more relevant to present-day situations than the activism shown in other more often quoted cases, such as the May Fourth Movement of 1919 or the Red Guards in the late 1960s. What the Chinese student case demonstrated is a type of activism that contrasts distinctly with both the various forms of radical activism periodically demonstrated by young Chinese students in the course of the twentieth century and the widespread stereotype of the so-called Chinese passivity, especially in the international arena. This latter tendency has been repeatedly criticized by many scholars, and by political elites, from within China for almost a century.

We can now find several books on other types of Chinese activism, such as the youth and labor movements during the early Republican periods, communist activism before 1949, and the Red Guards of the late 1960s. The Red Guards have been one of the most popular topics in the field of China studies that have looked at Chinese activism. Of course, research efforts have also been made in the recent past to examine a range of new forms of activism, such as Internet activism, consumer activism, labor activism and environmental activism. A careful examination, however, shows that all Chinese activism discussed in the existing literature has been based in large part on bigger sociopolitical events in China, which only had an effect on the lives of ordinary Chinese people in an indirect manner, in comparison with the multifaceted predicament faced by the 45,000 or so Chinese nationals studied in this book. The activism shown in this case resulted directly from the Chinese students' concerns for their own lives and futures in the immediate aftermath of June 4, instead of from their enthusiasm in and their devotion to larger issues that looked at political and ideological ideals. While more Chinese are adopting a pragmatic attitude toward their lives and their own futures, this book sets out to reveal the themes, patterns and characteristics of their activism that differs from the existing literature, including recent studies of various new forms of activism.

This study is essentially a reworking of my doctoral dissertation for a PhD in human geography at the University of Melbourne. I owe a great debt of gratitude to many people who have kindly helped and supported my undertaking of studying this large group of Chinese migrants coming to Australia in the late 1980s and early 1990s, and especially to those who helped me write up the study toward an earlier version of this book.

First, I am very grateful for the time, guidance and encouragement I received from Professor Jane Jacobs and Professor Ruth Fincher when I was studying for my doctorate on the subject of the Chinese student issue at the University of Melbourne. Without their great guidance and help, the social experiences of this particular group of Chinese migrants would not have been adequately analyzed and documented. I also want to thank Professor Mark Wang at the same university, who provided me with helpful comments on many parts of the earlier drafts. More than anyone else, Professor Jane Jacobs, who has since relocated herself to the United Kingdom, influenced this study and the writing. I will always be grateful to her for her tremendous intellectual support during my PhD years.

I could not have finished this research project and the writing of this book without the support of my family. I have to express my gratitude to my wife and son for their continuous support and inordinate amount of patience during my doctoral studies and the writing of this book. I am especially grateful to them for their encouragement and support when I was struck by a serious neck problem that was caused by my long time desk-bound work, especially since the subsequent neck surgery that I had shortly after I started working on this manuscript.

I would also like to thank the University of Melbourne, where I was not only provided with a chance to continue my postgraduate research, but where I also had the good fortune to be offered an academic position—one that I have held for almost 20 years. Among the many colleagues at the University of Melbourne, who have supported my work in various ways, I am particularly indebted to Dr Miriam Lang for her great assistance in editing the manuscript and useful suggestions for its improvement.

I am also indebted to the editors of the Social Sciences in Asia series for accepting the manuscript for publication in their series and the three anonymous reviewers for their helpful suggestions and comments on the first draft of this manuscript. I am particularly thankful to Dr Kelvin Low for his kind understanding of the circumstances that made me unable to submit the manuscript to his team and the publisher on time. I am also very grateful to Ms Patricia Radder of Brill and Mr Antony Green for their professionalism and efficiency in bringing the manuscript to press.

Most of all, my special thanks go to all the Chinese nationals coming and living in Australia in the late 1980s and early 1990s, but that debt is very difficult to acknowledge because I owe it not only to the kindness of many former students I interviewed, but also to the immense generosity of the entire former student community. A great debt of thanks is owed to all of them, and I hope that they fully understand and appreciate that their experiences have made an exceptionally important contribution to our understanding of Chinese activism and international migration.

Jia Gao, *PhD*
The University Melbourne

CHAPTER ONE

INTRODUCTION

In the early morning of Sunday, 4 June 1989, the newspaper posters displayed at news agencies and milk bars in Sydney and Melbourne (Australia's two largest cities) were still showing the headlines from the previous day. No newspapers were published on Sundays in these cities at that time, and the day was generally quiet and relaxing. On this early winter morning, however, there were more people than usual on the streets. Most of them were Chinese students. Horrified by the shocking news that had been reported by the local and international radio and TV stations—that troops had opened fire on hundreds of demonstrators that morning in Tiananmen Square and in other areas of central Beijing—they had flocked to the open areas in Melbourne's and Sydney's Chinatowns to hold protest rallies against the Chinese government's crackdown. Many wept and shouted angry political slogans. And it was there that some started, or in many cases were advised, to consider seeking asylum in Australia.

The 'June 4 incident,' as it is known in Chinese,[1] also marked the occasion when Australia joined other Western countries in the imperative to provide protection for nationals of the People's Republic of China (PRC)—living within their borders. Some countries, such as Canada and Japan, where there were a large number of PRC students enrolled in various language courses, made quick and clear-cut decisions on the Chinese student issue.[2] In Australia, however, the government's approach to the Chinese

[1] The 4 June 1989 military crackdown on long-running demonstrations in Beijing is also known as the Tiananmen (Square) massacre in English. It refers to events in which the Chinese government used military force to put an end to student-led popular demonstrations that had continued for many months in Tiananmen Square in the center of Beijing. These events are controversial, but they have been much discussed by participants (Li, 1990; Chai, 2011) and China observers (Pye, 1990; Wagner, 1991; Goldman, 1994; Miles, 1996; Barmé, 2000; Cunningham, 2009).

[2] Within a month of June 4, Canada decided to allow PRC nationals living in that country to apply for landed immigrant status on humanitarian and compassionate grounds through enacting a special program (known as OM-IS-339) (Liu and Norcliffe, 1996; Lary, 1998). The Chinese student issue in Canada was resolved within a year, a situation that has been criticized by some as an example of Canada's 'designated class' policy (Opoku-Dopaah, 2006: 73). Japan approached the Chinese student issue in a speedier, but less merciful, manner than Canada. 'Selected Chinese students' were quickly given visa extensions and

student issue was cautious, slow and tortuous, often beset by bureaucratic inflexibility and by hesitations and rivalries among policy-makers, which resulted in a situation in which the PRC students themselves organized and lobbied to be permitted to stay.

This book documents the process by which the PRC nationals living in Australia—a diverse group of students who came together to act for a common goal—fought for and achieved the opportunity, and the right, to stay permanently in Australia in the wake of June 4. Their efforts and strategies have been likened to the story of the 'Eight Immortals crossing the sea' (*baxian guohai*), the well-known Taoist story about Eight Immortals who journeyed to their destination over the sea (Knapp, 1999: 148; Seal, 2001: 64), 'each showing their special prowess' (*gexian shentong*, or *gexian qineng*) in pursuit of the common goal. To illuminate the 'special prowess' that enabled the Chinese students in Australia to achieve their goal, this book details their various initiatives and efforts to harness whatever resources they could in their campaign. It examines the particular type of activism in which they engaged and traces their collective efforts to understand, navigate and negotiate the Australian political environment. It also examines their collective adoption of a wide range of strategic approaches in their campaign for the right to stay permanently: the gathering and sharing of information, the formation of support groups, liaison with local agencies and individuals, the publication of political statements, rallies and demonstrations, and court cases.

All the above steps were complicated by the fact that the students were in a foreign country. They had few connections, limited experience of local institutions and procedures, and less than native knowledge of the local language. The students' efforts were also complicated by the fact that throughout their campaign, the Australian government kept changing its stance and its policies regarding its onshore humanitarian immigration program and the issue of asylum seekers. These changes of policy, it should be noted, were introduced largely in response to the activities of this student group and for that reason, it can be claimed that these Chinese students and their issue had a major impact on Australian humanitarian and refugee immigration policies from the late 1980s to the mid 1990s. As they constitute the majority of the new PRC migrant community

work permits (Bullock, 1993: 624), but the majority of the Chinese students were given no chance to seek asylum (Cheng, 2002) and many were even repatriated to China in early 1990 (Herzog, 1993).

in Australia up to the present (ABS, 2012; Gao and Kee, 2013), they are now also playing a crucial role in the contemporary relationship between Australia and China. It should also be noted that this generation of PRC nationals, born in the 1950s and 1960s, are the generation that now plays the leading roles in Chinese societies (both inside and outside China) and will lead China for the next two decades or more. For these reasons, the story of the Chinese student migrants and their collective campaign to remain in Australia is surely deserving of our research attention.

This book examines the collective activism of these students—of whom no less than half had already overstayed their visas—over a period of four or so years from June 1989 (when the June 4 events occurred in China) to November 1993 (when the decision was made to allow all of them to stay permanently in Australia). The policies and actions of the Australian government in response to the Chinese students and their quest to stay permanently in Australia were contradictory, dictated by both humanitarian concerns and national interests. In the end, the students were all allowed to stay permanently as a result of the so-called '1 November [1993] decisions' made by the Australian Labor government led by Paul Keating. The decisions honored a promise made by the previous Labor Prime Minister, Bob Hawke, that none of the Chinese students would be forced to return to China against their will.[3] To introduce the background of this book, the first and second sections of this chapter will outline the history of the new Chinese migrant community in Australia and provide a brief chronological account of the Chinese student protection campaign and the Australian government's policies that they responded to and, in a very real sense, shaped. The third section of this chapter will look at the existing literature and some theoretical explanations that are relevant to this study. The final section will briefly outline the organization of the book.

Chinese Students Living in Australia

For more than a century after the Australian Gold Rush of the latter half of the nineteenth century, the great majority of migrants of Chinese

[3] The '1 November [1993] decisions' will be detailed in Chapter Eight as part of the conclusion of the Chinese student issue in Australia (Birrell, 1994, 1996; Gao, 2001, 2009; 2011). It should be noted that these decisions should also be considered as part of Paul Keating's 'big picture' vision for Australia, which will be explained in Chapter Six.

ethnicity living in Australia had not migrated there from China. Prior to the mid 1980s, they came mostly from the so-called 'Nanyang' countries of Southeast Asia (Kee, 1992, 1995; Sinclair et al., 2000) to which their ancestors had migrated generations before. Historically, the Chinese had been seen as a problem in white-dominated Australia, but their numbers were not always significant, never higher than five percent of Australia's total population (Clark, 1969; Wang, 1978; Yuan, 2001; Gao, 2011; Sun et al., 2011). The Chinese community numbered less than 10,000 in the late 1940s and around 13,000 in 1954, because of the 'White Australia' policy (Kee, 1992)[4] but the introduction of the Colombo Plan in the early 1950s played a very important role in bringing in thousands of educated Chinese from various parts of Southeast Asia (Oakman, 2004).[5]

In the mid 1980s, migrants from the Chinese mainland, alongside those from Hong Kong and Taiwan, came to Australia in larger numbers. Yet before the arrival of the PRC students, the total number of people claiming primary and secondary Chinese ancestry in Australia in 1986 was still only around 200,000, resulting from the arrival of Indochinese refugees and many other immigrants from elsewhere in Southeast Asia (Coughlan, 2001; Jordens, 2001).[6] The resumption of direct immigration from the Chinese mainland in the late 1980s, however, took place in a rather unusual fashion. Tens of thousands of PRC nationals had come to Australia as stu-

---

[4] The 'White Australia' policy was introduced in 1901 when Australia became a federation, the policy being effected through two pieces of legislation: the *Immigration Restriction Act 1901* and the *Pacific Island Labourers Act 1901*. These two Acts restricted non-white immigrants from entering Australia. The policy was progressively abandoned between 1949 and 1974 (Yuan, 2001; Fitzgerald, 2007; Gao, 2011).

[5] The Colombo Plan was launched in 1950 as a post-colonial or post-war initiative to discreetly maintain British influence, especially its economic colonialism in South and Southeast Asian countries (Oakman, 2004), and 'to limit the spread of communism' in the region (Ninnes, 2005: 142). Part of the Colombo Plan was an overseas student scheme, which benefited the Chinese community in Australia. Unlike most of the Chinese who had arrived in Australia before this period, Colombo Plan students often came from middle-class backgrounds; they had high academic achievements and were able to speak English. While studying in Australia, many played an active role in negotiating cultural and social differences between Anglo-Australians and the Chinese (Yuan, 2001). More importantly, many of the students stayed on after finishing their studies, or migrated back to Australia after working in their home countries.

[6] Among tens of thousands of Indochinese refugees in Australia, Coughlan (2001: 730) estimated that more than one quarter of them, or according to Jordens (2001: 69), around half, were of Chinese origin. However, these estimates were made well before an identity shift started to occur among many Indochinese immigrants in the mid 1990s. On a very conservative estimate, therefore, the Indochinese arrivals probably added more than 50,000 new members to Australia's Chinese community (Ang, 1997, 2000; Gao and Kee, 2013).

dents. At the time of the military crackdown in Beijing on 4 June 1989, there were about 15,000 PRC nationals in Australia (Jupp, 1991; Cronin, 1993; Birrell, 1994, 1996). Almost all of them were given a four-year temporary residency permit for protection after June 4. When they were all finally allowed to stay permanently in Australia in 1993, they eventually became the largest intake of onshore asylum seekers in Australian immigration history (Jupp, 1991; Cronin, 1993; Gao, 2001). Therefore, their story is a significant part of Australian history, Chinese history and migration history.

A few days after June 4, in response to widespread concerns about its impact on Australia, the Australian government was forced to publicize figures relating to PRC nationals who were resident in the country at the time. Out of a total of 15,405, there were about 8,600 language students, 4,000 'visitors,' 2,000 students in other categories (i.e. those enrolled in university courses or programs), 475 individuals with temporary permits, and 330 individuals on other permits (Jupp, 1991; Cronin, 1993). In June 1990, when the Australian government announced its decision to provide the four-year temporary residency permit to all the PRC nationals who were in Australia before 20 June 1989, this number increased to about 20,000. The official statement said that there were 'some 20,000 Chinese nationals' in this special 'pre-20 June' category (Jupp, 1991: 93), and in addition, there were about 25,000 in a so-called 'post-20 June' category (Birrell, 1994; Gao, 2001). That is, the total number of the PRC nationals who were under protection in Australia had grown to about 45,000.

The presence of these PRC nationals in Australia was indicative of a new trend at the time. It was only in the mid 1980s that people from the Chinese mainland had begun to come to Australia in large numbers. The first sizeable group started to arrive as students in the mid 1980s when Australia set up its 'English Language Intensive Courses for Overseas Students' (ELICOS) scheme to export English-language education as a foreign exchange earner (Wang, 1987; Wang and Lai, 1987; Marginson, 1997). China was one of the main markets for the ELICOS courses. At almost precisely the same time in China, after the first major setback to China's economic reforms in 1984 and 1985, and also as a direct effect of China's open-door policy, a new social phenomenon called the 'tide of going abroad' was emerging (Hu, 1988; Luo, 1988; Gao, 2001).

The Tide of Going Abroad was originally the name of a long feature report published in 1987, which vividly described the attempts of young Chinese people to go abroad (Hu, 1988). The term was then widely used to refer to the many people who were hastening to leave China in the mid and late 1980s. The June 4 events would dramatically alter the nature of the 'tide of going abroad' by turning the great majority, if not all, of the Chinese students who were then studying abroad into a new generation of Chinese asylum seekers.

Once the ELICOS scheme in Australia had been put into practice in 1986, a few hundred PRC nationals came to Australia in the second half of that year to take various ELICOS courses. Although their number by no means dominated the overseas student market in Australia at the time, the renewed interest of many young Chinese in studying overseas, along with Australia's efforts to attract more students from Asian countries to take its ELICOS courses, resulted in a steady flow of PRC nationals to Australia. As potentially the biggest market in the world, China became a prime target for Australia's language export industry, and some ELICOS colleges began rounds of marketing there. Several colleges even set up consulting offices in the larger cities in China. Their message was very simple: a half-year term in Australia for AU$5000 (Wang, 1987; Wang and Lai, 1987).

In late 1986, within just a few months of the introduction of the ELICOS scheme in Australia, a so-called 'Australia fever' spread throughout China. The 'fever' first appeared in the southern province of Guangdong, where young people were receptive to influences from Hong Kong, and then it quickly spread to other big urban centers. The attention of a large number of young Chinese—especially many who were not qualified to study in the most preferred country, the USA—turned toward Australia. Australia, which had been known as the 'new gold mountain' (in contrast with the 'old gold mountain' of San Francisco, California) at the time of the Gold Rush (the first 'Australia fever') in the mid nineteenth century (Clark, 1969; Cronin, 1982; Rolls, 1992; Yuan, 2001; Fitzgerald, 2007), was rediscovered.[7] Because of these reasons, most of the PRC nationals

[7] Interestingly, Australian efforts to export language education even set two records in the history of the PRC. First, one ELICOS college became the very first foreign education institution to be permitted to advertise its language course in a reputable, official Chinese national newspaper (Wang, 1987; Wang and Lai, 1987; Yang, 1988). Second, and with far-reaching consequences, in order to cool down the 'Australia fever' quickly, the Australian Embassy in Beijing used the services of the official Chinese media. In June 1987, Australian officials held press conferences in Beijing, Shanghai and Guangzhou to refute the rumor that there would be an amnesty for all persons residing in the country unlawfully when Australia celebrated its bicentenary in early 1988. All the newspapers in those three major cities published similar reports advising that there would be 'no amnesty when Australia celebrates its bicentenary' (*People's Daily*, 26 June 1987). However, so unusual were the press conferences and the statement, and so practised were Chinese citizens at decoding

who were attracted to Australia to take ELICOS courses had not studied at a university in China, and many were not qualified to do so. Many of them were laborers or rank-and-file office workers while there were even some peasant farmers from rural or semi-rural areas. Most of them came from the coastal regions of Guangdong, Fujian and the Shanghai region, including the adjoining provinces of Jiangsu and Zhejiang. A few small-scale surveys conducted in Shanghai and Guangdong before the June 4 events found that almost all of them surveyed had strong intentions to stay permanently in Australia (Wang, 1987; Wang and Lai, 1987). Of the students who sought asylum in Australia after June 4, the majority (more than 70 percent) were ELICOS students.

The remaining 30 or so percent were postgraduate and undergraduate students (or, as they referred to themselves, 'degree students') and some visiting scholars. Most of this latter group had been sent to Australia under the official sponsorship of the Chinese government as part of its strategy to revitalize China through education, science and technology. Many of these students were also partly, if not fully, subsidized by the Australian government. All of them had gone through a tough selection process in China that involved English-language examination and training, political screening and further training (Orleans, 1988; Qian, 2003). As officially sponsored students, they all had to maintain their connections with their home institutions and government offices. Even the small proportion of the postgraduate students who had been permitted to study for a degree abroad on their own, thanks to various private sponsorships, had also to be registered with China's official overseas posts at that time. Despite their small numbers, the postgraduate students were to play an important role in organizing the protection campaign for asylum/residency because of their strong English-language and political skills.

It should be noted that there was a considerable social difference, or gap, between the ELICOS and the postgraduate students, not only because of differences in education, social class, institutional affiliations, and self-image, but also because of their different goals, career opportunities, and

---

political messages, that the announcement was read in an unanticipated way: many readers were convinced that its real meaning was that Australia needed Chinese labor. It seemed to them that Australia was different from other countries because it would—apparently—provide foreign students not only with an opportunity to study, but also with the chance of staying permanently (Yang, 1988; Gao, 2001). This misapprehension and other rumors had then made Australian language schools even more attractive.

different everyday experiences and social contacts while in Australia. These two categories of Chinese students did not necessarily mix well in Australia or meet each other very often, but together they made up a new community that looked like a microcosm of PRC society—a community on which this study of Chinese activism can confidently be based.

Geographically, the PRC students in Australia in the late 1980s and early 1990s commonly identified themselves with one of three broadly defined groups: Shanghai, Guangdong, or Beijing and other provincials. Within the groups, many students used their local dialects and tended to associate with people from the same region. The Beijing group, however, incorporated students from other regions and communicated in standard Mandarin Chinese, because they lacked a shared dialect. The Shanghai and Guangdong groups were the largest, and fewer in them had a higher education qualification than in the Beijing group (Wang and Lai, 1987; Yang, 1988).

It is also important to note that these students were not isolated from Australian society from the beginning, as some observes have suggested (Siu, 1987; Liu, 1995). The students from Guangdong initially relied on their links with the established Chinese migrant communities. While the degree students were connected to educational institutions, many other students had also tried very hard to connect themselves with the locals, through such avenues as churches and other community groups. Some of the earliest PRC students in Australia became members of the Chinese Alliance for Democracy (CAD), a political activist group formed among overseas Chinese, well before June 4 (Chen and Lu, 1994; Gao, 2006, 2009; Qin, 2012). The post-June 4 activism outlined in this book had its roots in these early political activities which worked for their chance, and the right, to stay in Australia.

The attitude of the Australian government toward the demands of the PRC students for residency or asylum was conditioned by its conflicting obligations to international politics and its own national interests. In line with the response from other major Western countries, Australia had to condemn what had happened in Tiananmen, and had also to consider providing protection for the Chinese nationals living in Australia. At the same time, public sentiment within Australia, together with Australia's emerging commercial interests in China, also prevented the government from doing these things in too direct a fashion. In the early 1980s Australia had already clearly seen greater trade potential in China than in other markets and by the mid 1980s, Australia had in fact integrated itself into the Asia-Pacific economy, with more than 60 percent of its total trade being conducted with Asia and the Pacific (Humphreys, 1985).[8] It could not afford to alienate China, but at the same time, it also could not afford not to give its protection to the Chinese students. As a result, two days after June 4, all the PRC nationals whose temporary entry permits had expired or were about to expire after 4 June 1989 were given short, temporary protection visas until 31 July 1989 (*The Australian*, 7 June 1989). The students were then given two similar temporary protection visas within six or so months of June 4. The purpose of introducing these bridging visas was to make some Chinese students eligible to apply for permanent residency on humanitarian grounds after 19 December 1989 when the *Migration Legislation Amendment Act 1989* was introduced and the onshore humanitarian program was abandoned (DILGEA, 1990; Jupp, 1991; Cronin, 1993; Crock, 1998b; Schloenhardt, 2003; Gao, 2011).[9] All of these issues resulted in a slow and complicated process in dealing with the PRC student issue.

At the time of June 4, the Australian government felt obliged to protect those Chinese nationals who were living in Australia. However, there was also another group of PRC students, whose position made the protection issue much more complex and difficult to resolve. These were prospective students in China, who had already paid their tuition fees to ELICOS colleges but had not yet arrived in Australia by 4 June 1989. The Australia government had no choice but to allow them to come to Australia, because none of the ELICOS colleges would want to refund the payments. The government therefore made a few changes to tighten the screening procedures for visa applications and to put a bona fide pre-visa assessment in place overseas (DILGEA, 1990: 67).[10] To help many new

[8] In 1980, Sino-Australian trade already 'amounted to US$1.27 billion, and Australia was China's fifth biggest trading partner' (Huan, 1985: 124). Also in 1980, Australia had already achieved a trade surplus of about AU$650 million with China (Fung and Mackerras, 1985: 262), and 'the annual growth rate averaged 24.5 per cent, almost twice Australia's total export growth rate' (Woodard, 1997: 147–148).

[9] The amendment to the *Migration Act 1958* in late 1989 was the most significant change to Australia's immigration administration since 1945, and it was the most important policy factor involved in the PRC student issue. This was because Australia planned to abandon the onshore humanitarian program and toughen the residency terms for all asylum seekers before the Chinese student issue was resolved.

[10] Australian consular posts in China seemed to have been more influenced by the ELICOS industry than other factors. The hundreds of Chinese who were staging small-scale protests outside Australian diplomatic posts in September and October 1989 to demand a speedy processing of their visa applications, something that was extremely unusual considering the tense political atmosphere in China at the time, did not appear to ring any alarm bells for them.

ELICOS colleges keep the money that the prospective students had paid, Australian consular posts in China resumed processing visas from early October 1989 for student visa applicants who had made their payments before 20 June 1989. Approximately 25,000 of these students arrived in Australia soon afterward.

Therefore, the PRC students who stayed permanently in Australia as a result of the June 4 events were made up of three major sub-groups: (1) the 'pre-20 June group' (who were already in Australia when the June 4 events happened); (2) the 'post-20 June group' (who were granted entry to Australia in or after October 1989, because they had already paid their ELICOS fees before 20 June 1989); and (3) the many later arrivals. The last group was also able to take up residency thanks to Australia's more relaxed government policies toward PRC students in and after the mid 1990s and the chain migration effect of granting permanent residency to the first two sub-groups.[11] All of the 'pre-20 June group' and the 'post-20 June group' (together totalling approximately 45,000 people) (Birrell, 1994, 1996; Gao, 2001, 2009; 2011) obtained the right to stay in Australia because of their activism analyzed in this book.

Pre- and Post-20 June Groups

The sweeping and significant changes to Australia's *Migration Act 1958* and the subsequent enactment of the *Migration Legislation Amendment Act 1989* brought changes in the government's approach to the issue of protection for the PRC students. Within the first year of the June 4 events (i.e. before June 1990), as noted, the students were granted four short, unconditional visa extensions and were allowed to apply for permanent residency on strong humanitarian grounds or to apply for refugee status. Of course, illegal overstayers were treated differently from legal visa-holders, and they were only allowed to seek permanent residency in Australia through applying for refugee status. With the changes in the *Migration Act 1958*—the first major and sweeping change to Australia's immigration administration since 1945—the country decided to abandon

[11] Evidence for Australia's more relaxed policies toward PRC students can be found in Chapter Eight, in particular the '13 June 1997 decision' made by the Liberal-National Coalition government led by John Howard. This decision eventually expanded the 'post-20 June group' to include the Chinese students who had arrived after 12 March 1992, but on or before 1 November 1993 (Birrell, 1994; Gao, 2001).

its onshore humanitarian program and toughened the residency terms for all asylum seekers. New asylum seekers would now only be given four-year permits rather than, as in the past or precisely before 19 December 1989, immediate permanent entitlement to stay in Australia (*The Australian*, 28 June 1990).

The second extension to the PRC students' temporary protection visa had been made on 16 June 1989 and was valid until 31 July 1990 but even before it had reached half of its term, the government announced (in early December 1989) that it would further extend the visa until 31 January 1991 (*ACD* [*Australian Chinese Daily*], 9 December 1989). The new cut-off date for the students to stay in Australia—and to apply for permanent residency on humanitarian grounds or refugee status from within Australia—was now 20 June 1989. Those who had arrived before this date were termed the 'pre-20 June group,' and the number of people in this category soon increased to 19,640 (DILGEA, 1989, 1990; Jupp, 1991; Cronin, 1993). Those who had arrived in Australia after 20 June 1989 were not eligible to apply for residency on humanitarian grounds from within Australia. This new policy initiative was designed to lay the legal foundation to allow the PRC nationals who had paid their fees to ELICOS colleges to come to Australia, without giving them an opportunity to seek permanent residency onshore on strong humanitarian grounds (*ACD*, 9 December 1989; Jupp, 1991).

Although these changes did not appear to directly affect the 'pre-20 June group,' the Australian government's rigid approach toward those who had overstayed their visa made many PRC students suspect that the government did not want them to stay permanently (Cronin, 1993). This insecurity mobilized them to take action. In 1989—that is, up until 19 December 1989—four categories of individuals were eligible to apply for permanent residency from within Australia: refugees (with recognized refugee status); the spouses, parents and children of Australian residents; people in certain occupational categories; and individuals with strong humanitarian claims. To allow the Chinese students to stay permanently on strong humanitarian grounds (as the Canadian government in fact did) would have been simple and easily applicable. However, the Australian immigration administration in the late 1980s was troubled with large numbers of overstayers and onshore residency claimants, whom it would be administratively impossible to process (Cronin, 1993). In fact, Chinese nationals constituted the largest group of overstayers. It was known that more than 70 percent of the 'pre-20 June group' had come to Australia to study in ELICOS courses, and no less than 50 percent were unauthorized residents when the June 4 event took place (*The Age*, 25 September 1993).

Under various strict regulations that were redrawn and adopted,[12] the Department of Immigration, Local Government and Ethnic Affairs (DILGEA) firmly insisted on treating legal visa-holders and overstayers differently, and would not allow anyone who had overstayed their visas to seek residency on strong humanitarian grounds. That is, no less than 50 percent of the students in the 'pre-20 June group,' totalling roughly 10,000 or so in the overstayer category, had only the refugee program available to them. Significantly, this meant that the students needed to be politically active if they wanted to qualify for refugee status.

As a result of the above policy changes, the students of the 'pre-20 June group' were given a fourth visa extension. It was announced by the then Labor Prime Minister, Bob Hawke, on a television program on 6 June 1990 (*The Sun*, 8 June 1990) and then officially confirmed by the DILGEA almost three weeks later on 27 June 1990 (*The Australian*, 28 June 1990).[13] This visa extension gave the students temporary residency for four years until 30 June 1994. Quite apart from the more than 2,000 PRC nationals of the 'pre-20 June group' who had already applied for permanent residency on strong humanitarian grounds before 31 March 1990 and were waiting for the outcome (DILGEA, 1991: 56; Le, 2001), about 17,000 Chinese nationals now applied for the four-year temporary protection permits. By the end of June 1992, around 8,000 spouses and dependent children were also granted special visas to come to Australia (DILGEA, 1992: 87). By this time, the PRC students in Australia had already kicked off a vigorous campaign for permanent residency/asylum. However, the four-year temporary protection visa meant a further period of uncertainty and left their long-term future insecure, and therefore the student community became increas-

---

[12] The High Court ruling on the Chan Yee Kin case in September 1989 was a very important factor behind these strict policies (Cronin, 1993; Crock, 1998b). Chan's case will be discussed in Chapter Five.

[13] This was often used as one of the examples to show that Mr Bob Hawke made some 'shoot-from-the-lip decisions' when he was Prime Minister (*The Sun*, 8 June 1990). In the same television interview, when commenting on boat arrivals from Cambodia, Hawke also said that 'Bob is not your uncle on this issue' (Brennan, 2007: 44; Kelly, 2010: 14). As will be detailed in Chapter Six, *The Australian* carried an editorial titled 'Hawke: why Chinese may stay, Cambodians must go' (7 June 1990).' It was also because of his comments that he was nicknamed Uncle Hawke by many members of the Chinese migrant community.

ingly mobilized into more organized and politicized action (detailed in later chapters).[14]

The 'post-20 June group,' i.e. the PRC students who had arrived after 20 June 1989 but before 12 March 1992, had come to Australia already aware that the refugee program would be their only avenue for seeking residency/asylum (*The Age*, 2 November 1993). However, as the great majority of this group had arrived more than four months after June 4 (in late October 1989), many of them had already learned something about the process of asylum seeking in Australia before they had left China. Some, in fact, had already taken part in small-scale protests outside Australian consular posts in China in September and October 1989 to demand that the processing of visas be speeded up (see Note 10 of this chapter).

In response to the strong demands and needs of ELICOS programs, the Australian government reviewed its ways of assisting the exportation of education without damaging the immigration program. On 30 August 1989, new arrangements were announced for overseas students wishing to study in Australia (DILGEA, 1990: 67). As mentioned, these changes were aimed at tightening the procedures for students from so-called high-risk countries, including China, and a pre-visa assessment process was also put in place overseas. More than a third of the visa applicants from the People's Republic of China who applied under the new policy did not pass the pre-visa assessments. This extra selectivity meant a higher level of qualifications and experience among the 'post-20 June group' than the 'pre-20 June group.' That is, more of them had university education and more had worked in China's larger cities and big institutions. Although they arrived in Australia a few months after June 4, this group sowed the seeds of skilful activism.

To guarantee that the ELICOS colleges had enough international fee-paying students and could reopen for business as early as possible, the Australian Embassy in China, and its consular offices in other Chinese cities, issued more than 21,000 visas in 1989–90 to 'non-formal' course applicants from the PRC (DILGEA, 1991: 75)—'non-formal' being a new technical term for ELICOS. Of these arrivals, 4,156 of them overstayed when their initial visas expired in April 1990; one year later, 6,042 overstayed (DILGEA, 1991: 89).

---

[14] The eventual acceptance of the 'pre-20 June group' as permanent residents took place in two ways. The more than 2,000 applicants for residency on strong humanitarian grounds took DILGEA to the Federal Court and the court ruled in their favor (discussed in Chapter Five). The rest of the group was allowed to stay permanently following the '1 November [1993] decisions' (DIEA, 1994: 6), discussed in Chapter Eight.

At the same time, the total number of PRC onshore asylum-seekers, which stood at 9,163 in October 1990, had climbed to 23,000 by December 1991. By the end of June 1992, over 16,000 onshore refugee applications (over 75 percent) were from PRC nationals who had arrived in Australia after 20 June 1989 (DILGEA, 1992: 101).[15]

In the end, the different groups acted together to seek a way for all the PRC students living in Australia to obtain permanent residency. The activism that is the subject of this book took many forms. It was shaped in response to—and in effect, and in turn, also shaped—the policies of the Australian government toward humanitarian migration programs and refugees in the late 1980s and beyond. The students' efforts were rewarded with the '1 November [1993] decisions' that allowed all of them, in every category, to remain permanently in Australia. Because of this particular issue, there has been a very rapid and considerable increase in the Chinese-language speaking population in Australia since then. The approximate number of ethnic Chinese living in Australia in 1992 was around 300,000 (based on figures for the language spoken at home) (Kee, 1992, 1995). After the '1 November [1993] decisions,' the 1996 Census found more than 343,000 Australians who identified themselves as speakers of one or more of 'the Chinese varieties' (Clyne and Kipp, 1999).[16] One of the foremost factors in this increase was the inflow of students from the mainland of China who are the subject of this book.

[15] This group was also allowed by the '1 November [1993] decisions' to stay permanently in Australia. Unlike the 'pre-20 June group,' the students in this category had to meet a set of criteria, including being under 45 years old, possessing a tertiary qualification, and having vocational English or being enrolled in an English course. Three types of visa were granted. The special onshore permanent visa (class 816) was given to 13,026 university-educated asylum-seekers. The 'highly qualified' permanent visa (class 818) was offered to 2,254 who had local postgraduate qualification. The third visa type was for people with refugee status (class 817). Some 5,000 to 6,000 from this group who did not meet the criteria were later granted residency under the '13 June decision' in 1997. For details, see Chapter Eight.

[16] Since the mid 1990s, the number of Australian residents claiming Chinese ancestry has been rapidly increasing. By 2001, Census figures indicated that the number of speakers of Chinese was 401,357 (ABS, 2001). Also in 2001, it was estimated that there were around 555,560 people of Chinese ancestry in Australia (Chan, 2005), the number of which had then risen to 669,900 in 2006. The 2006 Census also showed that although the largest overseas-born groups in Australia have continued to be those born in Britain and New Zealand, the People's Republic of China has rapidly moved up from seventh on the list in 1996, overtaking Italy, to third place (ABS, 2007). In 30 June 2009, the number of China-born residents in Australia had increased to around 351,000 (DIAC, 2010). According to the 2011 Census, there were about 866,200 Australian residents claiming Chinese ancestry; more than 74 percent of them were the first generation in Australia (ABS, 2012).

Chinese Activism from a Scholarly Perspective

The 'Chinese student case' initially attracted scholarly attention from the field of international migration and refugee studies, and it was from an international migration/refugee perspective that I first began this study. A spate of literature exploded into the field during the 1980s and 1990s, but there was little attention paid to one important factor: the decision-making processes of these onshore international migrants. Examinations of their unique case could therefore shed a little new light on the causes of global migration and the seeking of refugee status (Black, 1991, 1993; Robinson, 1993). For a few decades, there appeared to be a pattern in the research and writing on this subject, in both international migration and refugee studies (Findlay and Graham, 1991; Stillwell and Congdon, 1991; Fielding, 1992; Halfacree and Boyle, 1993; Skeldon, 1995). There was a predominance of macro-scale studies and model-building work (Stillwell and Congdon, 1991; Addleton, 1992; Berg, 1993; Cadwallader, 1993; Gordon, 1992; Massey et al., 1993; Gardner, 1995),[17] and most studies were either demographic or economic in their emphasis, while others tended to be descriptive in nature (Moon, 1995: 505).

As a result, international migration and refugee studies had tended to focus on the political and economic preconditions for those leaving their home countries, concentrating on various measurable characteristics of the socioeconomic or physical environment (Chant and Radcliffe, 1992; Hugo, 1992, 1995; Kee, 1992; Parnwell, 1993; Brown and Foot, 1994; Hardie, 1994; Iredale, 1994, 1997; Martin, 1994; Zlotnik, 1995). As a corrective to this macro level approach, numerous researchers have more recently turned to a micro level approach that concerns itself more with the individual's choice between alternatives in an international migration and refugee situation than with the macro-political economic conditions. The few researchers who have produced what is regarded as significant research in the field have largely confined themselves to a theoretical test of the problems that constrain choices of migrants and asylum seekers (Gardner, 1995; Papastergiadis, 2000; Geddes, 2003). Empirical studies of the actual decision-making process associated with refugee movement or international migration are still almost entirely absent. In the case of asylum seekers, a

[17] In fact, it has also been argued by some researchers that this body of work is still far from complete because of the importance of international migration or the migratory process (White, 1980; Moon, 1995).

widespread key assumption has been that they partake in forced movement through circumstances beyond their control, and consequently they are assumed to be passive in relation to their fate (Qiu, 2003; Gao, 2006, 2009, 2010). Much research in refugee studies has also tended to focus on political, humanitarian and cultural aspects of the refugee issue.

For these reasons, such research could not offer a basic approach that allows generalizations to be made about how international migration and refugee movement takes place. Many analysts have noted that existing migration theories and models are not sufficient for providing theoretical explanations for the causes of international migration and refugee flows, and have argued that migration studies in general is in danger of being left behind by recent theoretical developments (Moon, 1995; Brettell and Hollifield, 2000; Portes and DeWind, 2007; Lucassen et al., 2010). More case studies that give emphasis to the actual decision-making process of migration and refugee flows would contribute a crucial element toward explaining migration.

As one of the Chinese students studying in Australia at the time of June 4, it was not difficult for me to find examples of former PRC students speaking about the changing courses of their lives after that event. It was also very easy to describe how miserable their lives were if I were to approach the case in a descriptive way. Among the tens of thousands of the PRC students, there was a multiplicity of anecdotes about their lives and their decision-making processes, which were not only socioeconomically and demographically complex, but also sociopolitically and psychologically complicated. I was also surprised by the obvious mismatch between the existing literature on international migration and refugee studies and my preliminary observations of these students' decision-making processes (for example, the abovementioned feelings of passivity and isolation). My perception of this mismatch was based on my observations of this particular Chinese student community during those years as well as on the ideas articulated by the students themselves and the many reports published in Australia's Chinese community newspapers.

Even in the earliest stages of my research, this Chinese student case appeared to be very different in a number of ways from the experiences of international and refugee migrants outlined in the existing literature. First, the Chinese students were not passive in relation to their fate, a fact that runs counter to prevailing portrayals of ordinary Chinese people and international migrants, especially refugee migrants. Second, one did not need to talk to these PRC students for long, or to read numerous reports in Australia's Chinese community newspapers or magazines, to discover that their campaign to obtain residency or asylum in Australia was not so simple that it could be described by the commonly used push-pull model. Third, the students made their migration decisions within newly formed social groups. This runs counter to the existing literature, which identifies families as the key decision making unit in relation to global migration, whether voluntary or forced (e.g., Landale, 1997). A fourth complicating element was the fact their protection campaign to stay in Australia was not individual-based. These students were well networked both socially and politically, and they were relatively well organized both in Australia and internationally. Fifth, as onshore asylum seekers, the students were not separate from local Australian society and the political scene of the host country. Chinese community newspapers in Australia had recorded the students' intensive contacts with many local institutions and their active lobbying activities. The kinds of strategic actions that these students had undertaken had rarely been pursued by other onshore asylum seekers, or at least had not been adequately analyzed and documented as such in the existing research literature (e.g., Martin, 1994; Block and Levy, 1999; McMaster, 2001; Martin et al., 2006; Hatton, 2011).

It seemed to me that the students in this particular case had acted in unique ways under their own circumstances, namely the political crisis in China, their home country, and their temporary residency in Australia as the host country. The prevailing models for assessing migration decision-making did not seem able to account for their reactions and behavior. As patterns of group behavior and certain themes began to recur in in-depth interviews and in students' recounting of their stories and experiences, I began to shift my focus from international migration and refugee studies to consider the students' group behavior and their patterns of action as a type of Chinese activism.

My survey of the research literature on Chinese activism worldwide uncovered surprisingly little relevant research or theoretical material, and the active and strategic approach adopted by the Chinese students in their collective campaign to stay in Australia, therefore, seemed to provide an ideal case for an examination of Chinese activism. It has to admit that Chinese activism is one of the most studied topics in the field of China studies (Goldman, 1981, 1994; Rosen, 1989; Cherrington, 1991, 1997a; Wasserstrom, 2005; Ho and Edmonds, 2007; Yang, 201), but most of the research publications related to my focus on Chinese activism produced in the past three or so decades were historical studies. Researchers in the field of China studies seemed to be particularly interested in Chinese intellectual history, studies of Chinese political culture, communist activism throughout the Republican period (1911–1949) (Israel, 1966, 1998; Rankin, 1971; Pye, 1968, 1981, 1990; Pong and Fung, 1985; Schwarcz, 1986; Bailey, 1988). Research attention was also drawn to nationalism as expressed in student movements, the activities of the Red Guards in the 1960s, and the pro-democracy activism of the late 1980s and early 1990s (Granqvist, 1967; Rankin, 1986; Goldman, 1981, 1994; Rosen, 1982, 1989; Chan, 1985; Cherrington, 1991, 1997a, 1997b; Wagner, 1991; Levine, 1993; Yang, 1993; Levine and Chen, 1996; Pieke, 1996; Wright, 1999; Perry, 2001; Lai, 2004; Zanasi, 2006; Benton, 2007; Guo, 2008; Lanza, 2009).[18]

Significantly, in a way that is similar to the treatment of the topic of migration or refugee in studies of international migration and refugee flows of the 1990s, Chinese activism as discussed in the literature was always related to major sociopolitical events in China and examined through a fixed set of research themes. For example, it was often viewed through the lens of a broader sociopolitical structure in the twentieth century, with an excessive emphasis on certain conditions external to China. Analyses of Chinese activism as a sociopolitical process seemed absent from the literature and research methods were also limited in these earlier studies. Even though some studies tried to incorporate methods that involved the researchers in direct interaction with the events and the participants, as in participant observation or interviews (Chan, 1985; Nathan and Shi, 1992; Pieke, 1996; Lu, 2003), most earlier studies, in the words of Moody, 'abstract[ed] cultural generalizations from Chinese history, literature and contemporary politics' (1994: 733) and relied on secondary sources for information and analysis.

This tendency to focus on a few major historical events and a relative methodological narrowness has meant that many previous studies have reached a similar—if not identical—conclusion: namely that the post-1949 period, like pre-1949 China, has predominantly been 'marked by the growing radicalization of students' (Rosen, 1989: 77). Accordingly, many also believed that student activism has become a familiar feature of modern China. The students who are the subject of this book were at one

[18] It should be noted that since the completion of this manuscript, more studies on various forms of Chinese activism have been published, including consumer activism (Hooper, 2000), internet activism (Tai, 2006; Tok, 2010), labor activism (Hurst, 2004; Zhang and Smith, 2009), environmental activism (Yang, 2003, 2005; Wong, 2005; Ho and Edmonds, 2007; Wu, 2009), human rights activism (Copper and Lee, 1997; Ching, 2008), and grassroots economic activism of various kinds (Zhou, 2009; Bondes, 2011). More details about this growing research interest and these more recent publications can also be found in the early part of Chapter Eight.

time seen by many China observers and by the media as victims of state repression (Wright, 1999) or as an active part of the Chinese democratic movement of the late 1980s and 1990s (Goldman, 1994). However, their active, prolonged and strategic campaign for residency/asylum contrasted markedly with the various forms of Chinese student activism that had been staged periodically in the course of the twentieth century. Even the most cursory observation shows that their activities were strategic rather than ideological or radical.

Another aim of this study is to call into question the image of Chinese people as passive. This notion, which has co-existed along with various forms of Chinese activism, has been a major topic of discussion among many Chinese intellectuals and national activists within China for almost one hundred years, since the early part of the twentieth century. Many Chinese thinkers have regularly criticized this so-called Chinese passivity as a harmful tradition (Fung, 1966; Su and Wang, 1991; Waldron, 1993; Xu, 1999), or a feature of the national character (Guo, 2004: 70), imagining it to have run deep in China's national character since the late Qing period. Many have even used it to explain a wide range of issues associated with China's recent past and its supposed backwardness (Yang, 1996; Mosher, 1998; Gu, 2000; Guo, 2003; Su and Yang, 2005). Yet the approach adopted by the Chinese students in Australia as a response to the June 4 events and their strategic campaign activities were very far from the widespread stereotype of Chinese passivity (Metzger, 1980: 7; 2005: 618; Schwartz, 1985: 138; Alitto, 1986: 76; Fu, 1993: 21; Meyer, 1994: 142; Ebrey, 1996: 328; Hall and Ames, 1998: 151; White, 1999: 183; Ding, 2006: 156).[19]

[19] There are a number of ways to define the Chinese passivity and activism, ranging from cultural and historical to social and political. Culturally and historically, as pointed out by Kupperman, both Confucianism and Daoism have emphasized the importance of passivity through their 'preoccupation with politeness and ceremonial correctness along with the growing moral seriousness' (2006: 115). Perry once used what she called 'the alleged Chinese cultural of dependency' to explain the political passivity of Chinese labor because the culture 'proved powerful enough to act as an effective deterrent to popular resistance' (1997: 55). While earlier studies tended to emphasize that 'the servility and passivity of the Chinese might be racial traits and thus difficult to overcome' (Adas, 2003: 187), more recent studies pay closer attention than previous works to socio-political and political and economic conditions under which people participate in collective action, or in the exercise of political power in particular (Moody, 1988, 1994). From this new perspective, the notion of Chinese passivity has been used by some to refer to the condition in which the Chinese people's rights of political participation have been deprived by the authoritarian regimes (Spurr, 1993: 72; Gao, 2009: 435; Heberer and Gobel, 2011: 8). According to this trend of scholarship, the Chinese activism presented in this study may be defined as an active response by the Chinese students to opportunities available, under a democratic polity

The twin stereotypes of activism and passivity notwithstanding, the last few years have seen an evolving interest in newer forms of Chinese activism, such as China's increasing global activism (Foot, 2005; Shi, 2005) and civil activism in China (Hurst, 2004; Ho and Edmonds, 2007). The latter encompasses activism in the fields of law and human rights, which has made waves across a wide range of constituencies (Lubman, 1999; Ching, 2011; Bondes, 2011), and also China's home-focused and global environmental activism (Yang, 2003, 2005; Wong, 2005; Ho and Edmonds, 2007; Wu, 2009; Xie, 2009; Ebrey, 2010). Among millions of young Chinese, including university students, the well-known pattern of periodic bursts of radical student activity and pro-democracy activism is quickly being replaced by the pursuit of new interests and freedoms,[20] often of a materialistic nature and often on the Internet (Tai, 2006; Yang, 2009). At the same time, the history of activism within China and of pan-Chinese activism outside the country as an aspect of China's nationalism has become the focus of attention for several young researchers (Reilly, 2006, 2010; Tok, 2010).

Of course, the activism demonstrated by the PRC nationals studied in this book was prompted by their concern for their own lives and futures in the immediate aftermath of June 4, and their actions, both individual and collective, in Australia exhibited fundamental differences from the global and civil activism noted above. Perhaps their activism can be seen as characteristic of their generation—that is, relevant to the specificities of the situation in which they found themselves, and hence unlike either the communist movement before 1949 or the Red Guard activities of the late 1960s,[21] or even the activities of the Internet generation that came

---

and in concert with the international humanitarian regime, for achieving their personal goals and aspirations. According to this same trend, and also since this study is more about social behavior and interaction of the Chinese students, the passivity could therefore be considered as the state or condition in which Chinese people are rendered passive, rather than a particular and defining cultural or societal trait.

[20] In the past 20 or so years since June 4, Chinese students have not engaged in many large-scale collective political actions. Indeed such actions have never been seen in China since the May Fourth period of the early twentieth century. As a result, there is relatively little work on Chinese student activism, but some researchers have still identified and studied a number of post-1989 cases, including the anti-U.S. student demonstrations after the 1999 Belgrade embassy bombing (Parsons and Xu, 2001; Yu and Zhao, 2006; Zhao, 2009), and the 2005 anti-Japanese protests (Reilly, 2006, 2010; Tai, 2006; Weiss, 2008). During the same period, some researchers have also paid attention to re-analyzing the 1989 student movement (Yang, 2000; Zhao, 2009) and the political pragmatism emerged in China after 1989 (Chan, 1999).

[21] It is worth noting that in the past 10 or so years, the Red Guard activities of the late 1960s have not only been a topic of serious academic study, but have also resulted in interesting findings (Yang, 2000, 2011).

after them. As noted above, what the Chinese students demonstrated in their campaign to stay in Australia was a strategic rather than a primarily ideological kind of activism. In the field of China studies there has been, up to now, no adequate and systematic study of Chinese activism of this generation and this type. This study seeks to fill that gap.

Another issue for my study was Kelliher's concept of the elite-mass conflict that is caused by different goals of diverse groups of different social status (1993). As mentioned, the PRC students living in Australia came from different social groups. Most had come as English-language students, but a small group were specially selected postgraduate students. They had come from various different places in China, south and north, and from big cities and small towns. This was a Chinese society in miniature.[22] I need to make this clarification here as some researchers have warned against hypothesizing Chinese society based on overseas Chinese communities (Mackie, 2003). In fact, the Chinese students in this case were still part of Chinese society and they all maintained close links—not only with their families, but also with their friends and home institutions (Benton and Gomez, 2001; Ip, 2003; Gao, 2006b). Therefore, this disparate group was able to act together for a shared strategic goal, forming their own new networks and groups among themselves, learning to engage in lobbying activities, learning to politicize and strategize, and learning how to utilize various legal means—despite the fact that many or indeed most of the students had a very limited grasp of English.

Three questions took shape in response to my reading of the research literature. How could I approach this case study if there was as yet no similar study? How could I form a strong empirical basis for this case study? What features could be extrapolated from this case to argue for its uniqueness?

The first question was readily answered. My study could not be done by testing an existing theory or set of existing ideas on Chinese activism because there was no similar study. To pursue this case study, I would still need to find an appropriate set of organizing ideas elsewhere. Recent

22 As several Western countries introduced similar schemes to export language education and recruited many PRC students in the late 1980s, the Chinese student population in Western countries not only increased dramatically, but also diversified to include more people who were ordinary workers and peasants. Among English-speaking countries, Australia and Canada recruited more of what were called language students from China than did the USA (Orleans, 1988; Huang, 1997; Mann, 1999; Qian, 2003). Even considering an elite-mass dichotomy (Kelliher, 1993), the PRC student population in Australia was not simply an elite group.

thinking on identity, especially on strategic identity or performativity, showed itself to be a useful guide (Butler, 1993; Jacobs and Fincher, 1998). My preliminary observation of the PRC students tended to support the view that 'identity is not fixed but is historically determined' (Agnew, 2009: 387). Under certain circumstances, various parts of our identity could be negotiated and changed. The idea of 'strategic identity formation,' which I define as the process through which individuals, or groups, purposely identify themselves with certain sociopolitical groups or classes and sets of beliefs, allows me to productively examine the inside of the decision making process and convincingly reveal a set of meanings from within the social process of the student activism. As a central theme, the idea of strategic identity formation is therefore used to encompass processes of representation, signification and performativity as crucial components in the way identities are constituted—identities of 'refugee' and 'democratic activists' in this present instance. This approach also takes account of the fact that struggles over identity, especially political identity associated with political capital or certain powers, could be 'framed in and through differences that are variously constituted and contextually determined' (Jacobs and Fincher, 1998: 2).

The second question relates to what research method was to be used. As there were practically no pre-existing systematic studies, and as my research would be reliant on both the quality and quantity of empirical evidence, I decided to make use of a multimethod approach for depth, subtlety and accuracy (Hunter, 1983; Brannen, 2008). This approach is regarded as 'a strategy for overcoming each method's weaknesses and limitations' by combining different forms of research methods within the same study (Hunter and Brewer, 2003: 578). Given that I was one of the Chinese students studying in Australia at that time, I was familiar with many details of the student community and was able to collect data from the student activists themselves and their contacts.

This research was thus based on in-depth interviews, group discussion and participant observation along with documentary sources, especially Australia's Chinese-language community newspapers and mainstream English-language print media. I also made use of many policy statements of Australian government departments and agencies. Information gained from in-depth interviews forms the main source, and the data collected from participant observation are woven in among documentary sources (including those in print or in electronic form). Together, these provide a context for the interview-based data. In-depth interviews were conducted with about 60 Chinese students who arrived in Australia before 4 June 1989 and have lived there ever since, and with 50 or so students from the 'post-20 June group' who arrived in Australia after October 1989 and have stayed on a permanent basis. Interviewees were recruited using the snowball method, beginning with those contacts that I had established through my past involvement in the Chinese student community. Three main types of interviews were utilized: structured interviews, one-on-one interviews and group-focused interviews. A list of questions used in the first round of interviews is attached (Appendix B). All interviewees were informed at the start that the information they conveyed to me would be kept confidential and anonymous and it is for that reason that their identities have been concealed in this book.

As I pursued this multimethod approach and began to notice many repetitions of certain behavior patterns and themes in my interviews with students, an answer to my original third question began to take shape: the activism demonstrated by the PRC students was an instructive instance of strategic identity formation. The empirical evidence I was collecting indicated that their activism was characterized by six main features or patterns of behavior.

First: people taking action together to achieve a goal in a particular society will need to have extensive involvement with many parts of that society. They must find a way to contextualize themselves as actors in the situation. In the case of the PRC students in Australia, this involved selecting from various conceptions of refugee identity in order to be part of the refugee application process, which in turn brought about a series of changes to their primary social group structure and dynamics (as noted in Chapter Two).

Second: as these students were not recognized and aided by refugee agencies, they had to provide strong evidence to prove that they fitted the criteria for refugee status and were therefore qualified for protection as refugees. They needed to collect these various forms of evidence from within Australia. This is why they conducted so many self-consciously political activities, which in turn made not only their identity political, but also their identity construction strategic.

Third: when the Chinese students in Australia engaged in politicized activities as part of their efforts to seek political asylum in Australia, they did not act alone, but in connection with highly organized international networks. In fact, PRC students worldwide were organized before June 1989, but they were not yet networked globally. The new international network that formed after June 4 played a very important role not only in spreading information about seeking asylum, but also in coordinating a range of political actions by Chinese students in Western countries.

Fourth: some Chinese students even utilized their political and legal knowledge and skills to take the issue to court, setting a legal precedent for the entire student community and unleashing what was described as 'excessive use' of the court system by unsuccessful refugee applicants in Australia in the late 1980s and early 1990s (Fonteyne, 1994: 258). Yet, 'the most important starting point' occurred in late 1989, when the High Court of Australia made a favorable ruling on the residency case of Chan Kee Yin (Crock et al., 2006: 86). Chan was not part of the student group studied in this book, but a few students were encouraged by his case and worked to duplicate its success (discussed in Chapter Five).

Fifth: collective lobbying for the right to stay was an important part of the students' interactions with local institutions. This required not only political skills and high-level knowledge of government policies, but also organizational skills and strategies. Their approach to the student issue was conditioned by the fact that lobbying is interactive in nature, and the students strategized (successfully) to elicit commitment to their demands from local institutions (as noted in Chapter Six).

Sixth: the high point of this particular form of the Chinese activism is organized political action. In this case, organized political action was the direct result of organization by different student political groups. Such an organizational process effectively embodied the politics of performing refugee identity, but it also resulted in the politics of these groups, which drove the campaign in a way that was even more political than before. That is, this form of activism not only provided many students with more solid evidence for their refugee applications, but also further politicized the issue of their residency/asylum and brought it into the ambit of international politics. This political logic had not only made their asylum seeking in Australia a part of a democratic movement, but also the matter of their residency in Australia an issue of human rights.

Organization of the Book

The book is organized under thematic topics, but is also presented as a roughly chronological account of the PRC student protection campaign in Australia (although some of the activities outlined in different chapters—such as the collection of evidence to support their refugee applications—continued over time and overlapped with other stages of the process).

Chapter Two outlines and explains how the PRC student issue took shape in Australia in 1989. It builds on background information that has been introduced in this present chapter, and considers the students' immediate reactions to their predicament and the Australian government's initial approach to the issue. I discuss how the issue was raised in the student community and in Australian society at large. To illustrate the involvement of various Australian social agencies, I focus on six agencies (the Chinese-language community media; the English-language media; community services and agencies; the Australian government; Chinese community groups; and other community groups or organizations) and their interactions with each other. These interactions formed a context for the students' activism and familiarized the students with various aspects of their host country. The formation of the student protection issue brought about a series of structural changes for the student community in terms of the primary social groups that functioned as the basic units in this newly formed community. This micro-level analysis of the primary social groups, significant for international migration and refugee studies, traces how the basic social unit reacted to major socio-political changes and shows how the students' large-scale activism was initiated.

Chapter Three outlines and examines attempts by the students to transform their identity from international students to refugees and political asylum seekers—a process that they engaged in, both individually and as a community, before pursuing residency/asylum in an organized and politicized manner. The chapter begins with a review of the policy background to the residency/asylum issue, then provides an analysis of how Australia's criteria for refugee status were perceived by the students (noting the role of exaggeration in the students' discussions of the refugee criteria). I identify a collective identity construction process with multiple stages: information-gathering, information-analyzing and task-forming. The identity formation process culminated in purposefully directed tasks aimed at collecting evidence—locally within Australia, from family or friends in China or elsewhere, and even from the authorities in China—to support applications for refugee status. I summarize a number of the methods used by the students in the collection and presentation of various forms of evidence to perform the political identity they were seeking at the time.

Chapter Four deals with the students' organized international networks, an unusual element of the PRC students' activism that has hitherto received little scholarly attention. It examines the formation and utilization of international networks by the PRC students living in Australia and looks into their main international partner organizations and collaborators in the United States. The discussion begins with the role of independent student unions (founded on the officially controlled student unions that had existed prior to June 4 in PRC student communities abroad). The focus then shifts to the lobbying efforts of the PRC student community in the USA in 1989, led by the Chinese student unions, which helped to push the 'Pelosi Bill' through the U.S. Congress. Finally I examine the politicization of the student networks by two international Chinese student organizations: the CAD (Chinese Alliance for Democracy) and the FDC (Federation for a Democratic China).

Chapter Five looks at a court case brought against the Australian government (more precisely, against DILGEA, the immigration department at the time) by a group of PRC students over bureaucratic delays in processing their applications for residency on humanitarian grounds. The discussion begins with the case of Chan Yee Kin, an appellant for political asylum (though not a student). A few months after June 4, the High Court of Australia handed down a ruling on Chan's case. The ruling was favorable to asylum seekers, and helped to give a sympathetic definition to the 'well-founded fear' and 'real chance' of persecution that are prerequisites for refugee status (Crock, 1998a; 2004). Rather than challenging DILGEA over how refugee status was determined, some individuals in the PRC student community copied Chan's approach and took the government to court over the delays in handing their asylum applications. The chapter goes on to consider why these students opted to deal with the residency/asylum issue through the Federal Court, and how they prepared their cases. I discuss the impact of the Chan case on the student campaign, noting not only how it opened the door to the processing of many other residency applications on humanitarian grounds, but also how it further advanced the student campaign, especially the intensive lobbying activities.

Chapter Six deals with the fifth key feature of this Chinese activism: the way in which the student community as a whole lobbied intensively for the opportunity, and the right, to stay in Australia. I discuss how the first move was made, how the effort was maintained and manifested in interaction with various local institutions (following on from Chapter Two), and what strategies were employed. The chapter begins with a discussion of the channels of communication that the students formed with local institutions and the interactions between them. The close relationships between some student activists, student organizations and one publicly funded Migrant Service Center are analyzed in a case study. I also examine the strategies adopted by the students and the interactions with the media that were identified as 'the main battlefield' of their campaign (*China Spring [Australia Edition]*, No. 1, 1990; *FDC Newsletter*, 34, 1991; *The Tide*, 15 December 1992).

Chapter Seven extends the discussion to the organized, highly politicized actions taken by the students that finally won them their campaign for residency/asylum. I argue that this was a logical development of their strategic campaign. As noted in Chapter Four, the newly independent student unions and two political groups (the CAD and the FDC) played a pivotal role in internationalizing the issue of protection for PRC students and forming organized international networks of onshore asylum seekers. Chapter Seven investigates why the student community became so highly organized, then considers the role of the CAD and the FDC in leading the student lobby in the later stages of the campaign. The chapter outlines the various and changing strategies that were developed and applied in order to achieve the interrelated goals of the activist groups. It also discusses the emergence of internal factions, factional activities and the students' attempts to reorganize these groups. Although these incidents took the form of 'in-fighting,' the chapter argues that internal factions and factional activities as a special feature of the organized student groups, especially the resulting reorganization of the groups, eventually strengthened the overall fighting capabilities of the student community and changed the student groups into new political organizations.

Chapter Eight concludes the study with a summary of the main features of this case of PRC student activism and a general discussion of contemporary Chinese activism, moving its focus from the student case itself to a general consideration of the themes that emerge from this case study. There are three sections. After a summary of the main findings of this case study and an outline of the main features of the PRC student campaign for residency/asylum in Australia, I examine the theoretical significance of the empirical findings presented in earlier chapters of this book, most particularly the role of strategic identity formation. The chapter concludes with a brief discussion of future research directions and needs. A number of questions are then raised for further research, with a view to strengthening research on contemporary Chinese activism.

CHAPTER TWO

THE FORMATION OF THE STUDENT ISSUE

The fact that this group of Chinese nationals were away from their home country shaped their protection campaign in Australia in a number of ways. They needed to familiarize themselves with various aspects of their host society. They needed to find out about the local people's attitudes towards June 4. They needed learn what the locals understood a genuine refugee to be. They had to learn about the legitimate ways for seeking asylum. They needed to know how to interact with various sections of local Australian society that became involved with their cause. This chapter traces how the issue of asylum-seeking by Chinese students in Australia in 1989 took shape, and provides a context for the story of their political activism. It discusses how the Chinese student issue was first raised in Australian society in general and within the student community itself. The discussion goes on to identify the involvement of six local organizations or agencies and the interactions between them. It then examines the changes that came about in the newly formed student community as their residency or asylum-seeking issue took shape, noting the structural changes in the students' primary social groups in response to their changing circumstances.

The Student Issue after June 4

The first hint that asylum was being considered for the Chinese students living in Australia in 1989 appeared in the mainstream English-language print media as early as 6 June, only two days after the June 4 incident. A report titled 'Asylum likely for students,' published in *The Australian* (one of the most influential, and more conservative, English daily newspapers in Australia), included the following words:

> [The Australian Government] will consider granting asylum or refugee status to any of the 8,200 Chinese students studying in Australia who fear persecutions if they return home. The Minister for Foreign Affairs and Trade, Senator Evans, said he did not know of any applications from Chinese students, but each case would be considered on its merits (*The Australian*, 6 June 1989).

The next day, all the Australian English-language and Chinese-language newspapers contained lengthy coverage of the Chinese student protection issue. The *Australian Chinese Daily* (*ACD* or *Xinbao* in Chinese), the most-read Chinese-language community newspaper among PRC students at the time, carried the headline 'Chinese students seek political asylum, PM Hawke promises to consider' (*ACD*, 7 June 1989). At a time when many students were deeply worried by what had occurred in China, and especially by the rumors of a looming civil war, the media's focus on the issue of protection not only made them aware of a potential chance to stay, but also indirectly seemed to be urging them to consider taking this opportunity. In a sense, this was the beginning of a shift in the students' attention: from June 4 to their own protection issue, and from short-term student visa extensions to seeking asylum.

Even before the students' actions took the form of a campaign, their reactions to June 4 had changed in response to changes to the ways in which both they and local Australians understood the new issue of their chance—indeed their right—to stay in Australia and be protected. The media coverage seemed to be generating pressure on the government to offer them a visa extension. At the time, only a handful of students (those whose student visas had expired, or were close to expiry) were in need of a visa extension. Now, however, it appeared that a visa extension could potentially be made available to anyone who wished to have one without paying any tuition fees.

This change in perception became visible because thousands of PRC students rushed to the local DILGEA offices, desperately seeking application forms for either 'residency on strong humanitarian grounds' or refugee status. The largest convergences of students in several DILGEA offices occurred precisely, and ironically, on the day when a series of emotional memorial services were held throughout Australia for the victims of June 4 (*The Age*, 10 June 1989). By 14 June 1989, more than 5,000 Chinese nationals were reported to have presented themselves at DILGEA branches countrywide and picked up the application forms (*ACD*, 14 June 1989). According to an internal report prepared by a Melbourne-based Refugee Advice and Casework Service (RACS), so high was the demand for the forms that the DILGEA branches were rapidly running out of them, and some migration agents decided to sell them for AU$10 each so as to make as much profit as they could from these potential asylum seekers (RACS, 1990: 6).

The change in the local people's perception of the students was evident within just a few days in a shift in the focus of coverage, in both the

English-language media and the Chinese community media, from June 4 to the welfare of the PRC students living in Australia. Community service agencies, such as RACS, quickly took up the issue as part of their brief and became active in helping the students. Chinese community organizations spread the word of their concern about the students' predicament, bringing the issue to the attention of more students and to both Chinese and non-Chinese Australians (*The Sun*, 8 June 1990; *The Age*, 10 June 1989). The Australian government, under pressure from various local agencies, quickly promised to develop a policy to deal with the PRC student issue.

The extensive involvement of local agencies was an important feature of the formation of the student issue. In my interviews with students, six local organizations/agencies were identified as having contributed to shaping the entire process of the student issue. They were (1) the local Chinese community media; (2) the English-language media; (3) community services and agencies; (4) the Australian government and its departments; (5) Chinese community groups; and (6) other community groups or organizations. Among these six agencies, four were cited as having played particularly significant roles in shaping the issue: (1) Chinese community groups or organizations; (2) the Chinese community media; (3) the English-language media; and (4) community services and agencies.[1] However, the real driving force in the formation of the issue of protection for the PRC students did not come from any individual agency, but rather from the interactions between agencies. That is to say, their interactions not only made protection for the students into a serious issue, but also caused the organizations/agencies themselves to become deeply involved, and even morally committed. Thanks to the processes of interaction between these organizations/agencies, the PRC student issue became embedded in local institutions, local events and local political agendas. If there is one feature that typifies the context of the students' struggle to stay permanently in Australia, it is these interactions.

In my interviews with students, the embedding of the issue in the local context was presented as having seemed to be a natural and spontaneous process, 'a process-in-itself' as some described it (Group-focused interviews, 21 March 1998). Each organization/agency would react to the issue according to its own area of responsibility and its own perspective;

[1] It should be noted that this list is different from the previous one. The numbers (1) to (4) are in order of importance—number one being most important, and number four being least important in terms of their role in the formation of the student issue.

in other words, their involvements were not pre-arranged but took shape as required by their particular roles in the system. For example, the media had to report June 4 and the various reactions to it; the government had to react to community outcries and demands; community services had to offer their help to those who sought it. Each one was doing the right things according to its own point of view. The joining up of these different reactions formed the larger process. It should be stressed that in the immediate aftermath of June 4, all the local agencies reacted to the issue in a similarly emotional and political way. Despite an allegation by a couple of local Chinese community members that PRC students were taking advantage of June 4 to stay permanently in Australia (*The Age*, 8 June 1990; *The Australian*, 7 June 1990), it is crucial to note that the way in which the protection issue took shape was not a simple reflection of the intention of any one constituency, including the student group.

The interactive way in which the student protection issue took shape also reflects the dynamic and ongoing nature of the involvement of local organizations or agencies. Their involvement cannot be regarded as an 'external' factor bringing about an 'internal' process of student reaction reflected in organized, collective behavior. Any dichotomy of 'internal' and 'external' would oversimplify the case and hinder our understanding. The student groups were both an 'internal' force and an 'external' driver for the formation of the issue, and their roles were constantly changing. Given that many organizations/agencies were involved, the participation of each increased the likelihood that the others would react not only to the student protection issue itself, but also to how the other agencies were responding to it. These ongoing interactions between the various agencies gave the issue considerable momentum, and several activists regarded this phenomenon as a real force that kept the issue alive for several years (Group-focused interviews, 21 March 1998). To understand the phenomenon, one of interviewees reminded me of the importance of the event as follows:

> People need to put it [the formation of the student protection issue] back in the original context: we all were completely shocked, with fear and panic, by what happened then [in China] and the media coverage of the event.... all sectors of [Australian] society were mobilized to deal with the crisis. Yes, it was a very real crisis, and forced everyone to take action (Interviewee 11, 14 February 1998).

Momentum was created by the various agencies in relays. At first glance, it might appear that all the organizations/agencies were functioning at the same time, and all of the time. However, questionnaire-based surveys showed that though each one had an impact on every stage of the asylum seeking process, each one operated with different force at different times. Their importance rose and fell in different phases, and these 'ups and downs' perfectly matched the process of maintaining the momentum of the student protection issue. Some students suggested that the Chinese-language community newspaper were the most important agency in the process (Group-focused interviews, 21 March 1998), but my survey shows that their influence was less crucial over several short periods than the influence of the English-language media or the community services and groups (One-on-one interviews, 25 April 1998). However, it is still worth noting that, as several former students commented, the marketing strategy of the Chinese-language community media helped the student issue not only 'take root' locally in Australia, but also 'keep it alive.'[2] As will be discussed in Chapter Six, the community media gradually changed the focus of the coverage of June 4, and turned their attention to the protection issue. One interviewee made the following comment:

> The role of the Chinese [community] newspapers actually went far beyond what the newspapers should do.... they at least played three types of roles [in the student community]: providing them with a lot of information; helping them create evidence for their applications, and being a sort of organizer... in terms of helping achieve a consensus on the student issue in the ethnic Chinese community and among the students (Interviewee 39, 3 April 1998).

In the later stages of the process, human rights groups in fact played a leading role. Although less prominent than the other agencies at most stages of the process, they later helped to politicize the PRC student

[2] It is also worth briefly mentioning the role of the mainstream English media in influencing the formation of the student issue. A number of interviewees mentioned a very powerful comparison between June 4 and 'the fall of Saigon,' which was made by Peter Ellingson, a Fairfax journalist based in Beijing, shortly after June 4. On 8 June 1989, Peter Ellingson wrote that 'Beijing today resembled Saigon in the final days before the Vietcong rolled into the city' (*The Age*). His analysis appeared in *The Age* and *The Sydney Morning Herald* and created what a few interviewees called the 'Beijing version of the fall of Saigon.' This comparison was believed to have influenced many Australians at the time. In fact, one of Fairfax newspaper readers warned them of the possible negative effects of such media coverage and wrote that [the Western media would have to] 'take some responsibility for what has happened (in Beijing). Without the media coverage in the Western press the students would have gone quietly back to their universities or homes days ago' (4 June 1989, *The Age*). From the students' perspective, this 'Beijing version of the fall of Saigon' informed them that they were in a situation similar to 'the fall of Saigon,' which was the main reason behind the Vietnamese refugee crisis. In Australia, that particular crisis was resolved by allowing almost all of those boat people to stay in Australia.

protection issue, which gave a significant boost to their asylum seeking efforts when the other agencies were playing a less crucial role. No stage of the students' attempt to seek asylum was driven by any single agency; instead the students always felt the influence of all of them (Group-focused interviews, 17 January 1998). However, if we compare the roles of the various agencies in the formation of the student issue, the complexity of the process becomes very evident. Wave after wave of involvement by key local agencies meant that whenever the student issue flagged, it was repeatedly revived. So forceful was this whole, ongoing process that the student protection issue became intensely embedded in local politics and would become unstoppable.

At the same time, the students were familiarizing themselves with various aspects of their host country. This was a vital part of the process of embedding their asylum seeking initiatives within the local setting. They needed a deeper understanding and better knowledge of Australia in order to effectively wage their campaign to stay. Within a few weeks after June 4, the student community had carried out a range of activities to familiarize themselves with local opinions and with the options that were available for them to seek asylum. Chinese community newspapers and English-language newspapers recorded seven such activities: (1) students going to DILGEA offices; (2) the postgraduate student union representatives meeting DILGEA officials; (3) students going to the RACS to seek their help; (4) students soliciting help from local Chinese community organizations (5) students making inquiries by writing to newspapers; (6) students making contact with legal consultants; and (7) meetings being held by the student union to inform the students that they could apply for residency (*ACD* and *The Age*, 5 June–31 July 1989).

These activities encompassed three types of consultations. The first type occurred at an individual level, and included visits to DILGEA and RACS offices, to OSO (Overseas Student Office) offices by those holding or wanting to obtain a student visa, or to AIDAB (Australian International Development Assistance Bureau) offices by postgraduate students who were studying in Australia under AIDAB-subsidized programs. All these initiatives were followed by extensive exchanges of information and discussions between individuals (The IFCSSA seminar notice, 7 September 1989).

The second main type of consultation took place within these PRC students' primary social groups, and was focused on analyzing various pieces of information that they had collected from their visits to DILGEA, RACS, OSO and AIDAB offices. Given that these group discussions would in part reveal people's intentions to seek asylum, they can be considered as collective attempts at familiarization with local conditions for seeking asylum, especially with regard to policy relating to how to seek protection onshore from within Australia (Group-focused interviews, 14 March 1998; One-on-one interviews, 8 June 1998).

The third type of consultation took the form of meetings organized by postgraduate student unions, mainly the IFCSSA. There were two types: public meetings that were often held in a university classroom or theatre and open to all the Chinese students, including ELICOS students, and countless internal discussions or debates among the activists, which were often held in the student union office.

In all these initiatives, the focus was clearly on familiarization with four aspects of the students' host society. First, the students needed to be familiar with local people's attitudes to June 4. They needed to know how locals understood the issue of their opportunity or right to stay in Australia, and they needed to know what local people would expect them to do if they wanted to fulfill their hopes of staying. Information of this kind created a basis for deciding how to proceed—especially in terms of forming a new political identity. In interviews, students stated that these were the most important areas of familiarization not only in the initial stages, but also throughout the entire process (Group-focused interviews, 7 March 1998). One former activist noted that the students were well aware of changes in the local people's attitudes towards them in the aftermath of June 4 (One-on-one interviews, 25 April 1998). One example of such changes was a heated debate that arose in the English-language media when a few leading journalists argued that there had been no massacre in Tiananmen Square (*The Australian*, 6 September 1989). At this stage, many students had come to feel reasonably familiar with their host society and had begun collecting evidence for their asylum applications so the questioning of June 4 could have led local people to conclude that the students had no reason to seek protection in Australia. For their part, and by way of response, the student activists and their groups initiated many actions to protest against this heated 'no-massacre' debate (after a special public forum held by the IFCSSA on 7 September 1989 to respond to the debate)[3] (One-on-one interviews, 25 April 1998).

[3] This debate made the PRC students living in Australia even more worried than their counterparts elsewhere, because the 'no massacre' debate had been ignited by Hou Dejian, the famous popular singer, who had publicly stated that there was no massacre in Tiananmen Square after taking refuge in the Australian Embassy for a few weeks (Munro, 1990). The students became very anxious about the connection between the 'no-massacre'

The second task in the students' familiarization process was to learn more about Australia's humanitarian immigration program and refugee policy, in order to establish the policy parameters for their case and thus ensure that their residency applications would be appropriate within the specific context of Australian policies. This familiarization seemed vital given that the definition of what constitutes a refugee, even though laid out by the 1951 UN (United Nations) Convention on Refugees (Black, 1991), has been subject to differing interpretations at nation-state level (Kabala, 1993; Crock, 1998a, 1998b). A few early studies indicate that about 20 percent of the PRC students knew something about Australia's immigration policy before their arrival there (Sun, 1987; Wang, 1987; Wang and Lai, 1987), but they had to familiarize themselves with the policies in greater depth and at operational level when they all came to consider seeking asylum. This kind of familiarization was very practical: they needed to find out how many categories in Australian immigration policy could be applicable to them, and what the detailed criteria were for assessing residency claims under each relevant category. As already mentioned, these policy issues were rendered increasingly complex, and the students' familiarization efforts were even made more difficult, by the Australian government's frequent changes to its immigration policies at that time. Having learned about the categories and criteria, the students then also needed to learn every practical detail of the application process, such as how to submit an application form, which government office would assess their application, and how to appeal against an unfavorable decision should the application be rejected.

There were differences between what individuals and student groups wished to find out. Individual students simply wanted to know about the bureaucratic procedures for processing an asylum application. Student organizations, on the other hand, which intended to deal with the issue as representatives of the student community, sought to understand more than just the bureaucratic procedures. They needed to learn about the functioning of local agencies at administrative, legal and political levels. This was necessary because, from the very beginning, the student leaders and activists were prepared to act on behalf of the students at both legal and political levels.

debate and the Australian Embassy and the possibility that the Australian government had made a deal with China when Hou Dejian left the Australian Embassy.

The third aspect of the familiarization process was for the students to make themselves better aware of all the possible differences in approach between the various institutions, organizations and agencies mentioned above. Somehow, the student activists became aware that 'gaps' existed between the different agencies in terms of their attitudes and approaches to the student issue. From the second half of 1989, after several changes in DILGEA's policies, flaws and loopholes were uncovered in various immigration regulations and the legal system. As the student protection issue dragged on, it gradually became clearer to some students that there was an inconsistency between the political and policy statements made by politicians, bureaucrats and the media and the actual culture of control over the immigration. An understanding of these gaps and loopholes was especially critical for the student community's preparation of their own strategies for asylum seeking and the possibility of a prolonged struggle, in order to make a decision on how to approach their protection issue, and importantly, which sections of Australian society they should best associate themselves with.

The fourth and final familiarization imperative was for the student group, as onshore asylum seekers, to familiarize themselves with local people and networks in order to find a context for themselves and their quest for protection within the local scene. Activists and many other individual students devoted much time and effort to learning about local networks and organizations, and then to networking themselves with the Australians who were not only willing, but also able to help them. This initiative, which several former students regarded as a key characteristic of their activism (IFCSSA seminar notice, 7 September 1989), enabled them to turn their own issue into something that not only involved local people, but was also precisely attuned to local circumstances. The social networks that were formed through this process helped the students strengthen local support and sympathy for their plight (which had been the primary objective of the student unions from the beginning), as well as creating a level of understanding among local Australians that could form a starting point for asylum seeking.

In all, the familiarization initiatives achieved two major and mutually reinforcing objectives. First, protection for the Chinese students living in Australia was successfully made into an issue that the host country had to recognize and deal with. Second, practically speaking, throughout this contextualization process and because of it, the student community as a whole formed and developed a determination to seek the right to stay in Australia. That is to say, through the familiarization process, the students learned that there was a likely chance to stay permanently in Australia. Their determination to stay was reinforced by this anticipated chance.

Expansion of the Student Groups

While the PRC students in Australia were familiarizing themselves with the host society in the ways outlined above, they were also forming and expanding their social groups so as to prepare the ground for their protection campaign. As noted, the decision-making unit that is most commonly documented as the key one in migration decisions is the family (Harbison, 1981; Hugo, 1995; Zlotnik, 1995). Although some existing literature suggests, directly or indirectly, that the role of certain groups outside the family is important in different stages of migration (Hugo, 1981, 1995; Gold, 1992), our understanding of the functioning of primary social groups of migrants is very patchy. The Chinese students living in Australia in the late 1980s and early 1990s were far away from their homeland and families, and international telecommunications were not as convenient, cheap or sophisticated as they are today. When these students were making their asylum seeking decisions after June 4, it was to their newly formed social groups that they turned.

The formation and expansion of these primary social groups proved to be a significant element in the development of the student issue and laid a structural foundation for the students' activism (Gao, 2002; 2009). At the time of June 4, the majority of the PRC students in Australia had been there for only a short period of time, varying from a few weeks to several months. Only a small number, fewer than 10 percent, had already lived in Australia for more than a year (Wang, 1987; DILGEA, cited in *The Australian*, 8 June 1989; Slattery, 1991). This small group consisted mainly of postgraduate students and visiting scholars who, as noted above, had a significantly higher level of education, English-language ability and experience of political processes than did many language students who made up the majority. Of course, these Chinese nationals in Australia had formed social groups well in advance of June 4, through sharing houses, attending the same universities or ELICOS colleges or schools, working together and socializing together.

According to my questionnaire survey, more than 90 percent of PRC students in Australia at that time were acquainted with other Chinese students after arriving in Australia. For the purposes of this study, the students' newly formed circles of friends or acquaintances in Australia are defined as their primary social groups. Though these social groups were not originally formed for asylum seeking, the new circumstances in which the PRC students found themselves after June 4 required them to expand or develop integrative bonds in and through their primary social groups to serve their new purpose. June 4 created a unique and urgent situation: students needed to make migration/asylum decisions in the place where they were living, with the help of their newly formed social groups. As discussed later in this chapter, the students started expanding their social groups, or in some cases formed new ones, shortly before June 4. These social groups were to be the principal unit within which individual decisions about asylum seeking were made. Group expansion was extensive and forceful enough not only to initiate their protection campaign, but also to successfully embed their asylum seeking within a structured community context.

Immediately after June 4, these Chinese students had to rely on their primary social groups to help them to cope with their shock and horror, and to obtain information. However, once the local media had begun reporting the Australian government's intention—or, to characterize it more precisely, their promise—to identify so-called 'genuine refugees' in a case-by-case approach, they were greatly disturbed. The group atmosphere changed profoundly and internal tensions arose, because many individual students understood the implications of this: the case-by-case approach would mean that some could be protected while others would have to leave. In other words, they realized that they were all potential competitors and that only well-prepared cases would pass the screening. Similar remarks were made by an interviewee who had been troubled by the case-by-case approach for more than five years and who said that:

> It seems to me, as well all my friends, that the case-by-case [policy] was the real reason why there was a complicated process. What we heard was that [you had] 'to satisfy various criteria,' 'to prove that you are in real danger,' and so on.... to put it bluntly, you had to link yourself to politics, and you had to be 'reactionary.' The more sensational the evidence you could put in your [asylum] application, the better chance you seemed to have (Interviewee 5, 20 February 1998).

Accordingly, many students became dissatisfied with their original social groups, or at least felt a strong need to associate more closely with other students than before. In responses to the survey carried out for this study, these dissatisfactions with existing groups were articulated as stemming from three main causes.

The first was 'the secretiveness of people's intentions.' This referred to the unwillingness of some fellow students in the group to disclose to others any information or intentions with regard to asylum seeking. The second was 'the constant pressure to collect evidence.' This referred to the requirement that each individual student had to gather sufficient and strong evidence of an acceptable kind to support his or her refugee claim. As mentioned, it implied competition with other group members. The third dissatisfaction was 'unsustainable support,' and this referred to the unstable and constantly changing alliances between students as they deliberated and made their asylum-related decisions (One-on-one interviews, 11 and 25 April 1998, and 8 June 1998).

However, even though many students did not consider their social groups reliable or dependable, their groups, existing or new, were the only accessible and established social units they had in which to make their decisions as to whether to seek asylum in Australia and how to pursue it. The pressure to make these decisions made it impossible for them to dissolve their groups. The apparent solution to this problem of the unreliability of their existing social groups was to expand the groups, thus bringing in new individuals, new information, new opinions and new possibilities, until their social groups could actually meet their needs as onshore asylum seekers. In the days, weeks and months after June 4, the students' primary social groups were found to have kept expanding in response to the students' constantly changing circumstances, the most crucial part of which was the Australian government's decision to amend the *Migration Act 1958* while dealing with the PRC student issue.

The motivations behind the expansion of the students' primary social groups were complex. The empirical data suggest four main motives: fear reduction; overcoming uncertainties; comparing actions; and seeking information (One-on-one interviews, 11 and 25 April 1998, and 8 June 1998). Of course, there were some changes over time. Many students felt intense fear originally, but this subsided considerably after a couple of months. The sudden and sizeable expansion of the students' groups at the beginning was motivated by the need to calm their fear and overcome uncertainties, and in the early stages comparing actions was the least important factor although over the asylum seeking process as a whole it was seen as the strongest motivation (One-on-one interviews, 8 June 1998). 'Comparing actions' and 'overcoming uncertainties' appeared to be more closely interrelated than the other motives (One-on-one interviews, and 8 June 1998).

In those early stages, which were from early June 1989 to late March 1990, the groups expanded in several ways. First, and most visibly, the expansion was numerical. Of the groups surveyed in this study, three-fifths of those that had at first contained between nine and 12 people expanded to a size of 52 to 68 people. The remaining two-fifths of the groups grew from containing only five to eight people to a size of between 38 and 60 people (Gao, 2002: 384–386). While expansion was a common trend in most student groups, it should be noted that certain kinds of student groups resisted expansion in this initial phase. Groups that contained a significant number of students who had overstayed their visas expanded much less in the early stages after June 4 than they did later on, while groups that contained postgraduate students (that is, students enrolled in degree courses) actually shrank. This is perhaps an illustration of the 'secretiveness' discussed above, as neither of these two student types wanted others to know whether they were applying to stay in Australia or, more particularly, how they intended to do it.

Size was not the only significant change in the composition of the students' primary social groups. Four other important changes also took place at the same time. The first, and perhaps most obvious, change was the disappearance of geographical distinctions among the students. That is, associating with others from the same part of China became less a concern once the students' focus had quickly shifted to gathering information and ideas from each other to cope with the new situation in which they now found themselves. Second, the distinction between the students studying degree courses and those studying English weakened, and more primary social groups now included at least one postgraduate student (or a person with significantly better English-language skills). Third, and perhaps most significantly, groups began to form direct and close connections with the local Chinese community or other local Australian people. All the groups examined in this research project had formed such local connections, and no less than 75 percent of them were found to have acquired such local contacts shortly after June 4 (Gao, 2002). Fourth, 50 percent of the expanded social groups contained at least one activist ('activist' being defined as a person who had direct contacts with student organizations). Therefore, in addition to expanding numerically, most of the groups expanded in terms of becoming more diverse and connecting themselves with broader contacts outside their immediate circles.

As the students' groups expanded, there was a significant change in their daily discussion topics and activities. Before June 4, conversations had tended to focus on how to stay in Australia (legally or illegally), how to find cheaper ways of maintaining student status, and how to find a job in order to earn more money before leaving Australia. After June 4, their conversation was focused on the political situation in China, rallies or meetings against June 4 being held locally, and what other students were planning to do next (One-on-one interviews, 11 and 25 April 1998, and 8 June 1998). Within two or three weeks after June 4, their conversations revolved around changes in Australia's policy regarding the PRC student protection, individuals' plans for applying to stay, and how to go about applying. Individuals also became more dependent on their groups (Gao, 2002). They engaged in more group discussions about personal matters and decisions, and had longer and more frequent communications with others, often through phone calls that were made on a daily basis. This change laid the foundation for more intensive interactions among the students, which in turn developed the integrative bonds that united them in cohesive social groups that could play a role as the principal organizational units in their campaign.

Changes in Group Patterns

After June 4, two different forms of information regarding the issue of Australian protection for Chinese students were circulating.[4] First, there seemed to be a possibility, even an increasing likelihood that these Chinese students would be allowed to stay permanently in Australia. This could be inferred from the fact that a few months after June 4, the Australian government had extended the students' visas four times.[5] From mid June to late July 1989 alone, no fewer than 17 reports about the issue

[4] Four major newspapers (two English-language newspapers and two Chinese community newspapers) were important sources of information in this regard. The two important Chinese-language newspapers were *Xinbao* (*Australian Chinese Daily*, or *ACD*) and *Sing Tao Newspaper* (*Xingdao Ribao*, or *STN*); the two influential English-language newspapers were *The Australian* and *The Age* in Melbourne and *The Sydney Morning Herald* (*SMH*) in Sydney.

[5] As noted in Chapter One, the decision to offer the students the initial 'temporary protection' visa was made only a few days after June 4 (*The Australian*, 7 June 1989). On 15 June 1989, Bob Hawke, the then Labor Prime Minister, said in Parliament that 'the visa extension to 31 July announced a week ago was being kept under review' (*ACD*, 16 June 1989). On the same day, the minister for DILGEA, Senator Robert Ray, told the media that he would request the Cabinet to approve an intake of 'genuine refugees' to deal with the likely significant increase in the number of asylum applications from Chinese nationals living in Australia. On the following day, 16 June 1989, Bob Hawke announced the second

appeared in the four major newspapers (*ACD, STN, The Australian* and *The Age*, 8 June to 22 July 1989), 12 of which were about the PRC students' right to stay in Australia. These reports also informed the student community in more detail about four possible options: (1) short-term visa extension, (2) one-year visa extension, (3) 'genuine refugee' residency, considered on a case-by-case basis; and (4) permanent residency for all.

It was just because of this plurality of options that tensions emerged within the students' primary social groups. The students regarded the fourth option (the 'blanket approach,' as the media called it) as the ideal solution. However, because the media frequently invoked the scenario of 'genuine refugees' being granted the right to stay on a case-by-case basis, the students were well aware that this was the way that the government was likely to deal with their asylum applications. The case-by-case approach was troubling because, while they felt unable to return to China soon after June 4, it would be also very difficult to provide evidence within such a short period of time to demonstrate that they were 'genuine refugees.' Many students started preparing their refugee applications, but at the same time, many suspected that their fellow students were trying to conceal their plans as to whether to seek asylum and how to pursue it.

As the group atmosphere changed, tensions within the student groups combined with the students' unavoidable dependence on their groups created a dilemma. On the one hand, the students needed their groups, as they were far away from their families and friends, and in many cases, the group was their only social contact and network in their host country. On the other hand, if individual group members were competing against each other to prove that they were bona fide asylum seekers, this would mean that the group itself was not dependable. Interviewees indicated that the continual expansion of their primary social groups proved successful in compensating for these negative aspects of the group (Group-focused interviews, 7 and 14 March 1998). In theory, this finding generally agrees with the results of Simmel (2012), Lewin (1973) and those of Michigan School of group dynamics (e.g., Cartwright and Zander, 1968), but this study was more interested in how group expansion brings about more opportunities than it was in other aspects of how human groups might assist the students in coping with their asylum seeking.[6]

---

visa extension, in this case for one year. While the Australian government was busy dealing with the issue, the media gave it extensive coverage.

6 These scholars put forward such concepts as group cohesiveness, process, conflict, climate, expansion and dynamics, and formed the basis for multiple new academic fields

As George Homans, a founder of behavioral sociology, once pointed out in his pioneering study, *The Human Group* (1951), social interaction 'enables the group to evolve a more elaborate structure' (Mulkay, 1971: 139; Argyle, 1969: 224; Kornblum, 2008: 141).[7] During the formation stage of the PRC student residency issue, three main patterns of their group expansion also emerged as better structures to meet the requests of these students and their changing circumstances. The earliest one might best be described as the 'normal' or 'information-orientated' expansion pattern. When examining political decision making and action in small groups, Kirkpatrick et al. emphasize that 'decision-making is generally characterized by choice behavior. As such, it is necessarily information-dependent' (1976: 36). Therefore, the process often starts with a search for more 'information to reduce the individual's (or group's) uncertainty' (Robertson, 1980: 165). To gain sufficient information, this expansion pattern was a relatively even one, in which each group member would extend his or her contacts outside the group in order to collect more information on which to base his or her asylum seeking decisions. A similar pattern had been evident in the very earliest stages of the student protest against the June 4 incident, when the students needed to gather more information about what had happened in China. In the new context of asylum seeking, however, this expansion also conveniently served the students in other ways: it helped them to overcome a sense of secretiveness and mistrust, while gathering information about the Australia's policies on humanitarian immigration and refugees. All these compensated for any weaknesses or deficiencies within their social group. Because the goal of this type of expansion is to search for alternatives to the students' existing group, this pattern could also be called the 'alternative-oriented' group expansion according to the conventional academic use of the concept. This idea has not only been used in the study of activism (e.g., Taft, 2011: 154), but also in the Asian context (Magno, 1999: 156).

The second type of social group expansion took place in response to tensions within many individual groups. We might call this expansion the 'deviated pattern' or 'deviation pattern' as used by some sociolo-

---

that study small human groups. As a result, researchers have emerged from a variety of academic disciplines, and small groups can now be analyzed from several perspectives: functional, psychoanalytic, development, social identity, communications and systems (see Wheelan, 2005).

[7] For more information about group process, behavior and dynamics, readers are referred to the following: Fararo (2001: 231–243); Reynolds and Littlefield (2005: 115–120); and Allan (2011: 294–300).

gists (see Turner, 1969: 80; Weidlick and Haag, 1983: 170). Unlike the first group expansion pattern, this was an uneven and unpredictable form of expansion in which some members of a student group would extend their contacts selectively to members of other student groups. Two aims were believed to have driven this type of group expansion. First, individual students wanted to collect more—and also more solid—evidence for their asylum applications. Second, advantages could be gained by associating oneself selectively with activists (who not only knew more about politics than many other students, but could also offer stronger evidence for an asylum application) or even directly with certain student political groups and organizations that were emerging at that time. Many PRC students at this stage became members of groups such as the FDC (Federation for Democratic China) or developed closer ties with various activists. This caused the social organization of the student community to depart from its previous, evenly-connected group pattern and brought about changes in the interpersonal relations among students within their groups. In response, the groups expanded even further. Group expansion of this kind took place from mid September 1989 to mid February 1990 against the background of an increasing possibility that many PRC students would be permitted to stay in Australia but that their asylum applications would be dealt with case by case (according to DILGEA) (*ACD*, 14 September 1989; *STN*, 31 October 1989).

The third type of group expansion might be called the 'polarizing pattern,' which took shape when the PRC student community was clearly divided by two different kinds of approach: those who were vigorously preparing themselves to cope with a likely case-by-case approach by the Australian government, and those who were simply hoping for a 'blanket approach.' This pattern was no longer even; indeed, many PRC students became more and more selective in their associations with other students because some of them sought to connect themselves with activists and political groups. As observed in many early studies of group polarization, this type of expansion is a risky shift (Friedkin and Johnson, 2011: 232), resulting from 'social comparison among group members' (Davis and Buskist, 2008: 118). In this student case, this pattern emerged when the Australian government signaled changes to its humanitarian immigration program and refugee policy and decided on the widely expected 'blanket approach' to the student issue (*The Sun*, 8 June 1990). The students had intensified their campaign shortly before the general election was called on 16 February 1990 because they were worried that 'as soon as an election was in the offing, the [Immigration] Department [would be] told to sit on its hands' (*The Australian*, 9 June 1990). A new working group was established by a smaller body of activists who represented some existing student political organizations (including the FDC and the CAD, or the Chinese Alliance for Democracy, whose activities are discussed in Chapter Seven) to cope with the changing situation. Many PRC students regarded this new group, which called itself the 'Chinese Human Rights Investigation Working Group,'[8] as an effort by certain individuals to form a privileged group to secure their own chance to stay in Australia permanently, and this example led many students to seek closer and more direct contacts with activists who not only had stronger backgrounds in student politics, but would also be able to provide them with more written evidence—and evidence that was highly politicized—for their refugee applications.[9] Once this group pattern had begun to take shape, each student group eventually acquired an actual leader, who was in close contact with the leaders of other groups and activists in political groups.

This series of structural changes to the students' social groups was both a driving force in, and a response to, the raising of the PRC student issue in the community, its acknowledgment by many Australians, and its contextualization in the local setting. The newly formed and repeatedly expanding groups were the most important social contact and social unit for students facing the choice between returning home and staying in Australia. However, just like in many other cases, individuals in a group may make more risky and radical decisions, or may adopt more extreme behaviors than they would were they to act individually (Schwartman and Carlone, 2008: 22; Sinha, 2009: 160). This well-documented risky shift phenomenon was also observed in the Chinese student case, and the group-based asylum seeking process was found to be distinct from individual-based asylum seeking. The students' initial social groups were considered unreliable for the purpose of asylum seeking, and this resulted in expansions of the groups. The students' social groups then evolved into a form in which they were structurally fit to pursue a good solution for the

---

[8] When this group published its widely distributed report, titled *Human rights abuses in China: A survey of Chinese citizens in Australia*, in May 1990, it renamed itself as the 'Working Group for the Basic Human Rights of PRC Citizens in Australia' as discussed in the first section, 'Interactions with the Government,' of Chapter Six.

[9] As the student groups were becoming polarized, many students were not so much collecting evidence for their asylum applications as trying to forestall their rejection. According to the procedure for seeking refugee status, highly publicized and politicized documentation (such as anti-Chinese government statements or articles published in a newspaper) was the only guaranteed way to pass the screening.

students' protection and to engage effectively in an organized campaign. In fact, to a large extent, the asylum seeking activities of the Chinese nationals in fact depended on the repeated expansion of their primary social groups, because these expansion activities prepared the student community for the organized campaign they would successfully wage. Group expansion ignited collective activism. As the group structures evolved, the Chinese student community became increasingly organized and politicized in their approach to seeking protection in Australia.

CHAPTER THREE

STRATEGIC IDENTITY CONSTRUCTION

As the PRC student community went about reorganizing itself, it was also setting out on the next step in the process of forming a new refugee identity. From mid July 1989, in the personal advertisement sections of Australia's Chinese-language newspapers, statements opposing the CCP (Chinese Communist Party) and the Chinese government began to come out and then to proliferate; a few such statements also appeared in the English-language print media. This was not new: such statements had appeared in these Chinese community newspapers as early as May 1989, when the student demonstrations in China were escalating into large-scale mass protests. However, mid July saw a dramatic increase in the number of individual PRC students in Australia who chose to advertise their anti-Chinese government, anti-CCP political views.

Most of their published statements were relatively short and simple: a slogan denouncing the June 4 crackdown or the CCP, with one or even more Chinese names appended. The statements were written in both Chinese and English,[1] normally with a slogan or slogans in Chinese characters. Significantly, the names of the signatories were often given in the *pinyin* Romanization system rather than in Chinese characters.

Soon, a new and interesting phenomenon became apparent: the Chinese-language newspapers began to carry statements by individuals denying any connection with the political statements that had so recently been published. Initially, there were only a couple of denials, but over a few months, they proliferated until there were half a dozen in each edition of Australia's main Chinese-language newspapers. Then, from late November 1989, such strange statements appeared less frequently, and in smaller numbers.

Why would so many PRC students wish to spend their hard-earned money on advertising their political position, and thus risk trouble should they return to China later—and then spend more money to make another

[1] A simple survey showed that approximately 50 percent were in Chinese; 15 to 20 percent in English; and roughly one-third were in a mixture of the two (*ACD* and *STN*, 10 July to 16 September 1989).

statement denying their original one or their connection with them? In fact, all of these indicated an important change in the students' approach to their asylum issue. The publication of both the political statements and the subsequent denials was a strategy in the construction of an asylum-seeker identity. The asylum application process required that all asylum seekers would have to provide 'well-founded' evidence to back up their asylum claims. In the late 1980s, a public anti-CCP statement could be accepted as evidence, and these statements were to become a vital element in the formation of the students' new identity as refugees. Retractions, on the other hand, were a form of 'insurance' in case the strategies failed and those who had published anti-CCP statements had to return to China.

This chapter outlines the early stages of refugee identity formation among the PRC students in Australia in the immediate aftermath of June 4, relating the students' initiatives to the Australian government's initial responses to June 4 and the student protection issue. This chapter has the following three sections: (1) the Australian government's panic policy responses to the student issue; (2) the students' collective construction of a new identity; and (3) individuals' strategic identity construction.

The Government's Panic Policy Responses

The information cited in this brief overview of the policy background to the Chinese student protection issue comes from Australian newspapers (both Chinese community newspapers and mainstream English-language newspapers) and written materials provided to the PRC students by the Refugee Advice and Casework Service (RACS) at Migrant Resource Centres (MRC).[2] These two types of information were key sources of information that directly and greatly influenced and shaped the students' asylum-seeking behavior in the early stages. Official documents from DILGEA made little direct impact on the students at that time, given that many of them had a very limited grasp of English and public access to government documents was not so easy in the late 1980s.

---

[2] The Chinese-language newspapers surveyed here were the Sydney-based *ACD* (*Australian Chinese Daily*, or *Xinbao*) and *STN* (*Sing Tao Newspaper*, or *Xingdao Ribao*), and Melbourne-based weeklies, *The Tide* (*Haichao Bao*) and *Chinese Herald* (*Huasheng Bao* in Chinese). The mainstream English-language newspapers were *The Age* and *The Australian*. The names and dates of the newspapers and other details will be supplied wherever needed in later discussions.

As mentioned in Chapter One, the Australian government's approach to the student protection issue was characterized by frequent changes. These were guided by three major policy elements. First, unconditional visa extensions were granted to the PRC students four times. Second, all the PRC students were initially allowed to apply for residency on strong humanitarian grounds, or as refugees, and a change of policy meant that the refugee program became the only option for many of them, especially the 'post-20 June group.' Third, asylum applications from legal visa holders and overstayers had been dealt with separately throughout the entire four or so years of the Chinese student protection issue. I will discuss each of these in turn.

Visa Extensions

In the months following June 4, the Australian government's policy toward the PRC students underwent so many changes that the RACS pointed it out as a problem (in an internal report titled *History of Government Policy on PRC Nationals*). The report observed that the 'subsequent development of this [government's] policy [of dealing with the student issue], combined with major changes to *Migration Act* and new *Regulations*, resulted in confusion' (1990: 1). Initially, the Hawke Labor government offered four unconditional extensions to the students' visas in the first 12 months after June 4. The first visa extension, for less than two months (until 31 July 1989), was offered within just a few days of June 4 to all the Chinese nationals whose entry permits had expired or were about to expire on or shortly after June 4 (*The Australian*, 7 June 1989).

The second extension, reported on 16 June 1989 in Melbourne's main daily newspaper, *The Age*, was confirmed and announced by the Prime Minister, Bob Hawke, in a meeting with Chinese community leaders in Sydney. Like the equivalent policy measure introduced by the Bush Administration in the USA, this second visa offered all the PRC students a one-year stay (from 31 July 1989 to 31 July 1990).[3]

The third unconditional visa extension, first reported by the Chinese-language media on 9 December 1989 (*ACD*, 9 December 1989), lasted from 31 March 1990 to 31 January 1991. This visa extension allowed the Australian government to put off making a decision about the PRC student issue

[3] It should be noted that Canada's approach to its Chinese student issue differed from those of the Bush Administration in the USA and the Hawke Labor government in Australia (as mentioned in Chapter One, footnote 2).

for another ten months, with some commentators regarding it as a compensatory measure for the fact that the government had abandoned its onshore humanitarian immigration program shortly after June 4 by passing the *Migration Legislation Amendment Act 1989* (Cronin, 1993; Crock, 1998b; Schloenhardt, 2003).

The fourth and final unconditional visa extension was announced by Bob Hawke on 6 June 1990 (*The Sun*, 8 June 1990), and then formally re-announced by DILGEA on 27 June 1990 as one of a series of changes to the government's refugee policy. These changes were considered to have been 'designed to toughen the residency terms for refugees who would only get four-year permits rather than immediate permanent residency as at the time' (*The Australian*, June 28, 1990). Under these new rules, all Chinese nationals wishing to stay in Australia would need to apply for a four-year temporary residency visa before 31 January 1991 (the expiry date of the third extended visa), and this special permit would allow them to stay until 30 June 1994.

These constant changes brought added uncertainty and pressure to the Chinese student community, and the students were faced with having to submit application after application and meet deadline after deadline although, on the positive side, these visa extensions were all decided and announced well before the previous visa had expired. Furthermore, the time lag from the initial media report about the possibility of an extended visa to the implementation of the new policy measure grew longer with each new announcement.[4] In consequence, these increasing time lags gave the students more time to learn and understand the government's requirements and then to strategize for the preparation of their application in order to meet the application conditions and each successive visa extension allowed the students more time to complete the application process.[5]

Of course, some commentators in the mainstream English-language media thought that the sudden announcement of the third visa extension was a gambit related to the general election, called on 16 February 1990

[4] The second visa extension was decided upon within ten days of the offering of the first protection visa, and the last two extensions were announced well before the previous visas were halfway through their term. These time lags were interpreted by some as giving the appearance that the Australian government was gradually giving in to the students' demands for residency (*ACD*, 8 June 1990; *The Tide*, 15 December 1992).

[5] For example, the third extension, suddenly announced on 9 December 1989, gave the students an extra six months before the second protection visa expired.

and held on 24 March (*The Australian*, 21 February 1990). For their part, some Chinese students and Chinese community leaders believed that the third visa extension was offered in order to give the students more time to prepare their cases (*ACD*, 21 February 1990). At the time, the students had to choose between options, had a lot of information to deal with and needed time to consider their strategy and all these things were slowing the application process down significantly (*The Tide*, No. 3, March 1990). In the case of the third visa extension, the situation was further complicated by the introduction of a new policy to divide the students into the 'pre-20 June group' and the 'post-20 June group' (as explained in Chapter One). As well as signifying the government's intention to deal with legal visa holders and overstayers separately,[6] this rigid division also indicated to the student community that the Australian government really wanted to reduce the numbers of PRC nationals to whom residency/asylum needed to be offered.

Abolition of the Onshore Humanitarian Program

Before 19 December 1989, when the *Migration Legislation Amendment Act 1989* was enacted, 'persons eligible to obtain permanent residency from within Australia' could include refugees; asylum seekers; spouses, parents and children of Australian citizens or permanent residents; some professional and occupational categories; and foreign nationals with strong compassionate or humanitarian claims (Cronin, 1993: 91; RACS, 1990). Immediately after June 4, PRC students could apply for residency either on strong humanitarian grounds or through the refugee program. To obtain residency on humanitarian grounds, applicants were minimally required to establish that a natural disaster or political turmoil had taken place in their home country, and then the Minister for Immigration had to formally recognize that these situations 'severely and directly affected them' as individuals (*Regulation 141*, cited in Cronin, 1993: 94). Also according to the DILGEA *Instruction Manual* of 1989, applicants had to make or simply sign a number of statutory declarations stating that they had 'experienced or had a sound basis for expecting substantial violation of their human rights in their home countries' (Cronin, 1993: 97). This process was far

[6] As a bureaucratic measure, the new 829 and 434 TEP (temporary entry permit) visa categories were also introduced by the DILGEA for these two constituencies (*STN*, 9 December 1989; *ACD*, 20 December 1989; RACS, 1990: 2).

easier than the application process for residency under the refugee program, whereby people's circumstances had to meet the definition of 'refugee,' which is set out in the United Nations Convention on Refugees and to be accepted by an independent committee called the DORS (Determination of Refugee Status) (Kabala, 1993). The DORS, which contained representatives from a few interested Australian federal government departments and agencies, such as Foreign Affairs and the Attorney-General's office, made their decision 'very much on a case-by-case basis' (Bruer and Power, 1993: 116).

In 1989, both the humanitarian immigration and refugee programs in Australia were undergoing sweeping changes as part of a general review of the country's immigration policies. These changes, as mentioned, were aimed at controlling the increasing numbers of overstayers and onshore asylum claimants, among whom PRC nationals were a very significant presence (Cronin, 1993). As mentioned in Chapter One, there were 11 amendments to the *Migration Act 1958* and the subsequent *Migration Legislation Amendment Act 1989* between 1989 and 1992. There were 58 amendments to many regulations governing Australia's immigration programs, and more than half a dozen major changes to the humanitarian and refugee programs.[7] These amendments and changes, which may in fact have been prompted by their presence, narrowed the options for the Chinese students. The abolition of the onshore humanitarian immigration program meant that if they wanted to stay in Australia, they would need to apply for refugee status.

Of the six major changes to the humanitarian and refugee programs, four were made within a year from June 4, that is, before June 1990. The newly drafted *Migration Legislation Amendment Act 1989* took effect on 19 December 1989. Before that date, legal temporary entry permit (TEP) holders and overstayers had all been eligible to apply for residency on humanitarian grounds or as refugees (*STN*, 9 December 1989; RACS, 1990: 2). After 19 December 1989, the onshore humanitarian program ceased to exist, but the government introduced a provision to make two types of TEPs available to PRC students who had been in Australia on 20 June 1989 (TEPs 829

[7] For more information, readers are referred to the following publications: Hyndman (1989), Cronin (1993), Crock (1998b), McMaster (2001), Germov and Motta (2003) and Jupp (2003), especially 'A Culture of Control: An Overview of Immigration Policy-Making' by Katherine Cronin (1993), in James Jupp and Marie Kabala (eds.), *The Politics of Australian Immigration*. Canberra: AGPS, pp. 83–104.

and 434). This provision allowed them to apply for residency under the old *Migration Act 1958* before 31 March 1990 (*ACD*, 20 December 1989). In other words, the government brought back the humanitarian program for a couple of extra months to allow the PRC students to prepare their case. The slowness of the application process prompted DILGEA to introduce a new regulation (*Regulation 142A*) on 21 February 1990 that allowed 829 (legal) TEP holders to seek residency on grounds similar to strong humanitarian grounds before 27 June 1990 (RACS, 1990: 2). *Regulation 142A* was repealed on 27 June 1990 and the 'PRC (TEP),' introduced on 5 July 1990, gave all PRC nationals a protection visa until 30 June 1994 (Germov and Motta, 2003: 41). As a result, the humanitarian immigration program for residency claimants or other asylum seekers within Australia ceased to exist in Australia (Joint Standing Committee on Migration Regulations, 1990, 1992).

In addition to these new restrictions, other changes were also made to the onshore humanitarian immigration and refugee programs and these shaped the behavior of the Chinese students in response. Under the new *Migration Legislation Amendment Act 1989* and its related regulations, only refugee applicants—and not those seeking residency through the onshore, strong humanitarian program—had access to the judicial review system if their applications were not successful. Overstayers would be deported within 28 days of the rejection of their refugee application or their failure to appeal to a court or tribunal (Joint Standing Committee on Migration Regulations, 1990, 1992). At the same time, DILGEA decided to disallow onshore refugee applicants from regaining a student visa if their application for refugee status was refused. All these policies made the asylum seeking process not only rigid but also very complicated, and restricted the types of action the students could perform.

Legal Applicants and Overstayers

Also in 1989, those overseeing the Australian immigration program were concerned about the large numbers of overstayers and onshore asylum claimants. Numerous measures were drawn up and implemented in order to control people who entered Australia and overstayed the terms of their permits, and then applied from within Australia to stay permanently in the country. PRC nationals were 'the largest numerical group (7971) in the overstay population' at the time (Cronin, 1993: 86). One media report estimated that as many as 52 percent of PRC nationals had overstayed in June 1989 (*The Australian*, 8 June 1989), and a research-based estimate put the figure at 41 percent (Jupp, 1991: 93), while another leading daily newspaper reported that no less than 40 percent of them were overstayers (*The Age*, 26 July 1989). The RACS and student groups argued that, technically speaking, the high percentage of overstayers was caused by the Overseas Students Office (OSO), because they had stopped processing almost all visa applications from Chinese nationals after June 4. The problem was compounded by DILGEA's policy of treating legal permit holders and overstayers differently (RACS, 1990; *STN*, 22 March 1990). One year later, when the four-year special temporary protection visa was offered, the number of PRC overstayers was reportedly about 6,500 (*The Age*, 8 June 1990; *The Australian*, 9 June 1990); a Chinese community media source estimated that 42 percent of Chinese nationals in Australia had overstayed (*ACD*, 1 September 1989).

In actual practice, the Australian government, or precisely DILGEA, had put into operation a number of new polices and procedures in order to differentiate overstayers from legal visa holders. When the students applied for the four unconditional protection visas, legal applicants and overstayers were issued with different visas; more precisely, overstayers were not given any actual visa after the first extension, but had to register with DILGEA instead. This galvanized their attempts to form a case for refugee status and thus obtain a chance of residency equal to that of the legal visa holders. Arguing from the beginning that they were victims of a political disaster and should be identified and treated as refugees, they started to collect evidence earlier than other students did and sought the most solid evidence.

Changes to both the onshore humanitarian immigration program and the refugee program also made overstayers ineligible to seek residency in Australia on strong humanitarian grounds. This meant that the more than 40 percent of the PRC students who were overstayers could only apply for residency/asylum through the refugee program. The new DILGEA policy also prohibited applicants for either program to retain a student visa if their applications were unsuccessful. That is to say, unsuccessful applicants had to leave Australia when their applications were rejected. For this reason, the Secretary of DILGEA at the time described applying for residency through either program as an action that 'burns down the bridge to return to their own country' (*STN*, 31 October 1989). Also for this reason, the students were prepared do whatever they could to prepare a successful refugee case.

The Collective Construction of a New Identity

Before they could make any major decisions or take any further action in their protection campaign, the PRC student community had to devote an enormous amount of time to discussing and trying to understand each of these successive changes in government policy. They had to learn what the criteria were for each visa category or for asylum before they could know whether and how they could meet them.

As each individual student sought to meet the criteria, this disparate group formed itself into a community of asylum seekers—or, as I have termed it in Chapter One, they underwent a collective identity formation process to envisage and present themselves as political refugees. To form a coherent identity as a seeker of a protection visa and then of political asylum, careful reading and interpretation of media reports, in Chinese and English, and other types of information regarding the government's approaches and policies was required, and these also needed to be then translated into appropriate actions. The PRC students in Australia felt that they were 'caught between two fires' at the time. On the one hand there was June 4, which some Western media reports went so far as to describe as the start of a civil war in China (*The Age*, 8 June 1989). Reliant on such reports, these PRC students felt that returning to China would be impossible. On the other hand, the Australian government seemed to be very reluctant—if not unable—to make a speedy decision on whether, and how, to offer them protection. Throughout the government's many changes of approach, its principal position until late 1993 (i.e. until the '1 November [1993] decisions' made by the Keating Labor government) seemed to be a refusal to offer the students across-the-board protection and an insistence that the PRC student protection issue be dealt with on a case-by-case basis (*The Australian*, 6 September 1989; Slattery, 1991).

Faced with the specificities of individual asylum claimants rather than with collective opportunities to become protected in Australia, there were two fronts on which these students could make their own collective efforts. First, ongoing discussions could be carried out as to what in general needed to be done if individuals wished to seek asylum in Australia, especially if seeking refugee status. As the Australian government kept changing its strategies, approaches and policies on the PRC student protection issue, no information was considered officially final, complete and reliable. All discussions, therefore, seemed to be based on incomplete information, and information-gathering activities were hampered and prolonged.

Second, the PRC students had to make themselves eligible to apply for each new category of protection visas that were offered, including the offer of permanent residency—and they had to do this in time to meet the deadlines set by DILGEA. As the students' understandings of the asylum eligibility requirements changed, new government policies continued to generate ongoing discussion among the students, setting in motion the process of constructing the kind of identity—in line with the DILGEA directives—that the students urgently needed. The changing government policies and procedures shaped the formulas for the students to follow by telling them what they would need to do in order to make themselves fully eligible to be granted permanent residency or political asylum in Australia.

Based on information gathered from several groups of interviewees, I have traced the collective construction of the PRC students' new political identity as asylum seekers through three major stages. Some individual students used different expressions to name them, but the process seemed to include the following stages: (1) an information-gathering stage, (2) an information-analyzing stage, and (3) a task-forming stage. As one former student noted:

> Whenever we discussed our problems, we always asked each other a set of similar questions: whether they knew anything new about the government policy or decision, what their understanding of the new policy was, and what they were going to do after that (Group-focused interviews, 21 March 1998).

These questions were aired frequently and in every possible forum, from brief phone calls to long discussions among many groups.

At every stage, three features were particularly apparent in the PRC students' collective identity formation process, and a number of research questions were also used to target each one: (1) the involvement of every group member in the discussion (did each member have an equal chance to play a part in group discussion?) (2) the openness of the discussion (were members aware of secretiveness on the part of other members?), and (3) the dependence of group members on each other (what level of contact did group members feel they needed with each other in this process?). These features varied over time. However, most interviewees indicated that the earliest stage of this collective identity construction process (the information-gathering stage) was non-exclusive (that is, the students felt that they could take equal part in their group discussions), and that group members were not secretive and were interdependent. The second stage (the information-analyzing stage) was also considered 'non exclusive' and 'non-secretive,' but the students felt that they actually became 'less interdependent.' This was because more group members made their own independent interpretations of each policy change, relating each change in policy precisely to their own circumstances and considering the legal implications for their own case to decide whether they were eligible for each new requirement. Accordingly, the third (task-forming) stage was found by the majority of the interviewees to be characterized for the most part as exclusive, secretive and 'less interdependent.'

Some group-based research discussions brought forward two further aspects of the group discussion process, or the collective construction of a new asylum seeker identity. The first aspect relates to secretiveness, which particularly affected the students in the task-forming stage. Group members not only became more secretive themselves, but also felt the effects of this negative aspect of their social groups when they were all formulating an actual task related to their application to stay in Australia. Many former students admitted that although they all liked discussing various 'countermeasures' in response to policy changes, they kept their final decisions (regarding actions or tasks) to themselves. One student, who described himself as 'a victim of secretiveness,' believed that the connection between task formation and secretiveness was entirely due to the government's case-by-case approach, or their endless talk about it, which caused competition among the students. Many students appeared to have believed at the time that if they helped someone else to prepare a strong asylum case, then their own slim chance of staying permanently in Australia would become even slimmer. Because of this widespread and deeply rooted misconception, many PRC students continually assumed that others were concealing their own strategies.

Second, contrary to what is often assumed by some researchers about group behavior (e.g. Ellis and Fisher, 1994), information or knowledge appeared to be of secondary importance in determining the social capital of group members. Generally, information or knowledge is considered one of the most critical components of social capital in a group context. Members who command more social capital or knowledge than others are assumed to have a higher level of charisma, prestige or power based on their ability to enter into transactions or exchanges with others over that knowledge (Ellis and Fisher, 1994: 5). In this case of the Chinese students, however, where group members freely exchanged their opinions at the information-analyzing stage, but not at the task-forming stage, when an ability to develop some strategies was required, the ability to decide on an appropriate course of action was regarded as a more important form of social capital than the possession of information or knowledge. Some students became group leaders or community activists precisely because of their ability to decide on an appropriate strategy, make detailed plans, and identify a practical way to achieve their goals (for example, where to collect evidence, and how to interpret it sensibly and integrate it into an asylum application).

Another noteworthy and vital characteristic of the collective process of constructing a new socio-political identity as asylum seekers was the tendency to exaggerate the criteria for asylum that the government kept issuing and repeatedly revising. According to the interviewees, almost all discussions of the asylum criteria within student groups at every stage of their identity construction process ended with exaggerated interpretations of what the government required. The students' own perceptions of the criteria are crucial, because they affected the intensity of the collective effort to form a new refugee identity, prompting more students to go to greater lengths than might otherwise have been the case. In my research discussions, it emerged that exaggerated explanations of the criteria for refugee status in the information-gathering stage were simply the result of incomplete information about the asylum seeking process in Australia, which was compounded by the limited English language skills of most of the PRC students at the time.

There was widespread scepticism about the Australian government's motives in making so many, and such frequent, policy changes. Many students appeared to believe that there existed an extra—and unknown—set of criteria for assessing asylum applications, besides the criteria they knew about. Many students never considered the information that they had to be complete, always imagining that there was more information they needed to know or collect (for example, whether or not the level of education was to be considered). As will be discussed below, this scepticism led to the widespread assumption that they would have to collect more and more evidence, and also stronger evidence, for their asylum cases, or that they needed to take part in more and more extreme political activities in order to meet the criteria for political asylum. Early on, their scepticism fed their worries and anxieties; over time it then combined with the exaggerated explanations to become a way of thinking. It appeared that these students were always on the alert, and they all believed that they could not afford to ignore and misjudge the value of any asylum-related information because, in the immediate aftermath of June 4, they could not return to China.

The more serious the context of the information that the Australian government supplied, the more the students tended to exaggerate their interpretations. For example, many students became very worried when applying for one of the two bridging visas (829 TEP and 434 TEP). The purpose of introducing these bridging visas was, as noted above, to make the PRC students eligible to apply for residency on strong humanitarian grounds after 19 December 1989 when the old *Migration Act 1958* was to be amended and the *Migration Legislation Amendment Act 1989* was to take effect, with the onshore humanitarian program then being abolished. Despite this preferential treatment, many students, and in particular the overstayers, suspected that there were other motives behind the introduction of these special bridging visas. More information was then sought and a number of exaggerated interpretations were made (for example, these two visas were seen as a measure to identify and register thousands of overstayers who were hiding from the immigration department).

In fact, my in-depth interviews with the students indicated that even if information was clear and complete, the students still actively refused to consider it complete, preferring to 'leave leeway for further changes,' or 'better to overdo than underdo,' and 'substitute for the part of the policy that we don't know.' To explain why the students processed information in this way, one interviewee offered the following observation:

> We are a generation that knows a popular Chinese saying very well, which is 'be prepared for the worst.' Since we were thinking about something in that way, we formed our approach: 'leave leeway for further changes.' All our discussions of the government's policies and the [asylum] criteria were somehow exaggerated or left with 'leeway.' Our common understanding and practice were that if one item of evidence was required, you'd better provide them with two or three items.... We had to offer more evidence instead of waiting for a refusal (Interviewee 46, 30 May 1998).

Because of the scepticism about the two bridging visas, for example, a few student groups, such as the CAD, the IFCSSA and the FDC, were all asked to invite some 'people from the authorities' (i.e. DILGEA or other government departments) to attend their meetings and answer questions about their visa issues. To gather more information from the government, a group representing ELICOS students and overstayers (the Federation of Chinese Full-Fee Paying Students or FCFFPS) was formed in order to contact the government offices as a proper student organization (One-on-one interviews, 11 and 25 April 1998).

Of course, the personal background of each student was also a very important factor in the exaggerated interpretations of various policies.

Each individual's determination to seek asylum, or residency, and their personal situation vis-à-vis the eligibility requirements, also shaped their approach to the preparation and presentation their asylum case. It seemed that the stronger a student's determination to seek permanent residency in Australia, the more exaggerated would be his or her interpretation of the asylum criteria. The less a student's socio-political background met the asylum eligibility requirements, the more he or she would exaggerate the asylum criteria. It seemed that students, who belonged to social class groups that had been frequent targets of political repressions in China's recent past, including journalists and university lecturers, had less need to exaggerate than those who were from social class groups that had been considered politically loyal to the CCP (such as CCP members, workers, peasants, and soldiers of the PLA or People's Liberation Army).[8]

Strategic Identity Construction by Individuals

As the PRC students developed their understanding of what constituted eligibility for a refugee case, the next step was to form their new political identity as asylum seekers, or their 'singularised identity designation' as some scholars have called it (Jacobs and Fincher, 1998: 8). This involved a clearly defined task for each individual asylum claimant: to collect and present, or in many cases to create, evidence that they met the criteria for protection or permanent residency on strong humanitarian grounds, or for seeking political asylum through the refugee program. This evidence-gathering process did not finish until all the PRC students were granted permanent residency in 1994.

To apply for protection through refugee status in Australia or to seek permanent residency on strong humanitarian grounds in the late 1980s and early 1990s, applicants were required to attach at least one piece of evidence to their application to support their claims. Just a few days after June 4, in a message that was apparently intended to assure Australian people that those Chinese students were not automatically qualified to

[8] According to Lin (2006), there were two major social class groups in post-1949 China for many years. The 'people's' classes that the CCP relied on included party members, workers, peasants, revolutionary cadres, and soldiers. 'Class enemies' included a wide range of social groups, defined by their property and business ownership before 1949 and their political attitudes and affiliation after 1949. These two groups received different treatment in China (Lin, 2006: 182). For more information, readers are referred to the following: Bianco (2001: 38); Blecher (2010: 28); Li (2004: 86); and Pepper (2000: 297).

stay permanently and there would be no sudden large influx of refugees from mainland China that was then regarded as a very backward country, the mainstream English-language media mentioned the requirement for supporting evidence in the asylum application (*The Australian*, 6 and 7 June 1989; *The Sun*, 8 June 1990). However, staff of RACS and Chinese community organizations, and the ethnic Chinese community media at a later stage, urged all the Chinese students to take immediate action: to collect, or start to consider how to collect, evidence to support their applications for residency/asylum. The students were told to collect as much written evidence as they could that would place them in accordance with the second half of the UN's refugee definition, namely 'well-founded fear of persecution, for reasons of race, religion, nationality, membership of a particular social group, or political opinion' (cited in Black, 1991: 283). Many PRC students were also advised by the staff of RACS, and by JPs in local Chinese communities as well,[9] to conclude a statement in their applications, clearly stating that more evidence would be provided later.

Some of the students' evidence-collecting initiatives were evidently low-risk practices, where the individuals concerned would be difficult or impossible to identify and where involvement would be easy to deny if, in the end, they had no choice but to return to China. Low-risk practices included simply placing a public protest statement in a Chinese-language newspaper in Australia (as described at the outset of the present chapter), or taking photos during public protest activities held in Australia. More politically venturesome exercises included involvement in anti-CCP or anti-Chinese Government activities or organizations in Australia and, more particularly, being identified as an activist.

In general, the students were found to have, one after another, utilized about ten different methods of gathering evidence for their asylum application. These general methods are presented in Table 3.1, arranged into three main categories according to the source of the evidence: (1) locally collected evidence, (2) evidence from family, relatives or friends in China or elsewhere, and (3) evidence from relevant authorities in China.

[9] A JP or Justice of Peace is a member of the community who voluntarily plays a role in witnessing and signing statuary declarations, and certifying copies of documents. For more information, readers can visit: http://australia.gov.au/topics/law-and-justice/justices-of-the-peace

Table 3.1 General methods of collecting evidence.

Descriptions of Three Types	Number of Mentions*
Locally collected evidence	
1. Taking a photo in public protest activities in Australia	46
2. Advertising a public statement in a Chinese community newspaper	46
3. Asking a close friend to write something to support one's application	46
4. Having an article protesting June 4 published	37
5. Having a photo of oneself protesting June 4 published	37
6. Placing a public statement in an English-language newspaper	34
Evidence from family, relatives or friends in China or elsewhere	
1. Asking family members, or relatives, in China to write something supportive	46
2. Asking former colleagues to write something supportive	42
Evidence from relevant authorities in China	
1. Receiving a letter from one's former employer about deprivation of one's right to work	46
2. Receiving a letter from one's former employer about deprivation of one's right to have a house	42
3. Receiving written evidence from any other relevant authorities	38

* *Based on 52 applicable records of individual-focused interviews.*

The above three major categories of evidence for asylum seeking, and those ten or so general ways of collecting them, are discussed in more detail below.

Locally Collected Evidence

'Locally collected evidence' refers to the evidence that the students had collected from within Australia.[10] The first section of Table 3.1 is based on data from individual-focused interviews, in which former students were

[10] Here I have excluded certain types of evidence that some students collected through highly politicized and organized activities, such as membership and leadership positions in political organizations (these are examined in Chapters Four and Seven). I have

asked to comment on ways of collecting evidence at the time when they were preparing their asylum applications. Six commonly utilized methods were identified, but the first three methods were evidently used more commonly than other methods.[11]

Many students interviewed expressed a general belief that collecting evidence in Australia was much easier than collecting it from family or friends in China or elsewhere, or collecting it from institutions in China (discussed below). Many decided to gather this evidence locally simply in order to apply for a number of extended protection visas within a short period.[12] Collecting evidence within Australia was easier in three ways. First, it was quicker, more reachable and more convenient than gathering evidence from China or elsewhere. Second, it made it easy for evidence to be compared across cases. In Australia, the students somehow knew what other individuals were collecting and how they had been doing it. In order to present their own case with the same circumstances, or before finding out a way to collect solid evidence, many students had adopted the most conservative strategy, which was to do what other students had done. One interviewee made the following comment:

> Despite the secretiveness that we sensed in our groups at the time, we could actually observe each other, as we were well networked through sharing house, working together or participating the same activities. As a result, we all roughly knew what evidence the others collected. An approach that most of us had adopted in collecting evidence was to collect whatever other students were collecting and to show the seriousness of our own circumstances at whatever level as others (Interviewee 10, 12 April 1998).

As a result, this comparability of evidence initially became a source of security, allowing them to feel that they were all 'in the same boat' as the others. In fact, this comparability resulted in that the evidence collected by a large proportion of the students was more or less the same; and this, one Australian tabloid suggested, was what made the 'blanket approach'

---

also excluded other methods that were rarely mentioned by interviewees (see the next footnote).

[11] The seventh one, for example, was 'Asking an Australian citizen of Anglo-Saxon background to act as a witness to a statement.' The number of mentions of the seventh method was significantly lower than the sixth method (fewer than 50 percent of the students interviewed).

[12] Policy changes made by the Australian government at the time coupled with students' limited language skills meant that some had applied for six or seven different visa types—even eight in some cases—before all PRC students were given a temporary four-year visa in June 1990.

the only option to deal with the student issue in the end (*The Sun*, 8 June 1990). However, this ease of comparison also appeared to lead to competition among the students to collect more evidence, and more solid evidence, than the others and thus to strengthen their own case for asylum.

Third, collecting evidence locally was easier because it was, as many former students mentioned in many interviews, 'safer' than seeking evidence in China or even elsewhere. It was safer in a number of ways. Many students did not want to be found out by the Chinese authorities for collecting such evidence (One-on-one interviews, 11 and 25 April 1998). Some felt that local evidence could in fact signal a more convincing kind of political involvement. In Australia they could freely engage in activities that in China would be considered 'anti-CCP' or anti-Chinese government (and therefore coming to mean 'counter-revolutionary'), but which perfectly fitted in with UN's refugee criteria; and the fact that there was no risk in collecting such evidence outside China was a bonus.

Another factor that made local evidence collected in Australia less politically risky was the difference between Chinese and English scripts. If students published anti-CCP or anti-Chinese government statements in a newspaper with their names spelt in *Pinyin*, the Romanized Chinese phonetic system, rather than written in Chinese characters, it would be difficult or impossible to link the names with the Chinese characters and therefore identify the individuals concerned. Indeed, some students even reversed the Chinese name order (family name followed by given name) and put their names in the English order when publishing their statements. This method made it even more difficult to recognize particular individuals. Some students even advised their peers that it would make better sense to Australian officers, including DILGEA's refugee case officers, if their statements as well as their names were in *Pinyin* and not written in Chinese characters. In interviews, many students mentioned cases where people had published an anti-CCP or anti-Chinese government statement in English, then later published a statement in Chinese claiming that they had no connection with the original statement. The statement published in English would be used in their asylum application, and the statement in Chinese could be kept in case they needed to prove their innocence one day back in China when questioned.[13]

[13] Readers interested in reading such statements can consult the Sydney-based *Xinbao* (*Australian Chinese Daily*, or *ACD*) or the Melbourne-based *Haichao Bao* (*The Tide*), which started publishing these advertisements from late June 1989. It was only after early December 1989 that they became rare.

Students weighted different kinds of evidence differently in terms of their importance to an asylum application. On a scale of 1 to 5, the most significant and supportive type of evidence (5 out of 5) was published, photographic evidence or published articles protesting against the CCP or June 4. However, among the interviewees a greater number believed that photographs were considered more significant than any other published item. 'Publishing a statement in a mainstream English-language newspaper' was considered the second most valuable type of evidence (4 out of 5). The third best was 'Taking a photo at public protest activities' (3 out of 5). 'Publishing a statement in a Chinese community newspaper' was the fourth most valuable (2 out of 5) and 'Asking a close friend to write a supporting statement' was rated 1 out of 5 for importance.

Table 3.1 also records the frequency of mention of different types of evidence. Of the six commonly utilized methods identified, the first three were apparently more commonly used than the others. Students seemed also very aware of the distinction between the quantity and the quality of evidence from the very beginning, though some initially seemed to favor quantity and collected large amounts of evidence until they had acquired evidence that had 'real substance' (such as membership in the FDC or the CAD).

Evidence from Family, Relatives or Friends in China or Elsewhere

This type of evidence was collected in two ways and in a wide range of forms. Table 3.2 lists 11 sub-types and indicates the significance of each on a five-point scale based on in-depth interviews. Table 3.2 indicates that the former students interviewed for this research project considered evidence from China or elsewhere to be more significant than locally collected evidence, and they identified five types as 'very important' for their asylum seeking; average ratings on the five-point scale were clearly higher than for locally collected evidence which was discussed in the previous section.

Two reasons were put forward to explain why this type of evidence was rated more highly than local evidence collected from within Australia. First, it actually diversified what each asylum seeker could put into their application. Until June 4, the PRC students had not been well prepared for seeking political asylum in Australia, and it was difficult for many to gather evidence at the time. After June 4, many students quickly realized that the more types of evidence they could produce, the more 'complex' their asylum case would be. 'Complex' applications were believed to be

Table 3.2 Evidence from family, relatives or friends in China or elsewhere.

Descriptions of Evidence*	Significance on a Five-Point Scale
1. Suspension of one's right to work in one's work unit in China;	5
2. One's house taken back by his/her work unit;	5
3. The police investigating the issues relating to one's involvement in the protest in Australia;	4–5
4. Officers from one's work unit making the same inquires;	4–5
5. Officers from local neighborhood committee making the same inquires;	4–5
6. The same inquiries being made in family members' work units;	3–4
7. A member of one's family being arrested or removed from a job;	3–4
8. One's colleagues being arrested, exiled or removed from a job;	3–4
9. One's colleagues in China hearing of someone mentioning his/her involvement in the protest in Australia;	3
10. Officers from one's work unit naming his/her name at a meeting;	3
11. Letters telling of one's family's tragedies in the Cultural Revolution period or before	2

* *Based on 52 applicable records of individual-focused interviews.*

appealing to refugee case officers because most applications submitted by the PRC students were far too simple and short to be considered.[14] A longer, more complicated application was believed to be decisive for a positive outcome. Second, because this kind of evidence came from in-country, it substantially met the asylum requirements set by DILGEA, or it was at least very close to what RACS staff members and the Chinese community media had suggested that the students should collect. In other

[14] For example, some claims were simply based on the applicant's family background as a member of one of the so-called 'five bad social classes' (*hei wulei*) status. As Wang (1996) articulates it, 'Mao's China was divided into the revolutionary hierarchy of *hong wulei* (five red categories), *hei wulei* (five black categories), and *niu gui she shen* (monsters and demons)' (1996: 18). These Maoist policies had been abandoned in the late 1970s and early 1980s, and it seemed foolish to base an asylum claim on this. For more information about the Maoist era class categories, see Barmé (1996) and Schrift (2001).

words, after a short period of panic and confusion over the procedures and criteria for seeking asylum onshore and numerous policy changes, many Chinese students learned (from the media and from contacts with various institutions, including RACS and DILGEA itself) what kind of evidence would be expected to present a reasonable or strong case for refugee status.[15]

Evidence from China or elsewhere was collected both directly and indirectly. The direct way included making a few phone calls to family members or friends in China or elsewhere, or writing letters telling them that, for whatever reason, an application to continue to stay in Australia had to be handed in. The students might word their requests in various ways, but some of them often directly asked for materials to support their application. The interview results indicated that this direct way was most often used by the students from social classes that had arguably suffered little political persecution before the 1980s, such as workers, peasants or PLA soldiers. Students who came from major cities or had worked for large institutions before leaving China, and most particularly those from families that had suffered from political persecution, were less likely to have used this method to collect evidence. One interviewee offered the following explanation:

> This [method] was also in the main used by the students who were originally from rural areas or small towns and small cities, and they did not really believe that their families [in China] were monitored or under any surveillance. However, it seemed to me that the main reason was that they and their families had never experienced real 'Cultural Revolution-style' torture and persecution before. For the same reason, those [who were] from big cities and [worked for] big institutions did not do things in such a direct way because of what they had experienced in China in the 1960s (Interviewee 33, 13 April 1998).

As a result of the above difference in behavior, numerous students from revolutionary, 'fear-free,' family backgrounds (by Chinese standards) or from politically privileged families (of the Five Red Categories; see the very first footnote of this section) had collected more, and more solid, evidence for their asylum applications than those who had suffered from

15 Some student activists claimed in interviews that being told by organizations about what was required in an application had caused them to think that case officers would believe whatever evidence they were given, and that this in turn had led some students to believe that seeking asylum was not a process of showing their past political involvement, but rather a practice of proving their loyalty to a new country by producing a few items of evidence. This was another way in which the students' asylum seeking became a strategic process of forming a new political identity.

political persecution (One-on-one interviews, 11 and 25 April 1998). To a great extent, this was a significant change to students' qualification for seeking asylum, and the evidence collected by these different approaches actually redistributed what a number of students called 'political capital,' or social capital as lately used by many other researchers, among these PRC students (One-on-one interviews, 11 and 25 April 1998). Even if some students themselves knew that this type of evidence was not very reliable, they felt that the case officers would consider them differently because they were not from the place where they were then living. As a result, the students who had not collected solid enough evidence needed to work harder at collecting evidence. That is, it intensified competition among the students.

The indirect way of collecting evidence from some people in China or elsewhere was found to have been used by students whose backgrounds were sensitive to politics, who came from politically stigmatized families (such as the *hei wulei* or five black categories mentioned above) and by individuals who were concerned lest they give trouble to their relatives or friends. They needed to be skilful in writing to family members and friends if they wanted to obtain evidence from them without mentioning precisely what they wanted to have and why. One widely used method was to ask questions that would be definitely answered in a negative way with a few bad stories (for example, that the student's house or apartment had been taken back by his/her work unit, or that his or her position had been suspended). As to be detailed in the following section, answers to this type of question were normally negative in the late 1980s, which was believed to be very helpful, perfectly fitting the political definition of a refugee and guaranteeing residency/asylum. Such evidence was thought to be stronger and more objective than if it came from friends or, more particularly, former colleagues than from family members.

The indirect method of collecting evidence could also be deployed in either an 'obvious way' or a 'vague way.' The 'obvious way' was to write and ask former colleagues or friends in China several direct questions, without mentioning why they were asking and without making any direct request. For example, they might ask, 'Has anyone been questioned by police in relation to the trouble?' These questions could be expected to elicit something of a negative and political nature that they could then use in their asylum applications. At the time, the students had already learned from the media and refugee case officers that their asylum claims needed to be supported by negative comments on the political situation in China. The reality was that the students rarely received any positive replies from China in the aftermath of June 4.

The 'vague way' involved simply waiting to receive information from friends and colleagues in China that could be useful for an asylum case, without asking any direct questions. The political tensions in China after June 4 decided that students were very likely to receive bad news from China and pessimistic comments about what had happened there. Some students began to collect such written evidence or statements right after June 4, as soon as they understood that they would need them for their asylum applications.

Evidence from Relevant Authorities in China

As outlined in Table 3.1, this type of written evidence was collected in three ways. Mostly it came from the student's former *danwei* (work unit or workplace).[16] This method of collecting evidence was first employed three to four months after June 4, when the students were intensifying their efforts to collect written evidence for their asylum applications and their asylum-seeking activities were becoming more organized, marked by the establishment of an Australian branch of the FDC. Membership of this new anti-CCP organization was regarded as the strongest evidence to use in applications for political asylum, allowing many to claim that they had 'well-founded fear.' This changed many students' understanding of their eligibility for asylum, and it emboldened more of them to join in the process of strategic identity formation as refugees.

The direct collection of written evidence from Chinese institutions in China was a new method. The logic was simple: the students with FDC membership could argue that they would be persecuted if they returned to China, but it would be even stronger than the FDC membership if one could present evidence from China confirming that they had already lost their job or had lost the right to housing. In fact, receiving letters warning

---

16 The *danwei* was the basic social organizational form in China at the time, and the lowest level of China's multi-tiered governance system. *Danwei* or *gongzuo danwei* refers to the workplace—an organization, department, division, section, etc., where one works (He, 2001: 61). Until the early 1980s, urban residents of the PRC were normally assigned to a work unit on graduating from school or university. For more detailed information about the *danwei* system see Bian (1994), Shaw (1996), and Lü and Perry (1997), or the more recent studies by Cheek (2006), Keister (2009) and Gore (2011) that discuss the changes to the system since the 1990s.

that an individual's employment would be terminated, or that his or her allocated house, or apartment, would be taken back if he or she did not return to the home institution (as outlined in Table 3.3), was not necessarily evidence of any kind of political persecution since the late 1980s; rather, it was related to new policies and practices that were being introduced by many work units and local governments in China as part of their reform programs at the time.[17] If a person studying abroad decided to stay away longer than the time that had been allowed, their employment or job in their work unit, home institution, would be suspended if not terminated, and the house, or the flat normally, allocated to them would also be taken back by the work unit.[18] If a person sent or financially supported by the Chinese government to study abroad overstayed their term overseas, he or she would receive notification of this from their home institution or work unit in China and an overseas Chinese diplomatic post.

In September and October 1989, many students, including ELICOS students, had already been away from their work units for six months or longer, and some started receiving such letters from their work units or employers. After June 4, these mail communications were interpreted in some Western countries as forms of persecution, and thus they became valuable evidence in the preparation of asylum applications. This was why some students would joke to comfort those who had received such letters: 'They've taken your flat away, but they've given you evidence to stay in Australia.' While no one in the West was able to explain this part of China's reforms, no student attempted to explain the background behind this as everyone wanted their letters to be interpreted as evidence that

---

[17] Indeed, some students stated that they believed that this type of evidence had been collected purely by chance at this stage because of the many new reform programs introduced in China, as a result of which many work units developed a series of new policies to govern the terms and conditions of employees studying abroad.

[18] As well as paying employees' salaries, each work unit had to provide housing, medical care and some other daily-life needs for its staff members (Orleans, 1988; Bian, 1994). By the late 1980s, many work units were reluctant to provide for staff members who were studying abroad, but the government still required them to do so. This means that there were at least two systems operating in China at the same time. First, traditional social control measures were still in use, meaning that people studying abroad had to stay in contact with their work unit; if they did not, their work unit would contact them. This routine contact would be intensified if any sudden and dramatic change should occur in the political climate, and absent staff would receive a letter from the CCP branch of their work unit. At the same time, China's reform programs allowed each work unit to manage their staff members in a more modern way, which resulted in a range of new policies, such as the aforementioned new employment termination policy, and the new housing allocation policy (Lü and Perry, 1997; Blecher, 2010; Gore, 2011).

their right to work and their right to reside had been infringed, which was precisely in line with the UN's refugee criterion. Students regarded this as the best kind of evidence to support their asylum applications—much stronger even than the statements published in Chinese community newspapers.

In addition to the new policies of China's work units regarding allocated housing and study leave, their new terms and conditions for managing employees studying abroad also introduced a procedure for handling their personal dossiers. Under pressure from many work units to reduce the number of people on their list of employees and their list of payroll, the Chinese government decided to allow many work units transferring the dossiers of those who were on leave or studying abroad to managing agencies formed by the bureau of personnel or labor in each government division. Each work unit was therefore required to inform each person affected by this change in writing, and many PRC students studying in Australia received this notification. The very existence of personal files or dossiers was regarded by many in Australia and similar countries as a human rights violation; the receipt of notification of this policy change could simply be interpreted by some as evidence of deprivation of the right to work (One-on-one interviews, 11 and 25 April 1998).

Table 3.3 lists the kinds of evidence that students could collect from the relevant authorities in China in the late 1989s and early 1990s. All types were regarded as 'important' or 'very important' on a five-point scale, with the exception of the fifth type of documentation (rated 1 out of 5 by some, but 5 out of 5 by others), which related to suspension of CCP membership or union membership. Students' opinions differed on this issue. About half of those surveyed believed that it would be harmful their political asylum case if they revealed that they were members of the CCP, while the other half thought that revealing their membership would mean severe punishment if they were forced to return to China.

By now it was becoming very evident that the Chinese students' identity as refugees in search of asylum in Australia was being formed in the gap that existed between Western understandings of 'communist China' and what had actually happened in China, especially with regard to numerous new policy measures introduced by the Chinese government in the 1980s and early 1990s. Although many Westerners were fully aware of China's reform programs and their impact on its entire socioeconomic and sociopolitical systems, China was still routinely defined by a set of simple concepts and fixed judgements. Many Chinese students living in Australia were clearly aware of prevalent negative stereotypes about China, some

Table 3.3 Evidence from the authorities concerned in China.

Descriptions of Evidence*	Importance on a Five-Point Scale
Receiving a letter from a former employer about deprivation of one's right to work:	
1. Suspension of one's right to work in a work unit in China;	5
2. Warning that one's employment was to be terminated if one did not return;	5
3. Inquiry about one's student status if one continued studying in Australia;	4
4. Personal files to be transferred as a result of termination of one's employment;	5
5. Suspension of one's CCP membership or union membership;	1/5
Receiving a letter from a former employer about deprivation of one's right to have a house:	
6. A notice to vacate the housing allocated by one's work unit;	5
7. Warning that the allocated housing would be taken back if one did not return;	5
8. A refusal to consider allocating housing to someone studying abroad;	5
9. Other communications relating to the housing issue;	5
Receiving a letter from other concerned authorities:	
10. A letter from a police station about PRC citizen ID card;	5
11. A refusal to allow one's child to attend kindergarten or schools owned by the work unit;	4
12. A notice informing that one's personal file was transferred.	5

* *Based on 52 applicable records of individual-focused interviews.*

of which appeared to be so deeply rooted that any action taken by the Chinese authorities or Chinese institutions would be usually construed as torture, purge or persecution. After June 4, this dogmatic way of thinking about China, and its socio-political tradition, system and practice, became more entrenched, and this in turn created a political atmosphere in which any asylum seekers from China could invoke many kinds of documentation as evidence in their quest for asylum or political protection. As a consequence, it did not take the Chinese students long to realize that they could utilize some of their communications with their former work units or institutions to support their asylum applications, and that some of these communications could be easily interpreted as solid evidence and met the refugee criteria, because of the above-mentioned widespread and deeply rooted misconception.

A survey conducted by the 'Student Working Group for the Human Rights of PRC Citizens in Australia' in early 1990,[19] shortly after the official introduction of the *Migration Legislation Amendment Act 1989* on 19 December 1989, illustrates that strategic identity formation of the students was well underway by that point. As will be detailed, the survey itself was very much a community-wide education process, which helped to shape the further formation of the students' strategic identity (Group-focused interviews, 17 January 1998). The Group had published a short questionnaire in three Chinese community newspapers (*ACD, STN*, and *The Tide*). In the section relating to persecutions and risks that students might face if they were forced to return to China, they listed a number of key words: 1) detention, 2) deprivation of the right to work, 3) mental torture, 4) economic punishment, 5) restrictions on religious beliefs, and 6) other possibilities. A report was then written, published and circulated by a few activist groups.

According to the final written report based on the survey, 95 percent of respondents stated that it was 'likely' that if they were forced to return to China they would be persecuted for their political activities and other involvement in Australia, such as attending public protests against June 4. Over 50 percent of respondents stated that they were worried about possible detention; 63 percent stated that they were worried about the loss of the right to work; and 74 percent stated that they were worried by the possibility of mental torture. Economic punishment and curtailment of religious freedom were cited by 47 and 25 percent respectively. How accurately the survey results reflect real possibilities or real fears cannot be determined. Nevertheless, my interviews indicated that the survey and the report played a critical role by articulating a set of concepts for the PRC student community and guiding them to identify and articulate their concerns according to those concepts. Serious politicized claims such as

[19] As noted in the third section of Chapter Two, this group was also called itself the 'Chinese Human Rights Investigation Working Group.' More information about this survey and its report will be detailed in the first section of Chapter Six.

'deprivation of the right to work and live' might have been difficult to prove, but mail communications from their former work units about changes in workforce management, when read with the prevailing misconceptions about China and without an understanding of the real situation, delivered precisely such evidence to many students.

As each individual in the Chinese student community took on their new identity as a seeker of asylum and gathered evidence to support their application to stay permanently in Australia, national and international networks formed and re-formed to exchange information and to provide guidance and opportunities for involvement in making a successful case for residency/asylum. The following chapter will discuss these networks and their role in these students' quests for the opportunity, and the right, to remain permanently in Australia.

CHAPTER FOUR

ORGANIZED INTERNATIONAL NETWORKS

In studies of migration from China, and of some communities that early Chinese migrants formed in their host countries from the 1840s onward, networks, associations and organizations of various kinds have occupied a prominent place (for example, Skinner, 1958; Freedman, 1960, 1962, 1979; Topley, 1961; Fallers, 1967; Blythe, 1969; Yong, 1977; Wang, 1978; Thompson, 1980; Wang, 1981; Tsai, 1983, 1986; Wickberg, 1994, 1998; Li, 1998; McKeown, 2001). Three general types of network have been the focus of research attention in Chinese migration studies. The first is the association formed by people from the same home province, region, city or town. Studies of this type of network have tended to focus on traditional lineage systems, dialect groups or territorial bonds among early Chinese migrants, who primarily originated from the provinces of Guangdong and Fujian (Topley, 1961; Clark, 1969; Cartier, 1998; Li, 1998; Pieke, 1998).

The second is the international networks formed by commercial and professional associations of overseas Chinese. In examining this type of network, researchers have particularly focused on the links between the place of origin and the host country, and on the links between Chinese migrant associations in different host countries (Freedman, 1960; Topley, 1961; Fallers, 1967; Fawcett, 1989; Moore, 2006; Fitzgerald, 2007; Bowen, 2011). Like the first focus, migrant groups of Guangdong and Fujian origin have also been the predominant center of attention in this type of study.

The third type of Chinese migrant network comprises organizations or groups that are specifically devoted to a wide variety of purposes or involvements (sometimes of an illicit nature, for example, as in the case of secret societies among Chinese migrants). It includes organizations of overseas Chinese who trafficked in labor in the Chinese coolie trade in the late nineteenth and early twentieth centuries or, more recently, who have surreptitiously involved themselves in migrant smuggling (Smith, 1997; Chin, 1999; Chu, 2000; Lake and Reynolds, 2008; Meagher, 2008; Zhang, 2007, 2008). The category also includes organizations of Chinese people outside China who had involved themselves in Chinese politics, predominantly from the late Qing to the early Republican period, which was from the 1890s to the 1920s. During those two very chaotic periods in modern Chinese history, a number of secret societies or revolutionary organizations or groups emerged among overseas Chinese communities. Typical cases included the Society for Protecting the Emperor in the late 1890s and 1900s,[1] the Tongmenghui in the late 1900s,[2] and the Chinese Zhigongtang from the 1920s to the present time[3] (Liu, 1989; Huters, 2005; Scott, 2008; Barabantseva, 2011). Some studies of this kind of network have been preliminary studies of organized political activities (Wang, 1970; Yen, 1976, 2006; Yong, 1977; Wang, 1978; Wickberg, 1994, 1998). This third type of network—working for a particular political objective and cause—was the most significant network in the quest of the Chinese students to achieve residency/asylum in Australia, although native place connections and professional associations (student organizations) also played a role.

International networking was a crucial aspect of the PRC students' campaign to remain in Australia. The role of networks in the migration process is widely recognized, but (as noted in Chapter One) the major focus of scholarly attention has been on linkages between the migrant and the home country. This chapter discusses the third-country networks, specifically the linkages to the USA, which were very important to the Chinese student campaign. It moves forward from earlier scholarship that has presented the PRC student campaign as an instance of cross-national diffusion in social movements (Snow and Benford, 1999), cyber-politics (Matloff, 1997, 1998; Walsh, 1999; Wang, 1999; Grier and Campbell, 2000) or networked political activity (Li, 1990; Grier, 1998) to explore in more detail the significance both of migrants' international networks in the host country and of networking with third countries. It discusses how these networks functioned in PRC Chinese student community activities

---

[1] Also called Pao Huang Hui, this organization supported the young reformist Emperor Guangxu (Kuang-hsii or Kuang-hsu) of the late Qing dynasty. It was established in Canada first, in July 1898, after the failure of the short-lived 'One Hundred Days Reform' movement of 1898 (Zhou, 2006), and more than 170 branches were set up in Chinese communities all over the world (2006: 60–61).

[2] The Tongmenghui or T'ung-Meng Hui (known in English as 'United League' or 'Chinese Revolutionary Alliance'), led by Sun Yat-sen, was an anti-Qing secret society of Chinese revolutionaries which played a key role in the overthrow of the monarchy in 1911 (Levenson, 1986).

[3] The Zhigongdang (Chee Kong Tong, also known as Hongmen Zhigongdang, or Chinese Freemasons in English) was originally a semi-secret fraternal society in overseas Chinese communities, especially in America, Canada, Japan and Australia. It became a political party in 1925 and has since played a more active role in Chinese politics both inside China and, more importantly, in overseas Chinese communities (Wickberg, 1982; Fitzgerald, 2007).

and examines their organizational process and leadership. It also draws attention to the role of the *FDC Newsletter*, the *CAD Newsletter* and the online *China News Digest* in establishing contacts between PRC Chinese student communities worldwide, especially in their worldwide campaign to seek political asylum.

The discussion begins with an introduction to the Chinese students who were studying in the USA at the time of June 4 and their close links with their counterparts in Australia. The second section looks in detail at the independent Chinese student unions that lobbied to push the 'Pelosi Bill' through the US Congress, and thus provided an example for other PRC student communities outside China. The third section discusses the use of computer-mediated communication in forming and maintaining international Chinese student networks, enabling the students to stage what has been called 'the first major network political activity' (Grier, 1998: 137). I then call attention to the way in which the Chinese students' search for protection was first linked to, and then incorporated into, international politics—a step which led to the formation of strategies to guide their actions, and the involvement of the CAD and the FDC in the students' collective protection campaign.

The Chinese Students in the United States

The new Chinese student communities in the USA, like their Australian counterparts, were a product of the rapid sociopolitical changes that took place in China from the late 1970s and early 1980s and the subsequent 'tide of going abroad' (Hu, 1988) (see Chapter One). The USA was the most favored country for overseas study, and for this reason, the Chinese student communities there formed some years before those in Australia. According to a former Chinese ambassador to Washington (Yang, 2001), the USA accepted no fewer than 150,000 officially sponsored students from the PRC from 1978 to 2000. However, as Orleans (1988) points out, neither Chinese nor Americans knew accurately how many Chinese college students and visiting scholars were in the USA at any time after exchanges began in 1978. This was mainly because so many government agencies, colleges, universities and other institutions in the USA were actively involved in the Chinese student and scholar programs through a variety of exchange agreements and cooperative research projects.

When a sequence of student protests demanding greater democratic freedom erupted in China in late 1986, a published Chinese report (cited in Chen, 1987) estimated that some 25,000 PRC students and scholars were studying in the USA at the time. A year later, it was estimated that 56,000 American visas had been issued to PRC students between 1979 and 1987 (Orleans, 1988). Of these 56,000 PRC students, the majority—around 60 percent—were officially sponsored and had come to study in the USA on J-1 visas, which require the holders to return to his or her home country for at least two years before applying for residency in the USA.[4] The remainder, privately sponsored students, were on F-1 visas.

By the end of 1986, many of the PRC students in the USA, and visiting scholars as well, had already been studying there for about three to five years, and had completed (or were near to completing) their degrees or courses. While many were publicly talking about their plans to remain in the USA by enrolling in other courses, or were delaying their return by proposing conditions that their home institutions in China would find it impossible to meet, others simply left their universities (Orleans, 1988; Matloff, 1997, 1998; Qian, 2003). After almost a decade of allowing and supporting thousands of students and young visiting scholars to study in the USA, China was well prepared to face the fact that many privately sponsored students (F-1 visa holders) would remain in the USA for a longer period or would even stay permanently. However, it was hoped that the officially sponsored students and researchers, on J-1 visas, would return on completion of their degrees or courses.

Contrary to this expectation, however, it was becoming apparent in 1987 that 'an ever-larger proportion' of the J-1 visa holders from China were also seeking ways to remain in the USA, or at least to push back their return to China (Orleans, 1988; Matloff, 1997, 1998). One strategy utilized by many of them was to transfer to another university within the USA to study for another degree or take a technical course. Therefore, it was estimated that in early 1988 approximately 21,000 PRC students and scholars with J-1 visas and approximately 7,000 students with F-1 visas had enrolled in degree courses or were undertaking research in many US colleges and universities. Also 8,000 or so Chinese students or scholars had either lawfully changed their status within the USA or disappeared into 'the American melting pot' (Orleans, 1988: 9).

---

[4] The policy was apparently designed to ease the 'brain drain' suffered by the sending countries (Ling, 1998: 209). The 'brain drain' issue was of real concern for China when considering whether to send thousands of students and young scholars abroad (for more information see Orleans, 1988; Mann, 1999; Qian, 2003).

In terms of the 'tide of going abroad,' the USA and Australia differed in two major aspects. First, as mentioned in Chapter One, the USA began to accept students from China in 1978, while Australia only decided to open its doors in 1986, and received its first several thousand Chinese students in the second half of 1987. Second, the USA had more or less insisted on accepting postgraduate students only, while most of the PRC nationals coming to study in Australia came under the English-language intensive course scheme known as ELICOS (see Chapter One). Though some universities in the USA applied special selection criteria to Chinese students, for example, by waiving some of the standard admission tests, such as TOEFL (Test of English as a Foreign Language) and GRE (the Graduate Record Examination), most of them insisted that every student meet minimum English-language requirements before allowing them to enroll (Qian, 2003). As a result, the new PRC students studying in the USA were, in general, 'academically competitive and highly motivated individuals' (Orleans, 1988: 11) and most were carrying out research or doing their course work at doctoral or postdoctoral level (Orleans, 1988; Matloff, 1997). As the number of Chinese nationals going to the USA increased, the age profile also changed; by 1987, scholars leaving China to undertake PhD and postdoctoral research were significantly younger than they had been at the time when a few Sino-American scientific and educational exchange programs were first introduced in the late 1970s and early 1980s (Harding, 1992; Qian, 2003). The relative youth of the students may also have increased the likelihood of their staying on in the USA to study for a further degree or take another technical course. In line with China's long-term national policy and strategy to revitalize its education, science and technology, a high proportion of the government-sponsored Chinese students in the USA were taking courses in engineering and science, or related fields (Orleans, 1988; Qian, 2003). This obvious predominance of technical fields of specialization may help to explain why these PRC students were able to stage such an effective campaign using computer-mediated communications (as to be discussed below), before ordinary Americans, and ordinary Australians as well, started using computers for their communications.

As ever-larger numbers of PRC students and visiting scholars sought ways to remain in the USA, some were becoming actively involved in various political activities in the USA. The best-known example in this regard was Wang Bingzhang, with his US-based magazine *China Spring* and the Chinese Alliance for Democracy (CAD) that he and his several supporters and associates established in New York in late 1983 (Chong, 1989; He, 1996; Qian, 2003). After completing his medical PhD degree in pathology at McGill University, Canada in 1982, Wang moved to the USA and actively engaged in political activities there. To his supporters and sympathizers, he was a founder and organizer of the Chinese pro-democracy movement abroad in the post-Mao Chinese politics. To his opponents, he was pursuing anti-Chinese government activities. In the eyes of many in the PRC student community in the USA, however, the ventures of Wang and his associates represented nothing more than an extreme example of finding a means, or an excuse, to prolong their stay in North America after graduation (Group-focused interviews, 17, 24 and 31 January 1998; Qian, 2003).

The publication of *China Spring*, the so-called first pro-democracy Chinese magazine overseas, in New York in 1982 and the founding of the CAD in 1983 were turning points in what has since been termed the Chinese democracy movement overseas. As students switched courses or postponed the completion of their degrees, more and more of them began to include political elements, or democratic demands, into the conditions for their return that they put forward to their employers in China. Several weeks after the student demonstrations held in several Chinese cities in late 1986, Hu Yaobang, the General Secretary of the CCP, was forced to resign for supposedly supporting or even instigating them. This provided some PRC students living in the USA with a justification for wishing to stay in the USA, and it increased their resolve. The conditions that some PRC students and scholars were placing on their home institutions for their return, already impossible to meet, were then upgraded to include intangible expressions and conditions—such as democracy, freedom of speech and personal freedoms—that it would be impossible for China to meet in the foreseeable future. There was a broadly shared understanding among PRC students that the failure of their employing organization in China to meet these demands would mean that they could prolong their stay in the USA (Orleans, 1988; Qian, 2003).

From late 1986 to 1987, more PRC students and scholars living in the USA were spurred into active political action by numerous small-scale university student protests in China. On 19 January 1987, approximately 1,000 students from 51 US universities publicized an open letter to the CCP Central Committee and China's State Council (or China's cabinet) expressing their serious concerns about the political situation in China and putting forward demands for demanding political reform. The letter was then published in the *New York Times* on 23 January 1987 (Orleans,

1988) and in the March edition of *China Spring* (No. 45), with 482 PRC student and scholar names affixed. Many Chinese students believed that this highly politicized action had been organized by the CAD (Chen and Lu, 1994), and it proved to be a watershed in the Chinese student pro-democracy movement, moving the PRC student community towards a consensus about how residency in the USA might be pursued.

As outlined in the third section of this chapter, technology played an important role in the formation and implementation of this consensus. Given that the students were scattered at universities across the USA, the utilization of computer-mediated communications was crucial (Li, 1990; Grier, 1998). This new PRC student and scholar community as a whole began to make use of coordinated computer-mediated communications in the second half of 1986, and by April 1989, there were three electronic groups: CHINANET, soc.culture.china and Electronic News for Chinese Students. The utilization of these network forums was initially related to political events occurring in China, and had little reference to what was going on within the PRC student community in the USA. CHINANET, a listserv group, was the first network forum. It was used for PRC student and scholar discussions from December 1986 to November 1987, and it helped to form the Usenet group soc.culture.china in late 1987. Based on the latter group, the Electronic News for Chinese Students also became part of the community-wide network in the USA, which played crucial roles in 'debating issues, educating themselves, making decisions and working together' (Grier, 1998: 138) to form a consensus among the PRC students and scholars and take further political actions.

June 4 turned almost all the Chinese nationals living in the USA or Australia in the late 1980s into a new generation of asylum seekers. As Grier (1998) has noted, the summer of 1989 was a period of intense political organization for them. Shortly after 4 June 1989, the number of Chinese nationals studying in the USA was normally cited as 43,000 (Li, 1990). According to the assessment made in the *Chinese Student Protection Act*, however, which was passed by the US Congress in late 1992 (Matloff, 1998), no less than 80,000 PRC nationals were in the USA at the time, whether on J-1 or F-1 visas. After June 4, these PRC nationals lobbied the US government intensively to offer them protect from being forced to return to China. Their lobby resulted in the *Chinese Student Protection Act*, also known as the 'Pelosi Bill,' which gave them the right to apply to stay permanently in the USA. Under this pressure, the US government decided not to deport any Chinese nationals. Although President Bush vetoed the

'Pelosi Bill' on 30 November 1989 (Suettinger, 2003: 96), his administration issued an Executive Order on 12 April 1990 that protected all PRC citizens in the USA on or after 5 June 1989 from deportation to China and affirmed their right to be employed (Ling, 1998).

This victory was a very positive sign for PRC students elsewhere. As noted, however, the majority of PRC students in Australia (more than 70 percent of them) were language students rather than graduate students or visiting scholars as in the USA, and an estimated 50 percent were already overstayers at the time of June 4 (Easterbrook, 1993). According to two surveys conducted in Shanghai and Guangdong (Wang, 1987; Wang and Lai, 1987), even before June 4, a large proportion of these students had already decided to stay in Australia. Furthermore, the major changes that Australia made to its onshore humanitarian and refugee immigration policies at that time (noted in Chapters One and Five; also see Cronin, 1993) placed them at a disadvantage compared with their counterparts in the USA. For these reasons, international networks were of critical assistance in their collective efforts to seek residency/asylum in Australia after June 4.

International networking was facilitated by the fact that PRC student communities all over the world were already relatively organized before June 4, even though they were not fully or independently networked, let alone networked internationally. First, PRC students at each university abroad were organized through the Chinese education consuls in their country of residence into an officially controlled student union. Before June 4, this was universally called the Friendship Association of Chinese Students and Scholars (FACSS) (Li, 1990), and it followed China's long tradition of governing students and scholars studying abroad from the late Qing and as a standard practice of political governance in post-1949 China (Fitzgerald, 1972; Yen, 1976; Wang, 1980). Second, these PRC students were also organized in their own primary social groups, and as discussed in Chapter Two, these social groups helped students to become partly networked as an alternative social formation to the student union (Li, 1990; Gao, 2002, 2006). Third, the Chinese Alliance for Democracy (CAD), a US-based Chinese opposition organization, formed branches in major cities if not at each university (Nathan, 1992; He, 1996; Chen and Lu, 1994). All these groupings facilitated the transformation of the PRC student communities into asylum seeker networks.

The Role of Independent Student Unions

In May 1989, in support of the student demonstrations in Beijing and a number of other Chinese cities, branches of the Friendship Association of Chinese Students and Scholars (FACSS—the PRC overseas student union) in several major Western countries declared independence from the Chinese education consuls, thus openly terminating their political, organizational and financial associations with the Chinese consulates. Numerous FACSS branches began to reorganize and a new union was formed in the USA: the Independent Federation of Chinese Students and Scholars (IFCSS). Its first convention was held in Chicago from 29 to 31 July 1989, and was attended by representatives from several Australian universities.[5]

This newly independent PRC student association organized most of the early protests against the Chinese government outside China. In May 1989, as part of the IFCSS's activities, CHINANET was transformed by a group of volunteers to become a communication channel for student communities scattered all over the USA and in other countries, including Australia.

These were not the only missions that the IFCSS was to fulfill. It also played an active and central role in internationalizing and coordinating the student residency/asylum campaigns worldwide. Even as the students were cutting their ties with the education consuls in May 1989, their own networks were internationalizing in order to overcome both their former dependence on official connections and their own isolation. However, importantly, many PRC students and visiting scholars had already clearly identified common tasks that should be pursued not only collectively, but also internationally as a united force. These were the issues of whether they should return to China, and how to seek protection, as expressed at the time, outside China if they decided not to return.

Their reorganization process went through two stages before the new unions clearly directed their focus to organized lobbying for residency. The initial stage began only a few days after June 4 and lasted until 31 July 1989, the finish of the first convention of the IFCSS, at which the organization was formally constituted.[6] This first convention succeeded in merging all the existing Chinese student unions and establishing itself

---

[5] Several studies have addressed the role of the IFCSS in the USA (including Li, 1990; Grier, 1998; Mann, 1999).

[6] The number of people who attended the convention has been variously reported as between 350 PRC students and scholars representing 105 universities (Ma, 1989) and 30 or so student activists representing a dozen universities (Li, 1990).

as the only organization coordinating student activities. The convention also set a positive example of how PRC students living in other countries might form groups. It incorporated the three Chinese electronic network forums, which would now merge into a single forum called *China News Digest* (*CND*). The individual subscriber lists—of over 4,000 names—were pooled, and the merger of the three lists was completed by the end of August. With the founding of the IFCSS, there was a rapid shift in the focus of the students' activism from China to immigration offices (Mann, 1999: 210). In Australia, for example, thousands of PRC nationals rushed to immigration offices to ask for application forms for residency (*The Age*, 10 June 1989).

The second stage of the new networking also began at the first IFCSS convention in late July and lasted until the constitution was amended and passed almost three months later on 27 October 1989. The constitution stated that:

> [The association] 'shall (i) disseminate information and educate the public regarding the democratic movement in China, (ii) promote freedom, democracy, the rule of law and human rights in China, and (iii) represent the interests of Chinese nationals, especially students and scholars, residing in the United States' (IFCSS, 1989).

The IFCSS and its manifesto were considered by many Chinese students and scholars to be less ideological, and less radical as well, than the CAD and its manifesto. Some scholars, however, have suggested that many pro-democratic activists (Ma, 1989) and pro-China students (Qian, 2003) regarded the IFCSS as a politicized group whose practical interest was residency for the students in the countries in which they were living. Yet, many PRC nationals in both the USA and Australia also felt frustrated because the IFCSS did not reach any consensus, at least not in its first manifesto draft circulated at its first convention, on how to pursue their protection issue (One-on-one interviews, 11 and 25 April 1998). In the USA, student leaders and activists succeeded in arranging meetings with several members of Congress, and both sides decided to work jointly on a number of bills that would protect the students from being required to return to their home country (Mann, 1999). One such bill was introduced by Nancy Pelosi on 21 June 1989 and this became not only a key vehicle through which the IFCSS sought protection in the USA but also the setting for a major confrontation between Congress and the Bush administration over control of China policy.

It was also because of the support from several members of the US Congress that the IFCSS established a lobbying committee to coordinate activities by the students at over 160 colleges and universities (Ma, 1989; Li, 1990; Bonchek, 1995). These committee members organized a series of meetings with other Congress members. Their efforts were so intense that there was virtually no member of Congress in America who did not receive faxes and other printed materials from the Chinese students or was not visited by them (Matloff, 1998; Mann, 1999). The PRC student activists also took their claim that they would be in political jeopardy if they were forced to return to China to the House Judiciary Subcommittee on Immigration.

Like their counterparts in the USA, the Chinese student leaders and activists in Australia also established contacts with government officials in Australia as early as May, and remained in regular contact with them throughout their protection campaign. In mid June, they wrote an open letter to members of Parliament and government departments appealing for protection (*The Tide*, 15 June 1989). The ELICOS students began to organize their own associations in each city, and they advertised a series of seminars and meetings on how to seek protection in Australia (*ACD*, 17–18 June 1989). Over 80 percent of those surveyed for this study had sought to learn to what extent they could seek protection in Australia in the first couple of weeks after June 4. They hoped that the IFCSS would help them to seek residency openly; if not, as several of them said, there was no point in forming a new union. Of course, the IFCSS manifesto and its original constitution draft did not reflect the students' concerns with residency, in either the USA or Australia.

There were plenty of signs, however, of local support for protecting the PRC nationals living in both the USA and Australia. Activists in both countries remembered the clear and strong words of members of the US Congress, the tears shed by Australian Prime Minister Bob Hawke, and the granting of permanent residency to the female student who made a tearful speech at a memorial service in the Great Hall of the Australian Parliament for those killed in Beijing. These were all clear signals that Americans and Australians cared about the students' plight, even without the hints that a handful of student activists received in private meetings with politicians and senior government officials. These signals triggered intense debate among the student activists,[7] and internal debates about

[7] Of the activists surveyed for this study, more than 50 percent recalled the debates at the time focusing on the students' difficulties in articulating their need for protection (i.e. permanent residence); about 30 percent recalled the debates focusing on strategies; less than 20 percent recalled them as focusing on the union's priorities.

the IFCSS's key priorities and strategies characterized the second phase of organizing and politicizing the international IFCSS-networks.

As one U.S.-based activist pointed out, many PRC students regarded June 4 as a 'one-off' opportunity to seek residency outside China, and they wanted this to be dealt with strategically (Ma, 1989; Matloff, 1997, 1998; Ling, 1998). The IFCSS was the only organization that was then supported by the majority of the students, and it appeared to be capable of dealing with such a complicated matter. Although the CAD wished to play an active role in organizing the students, many students seemed not to be interested in being part of what the CAD often called the Chinese democracy movement, seeking only to actively pursue their protection issue or their residency issue in other words (Ma, 1989). This was partly based on their understanding of the seriousness of June 4, which in effect united almost the entire Chinese student and scholar community for one common goal: to seek asylum outside China.

The visa issue was the common ground on which the students were united and was a direct spur to the rapid and complete reorganization of the PRC student community worldwide. As noted, about 60 percent of the PRC students and scholars in the USA were officially sponsored on J-1 visas, meaning that they were not permitted to remain in the USA on completion of their studies or research projects (Orleans, 1988). Many PRC students and scholars in Australia were in a similar situation: they had been selected and sent by Chinese institutions, but many had been subsidized by the Australian government, and they too were required to leave Australia for at least two years after completing their studies before they would be eligible to apply for residency in Australia. Many PRC students and scholars in both countries were also holding expired or nearly expired visas around the time of June 4.

It was an urgent priority for those who were seeking to form a unified and internationalized student organization that it should include the PRC students who were not associated with the officially sponsored students and their organizations. In the USA, these were F-1 visa holders: they were privately supported by family, relatives or friends, and accounted for some 40 percent of the total number of students and visiting scholars from the PRC. In Australia, they were ELICOS students (more than 70 percent of the total number of PRC students). As noted, about 50 percent of the PRC nationals enrolled in various ELICOS courses in Australia had already overstayed their visas on 4 June 1989 (Easterbrook, 1993) and these several thousand overstayers also needed the help of the new union to deal with their visa issues. There was also a concern among many legal visa holders that the language student union would run its own separate lobby for its members (*ACD*, 17–18 June 1989). Many PRC activists and leaders were worried that an uncoordinated lobby might be damaging to the outcome of a community-wide effort (Group-focused interviews, 17 and 24 January 1998). As a result, a nationwide coordinating body called the IFCSS in Australia, or the IFCSSA, was established on 27 August 1989 and held its first meeting in Sydney (*ACD*, 28 August 1989).

At the same time, international relationships and cooperations among the students were being transformed into organized networks. Before the IFCSS was formally established, there were numerous contacts between PRC students and scholars living in the USA and their counterparts in Australia. Links existed through the officially controlled Chinese student and scholar unions, the informal networks formed by students' primary social groups (including colleagues, class- and schoolmates, or friends) and the political association organized by the CAD. From early 1989, computer-based networks also came to play a critical role in connecting the PRC student and scholar community worldwide (discussed below) and even before June 4, much of the international networking among PRC students overseas had been formed and was frequently used precisely for the purpose of exchanging information about how to prolong their stays in the West. Students resorted to a wide range of ploys for this purpose: switching courses or majors, transferring to other universities or colleges, or extending the term of their graduate work or research project. All of these tactics forestalled their being classified as having completed their studies, upon which they would be required to return to China for at least two years (Mann, 1999: 211). However, the June 4 events were still seen as the main driver behind the organization of the students' international networks as one interviewee explained in an interview:

> June 4 changed our relationships with our old friends, schoolmates, or even colleagues, studying there [in America]. Before it, we had many topics to discuss, but no such serious opportunity. June 4 was both a serious topic and a serious opportunity for us, and it turned those who were simply our contacts into *zhanyou*, battle companions. Not just that, we were also very much 'fighting in the same trench,' [which was] finding our way to stay protected (Interviewee 8, 24 January 1998).

Once the Chinese student and scholar unions had successively declared independence from Chinese official control, and after many rounds of international discussions, consultations and negotiations, the IFCSS took over their role of community organization and communication. Each of its branches in the USA was required to have a few 'liaison officers' in charge of liaising and communicating with students and scholars at other universities and in other countries (Ma, 1989; Li, 1990), while all the previously existing types of contact network were at the same time still functioning.

In addition, almost every IFCSS branch had a few computer experts who maintained efficient communication electronically, both nationwide and internationally. As a very high proportion of the officially sponsored Chinese students, and visiting scholars as well, in the USA and Australia were in technical courses, there was no shortage of technical expertise (Orleans, 1988; Huang, 1997). An internal reporting system was also introduced in each IFCSS branch as an organizational measure, and any information received from the networks, including computerized networks and personal contacts, had to be passed on to either general or special meetings of the local branch. This internal communication mechanism guaranteed the speedy spread of information among not only student leaders and activists but also ordinary members of the community.

Computerized Networks and the 'Pelosi Bill'

Republican Senator Alan K. Simpson from Wyoming, who was also the Republican whip in the U.S. Senate from 1985 to 1995, told the Senate on one occasion that the Chinese students

> ... are tough. They have people who are really setting them up [in their lobbying techniques]. They have fax machines, they have used the computer systems of every major university. I received 1,000 Christmas cards [from Chinese students], and that is more than I get from Wyoming. They are good and they know exactly what they are doing (cited in Matloff, 1998).

In fact, a study by Grier and Campbell (2000) notes that some Chinese postgraduate students in the USA had set up a network-based discussion group as early as 1986, and that online news groups were also 'a useful means of disseminating news within the Chinese student community' (2000: 38). Matloff (cited above), himself a computer science professor and a passionate participant in the immigration debate in the USA, draws attention to the Chinese students' skillful use of computerized networks, as have Li (1990) and Grier (1998); indeed the PRC students' campaign is regarded by some scholars as the first major network political activity (Grier, 1998).

The PRC students studying in America were among the first small group of university professors, researchers and graduate students to have access to electronic communication when 'most of America had not yet discovered the Internet' (Mann, 1999: 201). They had learned how to use the Internet in the course of their research work, and a group of Chinese students and visiting scholars at Texas A&M University had created the CHINANET computerized forum, for exchanging news and information and debating a wide variety of issues. As noted, three already existing computer-mediated forums set up by the Chinese students before June 1989 were merged into one at the first IFCSS convention in July 1989. In his pioneering study of the PRC students' use of computerized networks to communicate and engage in political actions, Tiger Li (1990) found that 43,000 PRC students and scholars in colleges and universities across the USA, organized into 160 campus IFCSS branches, were using two forms of computer-mediated communication to communicate. According to Wu (1999), the students were scattered among several hundred higher education institutions: 28.5 percent in the Northeast, 26.9 percent in the Midwest, 16.9 percent in the South, 15.4 percent in the Pacific region, and 8.4 percent in the Southwest.

The first form of computerized communication that the PRC students used was a newsgroup called Social Cultural China on Usenet, one of the oldest computer network communication systems, which was first put into use in the early 1980s (about a decade before the World Wide Web came into existence). All students with a computer account at a university had access to this newsgroup, and during the residency campaign in the USA, approximately 40 articles were posted to the newsgroup per day, with an estimated 20,000 readers, making it one of the 20 most active, or the most frequently-used, of the 1,500 groups on Usenet at the time (Wu, 1999). The PRC students also made extensive use of electronic mail, which was accessible through each university network and played a very important role when 'the students turned to Capitol Hill for legislation that would grant them new legal guarantees against being required to return home' (Mann, 1999: 211).

To implement the decision made at the first IFCSS convention in the USA in July 1989, a number of IFCSS branches in Australia also made a similar arrangement to have a few 'liaison officers' to receive and relay information regularly. Thus, the students in Australia were fully aware of what IFCSS activists in the USA had discussed with some members of the US Congress and what their counterparts in the USA were doing in their protection campaign. It helped them develop a better and more detailed understanding of the highly politicized and complicated issue of seeking asylum in the West. That is, this helped open up opportunities, or new horizons, for the PRC students living in Australia, who were in general less sophisticated, less politically skilful as well, than their counterparts in the USA. One interviewee recalled:

> I definitely agree that the new technology helped the students a lot. A friend of mine knew a postgraduate student, and he often brought back printouts of news articles that his postgraduate friend found from a computer search and printed out.... We could not find that sort of information from Australian newspapers. Because of these printouts, we often knew 'something' earlier than a friend who kept listening to the VOA Radio [Chinese] program every day [in order] to learn what happened there in the USA (Interviewee 20, 17 January 1998).

Some Chinese activists in Australia even knew that several congressional bills were drafted in the US Congress to address the PRC student issue. There are seven versions of the congressional bill numbered HR2712 in the record for the 101st United States Congress and these various versions were introduced by members of Congress from both political parties. The first version, proposed by Republican Senator Slade Gorton, advocated granting all PRC students and scholars permanent residency in the USA. Another, proposed by Nancy Pelosi (a newly elected member to the US House of Representatives), suggested legislating a temporary suspension of the requirement that the foreign students return home on completion of their studies, giving them four years before they could apply for new visas or residency. All of this took place well before the IFCSS held its first convention in Chicago in late July 1989, but the IFCSS preparatory committee already had a team to lobby Congress on the students' behalf. On 20 July, when the House Judiciary Subcommittee on Immigration started a public hearing and the PRC student representatives expressed support for the 'Pelosi bill,' the lobbying committee was given four days to conduct a survey among the PRC students. The lobbying team used email to distribute and collect the surveys in time for the hearing and email communication was also used to report to the students on the progress of the bill. The newsgroup was used to publish drafts and detailed analyses of the proposed bills and to list those Senators and Congresspersons who were 'good prospects' for lobbying, along with their phone numbers and addresses (Bonchek, 1995: 9).

Since there was practically no member of the US Congress who did not have a few PRC students at colleges or universities within her or his district, the IFCSS committee even drafted and circulated a template to suggest the wording to use in messages to Congresspersons and Senators and urged their members to send them. The instruction from the IFCSS lobbying committee was loud and clear: Flood every single Senator's office with phone calls and faxes (Matloff, 1998).

Tiger Li (1990) has noted that computerized networks were used as a tool to organize and coordinate a public campaign and a public forum and as a news distribution channel as well. As Bonchek (1995) points out, the network reduced communication and coordination costs for the PRC students, who had limited time and small budgets, and that this had a direct impact on group formation, group efficiency, group recruitment, and group retention by the IFCSS (Bonchek, 1995: 6). Without such a network, the Chinese students and scholars—who were widely dispersed geographically—could not have formed and organized as a group, would not have been able to maintain group size and cohesiveness, and would not have been so effective (Bonchek, 1995: 10).

In relation to the political impact and nature of the newly emerged computerized networks, Grier (1998) points out that the success of the PRC student lobby resulted from both the decentralizing and centralizing tendencies of the networks. Because of their decentralizing tendencies, the networks could be utilized for promoting easy access to information and the participation of individuals in networked activities. On the other hand, computerized networks centralize power by allowing a leader to inform, and potentially control, a group of supporters. In the case of the PRC student lobby, these opposing tendencies were the cause of tensions within the IFCSS, but the centralizing tendency facilitated the formation and implementation of collective strategies in their campaign by telling supporters how to act, what to do and where to go, rather than promoting open and endless debates. Professional political advocators, lawyers and, more importantly, the Democrats were able to influence a range of vital decisions of the student campaign in this way.[8]

Nancy Pelosi was first elected in 1987 to represent the congressional district of downtown San Francisco, which is well known as one of the highest concentrations of Asian-Americans in the USA. Perhaps because of this, her first proposed legislation in relation to the PRC students, the *Emergency Chinese Immigration Relief Act of 1989*, was considered a

[8] One mystery that remains unexplained to the present day is why the IFCSS lobbying committees of 40 or so members, headed by Harvard biochemist Zhao Haiqing, believed that the bill put forward by Republican Senator Slade Gorton was so far-reaching that it could never be enacted, and decided to support the moderate bill proposed by Nancy Pelosi (Mann, 1999). Although some, for example, Republican Senator Alan K. Simpson, regarded it as an attempt to embarrass President Bush (Grier, 1998: 144), it apparently reflected strategic thinking on the part of the IFCSS (Mann, 1999).

low-key effort on behalf of a constituency important to her San Francisco district. Thanks to the strong, widespread sympathy in the USA for the students, the 'Pelosi bill' became a high priority for Congress and won quick approval from the House Judiciary Subcommittee. After various necessary amendments, the bill passed the House simply by voice vote on 31 July 1989 and moved quickly to the Senate, where it was delayed for a few months for a number of technical reasons. On 19 November 1989, the House once again passed the Senate-amended version of the 'Pelosi bill' by a vote of 403 to 0. On the following day, the Senate also passed the legislation by a voice vote.

About two weeks later, on 30 November 1989, President Bush vetoed the bill because it constituted congressional mismanagement of foreign policy. Of course, Bush also believed the legislation was not necessary because he had taken a number of actions to protect the PRC nationals (Mann, 1999). To prevent Congress from overriding his veto, President Bush then announced an executive order to provide the PRC nationals with the same protection that they would receive from the bill that Nancy Pelosi sponsored. Through her support of legislation to allow the PRC students and scholars stay in the USA, Pelosi emerged as the Democratic Party's leading critic of the Bush administration's China policy, which provided her with a perfect platform on which to further consolidate her electoral position and to start playing an active role in both national and international politics.

The politicization of the PRC student issue in the USA had a direct influence on the Australian government's approach to the same issue in their own country. Although Australia's response to the issue took the form of the amendment of its *Migration Act 1958* and the abandonment of its long-term onshore humanitarian immigration program, the timing and frequency of its policy changes were found to be perfectly matched with what happened in the USA. As one former student noted:

> Australia is closer to America than Canada in every aspect [of its Chinese student policy], although Canada is geographically close to America. A group of friends of mine paid a lot of attention to every decision made by the US government on the [student] issue, and we all realized that Australia followed American policy almost item by item, including their problems, such as repeated delays, frequent changes, and internal disagreements, and so on. This was why we had to learn how the [Chinese] students in America handled these problems, and learn their skills, especially how to organize a media campaign and talk to MPs (Interviewee 7, 11 April 1998).

Having been professionally guided by the Washington-based law firm, Arent, Fox, Kintner, Plotkin and Kahn (Grier, 1998: 137; Mann, 1999: 213), IFCSS activists had acquired more skills for lobbying Congress, and started running a media campaign. One characteristic of its lobbying strategy became clear: to relate itself with the Democrats. Nancy Pelosi became a leading sponsor and in early January 1990, when the IFCSS held a conference at Harvard to discuss the president's veto of the 'Pelosi bill,' Pelosi was the only Congressperson in attendance. The meeting turned out to be a turning point for both the student lobby and Nancy Pelosi's political career. The student activists knew that a congressional vote on whether to override the veto was scheduled for later in January 1990, and they wanted to use the conference to push Congress to make efforts to override it. In case this should fail, the conference at Harvard identified another central issue or topic that they could utilize to keep Congress's attention focused on China, Congress being the place with which their protection was associated. At the end of the Harvard conference, they found their solution, which was to purposely target China's most-favored-nation (MFN) trade status, which was first granted by the USA in 1980, but needed to be renewed each year thereafter (Menges, 2005: 465).[9] From Pelosi's point of view, her bill was not purposely designed to cause a major showdown between Congress and the Bush administration over control of foreign relations, and in particular, over China policy, but Bush's veto had elevated both the importance of her bill and her position in Congress.

Having triggered off a major collision between the executive and the legislature, Pelosi was now looking for other ways to fight back against President Bush's veto of her first bill (Mann, 1999; Suettinger, 2003). China's MFN status was a promising topic over which to attack the Bush administration; more importantly, this was a legislative means to counter the Bush administration's approach to China. According to Mann (1999), few in the USA at the time still remembered the controversies of the late 1970s, in which the Carter administration had decided to extend MFN

[9] According to Arce and Taylor (1997), the annual MFN status review process was conducted as a relatively low profile event up until 1989. However, from 1989 onwards, each time the process for China's MFN renewal had occurred it did so under strenuous discussion and debate between US policy makers. Both the Bush and Clinton administrations also decided to link it with China's human rights record, and its domestic and foreign policy behavior as well, making the MFN a highly contentious and debated issue. Nancy Pelosi played a very important role in linking China's future MFN renewal with its human rights. For more information about the issue, readers are referred to the following publications: Lampton (1994: 9–27); Nakatsuji (1999); Suettinger (2003: 161–174); Xie (2009: 104–113).

status to China while completely denying it to the Soviet Union. Since the first congressional approval in 1979, China's MFN benefits had been repeatedly renewed on an annual basis without debate, to the point where they were taken for granted. The IFCSS's Harvard meeting kicked off a series of annual legislative battles that lasted for more than one decade; ironically, they proved more enduring than the student movement itself.

Connecting to International Politics

Although Nancy Pelosi wrote to her colleagues in March 1990 to invite them to establish a congressional working group on China's MFN status, the Harvard meeting in early January 1990 marked the point at which the student lobby became part of international politics. The Chinese students had long since realized the usefulness of international politics in dealing with their protection issue, because they were very familiar with ideas such as economic sanctions against China, human rights issues and the promotion of democracy. The formation of the strategies adopted by the IFCSS and other PRC student organizations was a bottom-up process in which local student groups took innovative approaches such as linking their residency issue to international politics at a macro level. Though the IFCSS had developed and adopted the strategy of making the students' right to stay into a human rights issue within weeks of June 4, it was only at the Harvard meeting that the issue finally became firmly connected to international politics in cooperation with one of the two major American political parties.

In fact, the idea of dealing with their own protection issue as a matter of human rights was one of the critical issues that prevented the first IFCSS convention in Chicago from reaching a consensus about how the situation in which the students found themselves was to be pursued. Because many students felt frustrated that the IFCSS convention did not reach a consensus, the IFCSS constitution had to be repeatedly amended and was not passed until three months after the first convention. This was a source of anxiety for many student groups in both the USA and Australia. In Australia, for example, a group called the Chinese Association for Safeguarding Human Rights (CASHR) was set up as early as July 1989, hard on the heels of the IFCSS convention in the USA. As will be discussed in Chapter Seven, the CASHR—thanks to its human rights strategy—became a driving force for pushing the FDC and the CAD, two highly politicized organizations in Australia, to deal with their member's residency claims.

Once the issue of protection or residence for the PRC students had been connected to international politics, there was a fundamental change in the strategies of the IFCSS, and of the CAD and the FDC as well. This strategic change comprised three concurrent shifts.

The first was a change in the focus of the students' demands, from 'small claims to bigger ones,' in the words of many former activists. This change was expressed in different ways in the student union newsletters and Australia's Chinese-language newspapers. For example, according to the *Australian Chinese Daily*, the PRC student community had made nine demands in several stages over time. In chronological order, their demands were: (1) unconditional extension of visas; (2) a short period of protection against sociopolitical uncertainty in China; (3) that all students be eligible to apply to stay; (4) a long period of asylum for some student activists; (5) a long period of asylum for all PRC students; (6) that the Australian government be pushed to process all the asylum applications; (7) residency for the student activists; (8) residency for all members of the student organizations; and (9) that the government regard—and solve—their issue as a matter of human rights (*ACD*, 28 August 1989). Obviously, the focus of the demands can be seen to move from individual cases to the highly politicized human rights issue. Initially, protection was only called for in the case of those PRC nationals who had an expired or nearly expired visa. Then the activists of student unions and the members of political groups were included until, ultimately, protection was demanded for all students.

It became the students' shared goal that a blanket approach be sought, although many were unsure whether this collective objective would be achievable. In the USA, the differences in individuals' situations were not as apparent as in Australia, because most of the PRC students there were postgraduate students and the great majority had legal status there. Even so, the IFCSS leaders in America disagreed with each other from the start. Quite apart from disagreements over what the IFCSS manifesto and its constitution should be, the activists spent most of their time at the organization's early meetings debating their key strategies. When they first sat down to think about and formulate their key tactics, they put forward three objectives (Mann 1999): to push for economic sanctions against China; to advocate a boycott of international events held in China; and to seek legal changes that would protect them from being required to leave the USA. These objectives were not essentially in conflict, however, so the IFCSS had the option of pursuing them simultaneously.

In Australia, the various PRC student groups—including the IFCSSA—appeared to be less strategic at the start, because they placed too much emphasis on the demands of different types of students and the need to identify a right strategy to meet all the demands. In 1989, the Australian government restricted those already within Australia, including many university graduates, from applying to stay (Iredale, 1997). As noted, after June 4, many PRC students, who either held an Australian higher degree or were studying for one, wanted to lobby the government to waive this policy. This was perceived by the majority of PRC students (especially those ELICOS students, let alone the approximately 50 percent who were overstayers at the time) as a 'separatist' approach. Once the community was coordinated by the IFCSS and its networks, however, it was found to have moved quickly toward a unified approach.

The second main change in the students' approach was the change from one that was passive to one that was more active. Many Chinese students initially regarded themselves as victims of June 4. This sense of themselves as 'victims' was identified by some activists as a problem in their campaign, and was changed after October 1989, when the IFCSS constitution was finally amended to explicitly combine the protection of the students and scholars studying in the West with the promotion of democracy in China. More efforts were now made to turn the student protection issue into part of international politics. The first attempt was the establishment of the FDC. From October 1989, the FDC set up branches around the world, publicly stating its aim to be the pursuit of both the Chinese democratic movement outside China and the protection of its members' welfare (He, 1997). Having been re-emphasized by the FDC, the combination of the protection of the PRC nationals and the Chinese democratic movement was also finally accepted by more students as a perfect strategy: it would allow them to be defined as people fighting for democracy for China, and therefore as either democratic activists or political asylum seekers. This rationalization was then circulated widely among the students, with the expectation that governments in Western countries such as the USA and Australia would give short-term visa extensions to all PRC students and scholars if they presented themselves as the victims of a political event.

In the course of the international politicization of the Chinese student issue, the IFCSS also successfully obtained financial support from the US-based National Endowment for Democracy (NED), one of the most powerful 'non-governmental' organizations to pursue the global agenda of promoting democracy (Barker, 2008). The NED, like the US Institute for Peace (USIP), was established in the early 1980s as part of the formal institutionalization of the promotion of democracy in US foreign policy. In the early years of the PRC student campaign, the NED supported the publication of the IFCSS newsletter, which was distributed to more than 40,000 students and scholars studying in the USA. It was through this connection that the IFCSS became part of the global effort to promote democracy, which in turn qualified a large number of individual students to apply for political asylum.

In Australia, this strategic change soon proved successful. When the government abolished the onshore humanitarian immigration program in 1989, this meant that all onshore residence claimants for residence had to apply through the refugee program. At the time, the value of an activist approach had already been demonstrated by IFCSS activists in the USA several weeks earlier. Having read and observed the strategies of their counterparts in the USA, the PRC students in Australia likewise adopted active and strategic approaches to pursue their right and opportunity to stay in Australia, and started lobbying intensively on the new migration regulations. For their part, Australia's Chinese newspapers gave significant coverage to their activities. As will be detailed in Chapter Six, The *Australian Chinese Daily*, for example, published 194 items on the subject in 104 issues in the 24-week period from 13 October 1989 to 31 March 1990, an average of about two items per day. These 194 items reported on 48 meetings of the Chinese student activists with senior government officials, including 15 meetings with the Minister for DILGEA and nine meetings with the Prime Minister—an average of two meetings a week.

The third change in the key strategies of the student campaign was to turn their issue from one of politics controlled by someone else to one of politics that could be effectively controlled by them. As several activists noted in interviews, the Chinese student issue was a 'card' played by the main Australian political parties, and the students also needed to seize the initiative and 'grab the card in our hands,' as some put it then (One-on-one interviews, 8 June 1998). More specifically, the need to submit a strong asylum application was the main driving force behind this third shift. The students in Australia realized that they had to learn from their counterparts in the USA how to deal directly with the government in a highly politicized manner. They had become aware that the evidence for their applications to stay as refugees might be not sufficient to meet the government's criteria. Many also realized that the Australian government had its own political interests, having already taken away their chance of staying in the country on humanitarian grounds by abandoning its onshore humanitarian program and introducing many new migration regulations (Cronin, 1993). Many PRC students in Australia asked why the onshore humanitarian program had been swiftly removed from the immigration program at the time when they had strong humanitarian grounds to apply to stay. Many could not answer this question at all, but their community was fortunate in having some highly motivated and skilled members. The above-mentioned interviewee still remembered the conversation he had with one student activist in late 1989, and said:

> He said we had no time to explain why the [Australian] government decided to dump its [onshore] humanitarian [immigration] program. What we now needed was to play a real game, and to have a head-on campaign for our opportunity, not even against anything. Look at the games played by the students in America: they were playing the Chinese *shanggang shangxian* [to magnify some problems into serious political issues, i.e. to politicize some issues] with Yankees now (Interviewee 2, 31 May 1998).

Since there was no hope to be treated like their counterparts in Canada (as explained at the start of Chapter One), the PRC students in Australia paid very close attention to what had happened in the USA. However, because of a low level of readiness for their campaign as compared with their counterparts in the USA, the PRC student community in Australia went through a more rapid politicization of their campaign than any other PRC student community in the West (see Chapter Seven; also see *STN*, 19 December 1989; *FDC Newsletter*, No. 32, 1991; He 1997: 92). They organized countless rallies, press conferences, public seminars, touring photo displays, sit-ins and protests outside China's overseas posts, and commemorations of the students killed during June 4 on every possible occasion—monthly, on the hundredth day after June 4, annually and so on. All these activities were highly organized, and strategically coordinated by the student networks internationally.

There were two other reasons why the IFCSS and other groups all adopted the human rights strategy. In addition to allying themselves with Western criticism of China's human rights record, they understood the strategic value of the term human rights in itself. Playing the human rights card turned out to be more strategic than some of the other, more easily achievable demands put forward in an *ad hoc* way by many PRC students then. For instance, a number of students argued that they wanted to remain in the West until the Chinese government was overthrown, or until certain senior Chinese leaders stepped down. All these were seen as childish and immature. An emerging consensus held that, as their issue dragged on, the students could not stake their future on a few short-term goals tied to quite separate arguments about political fears. International politics became a way to handle any possible changes in both Chinese politics and international politics in the future, and this could create the conditions for their demands to be ultimately fulfilled. Under this refined strategy, a series of political games were played out more skillfully than in earlier stages of their campaign. These will be outlined in the second half of this book. While engaging in lobbying activities and taking a range of organized political actions (see Chapters Six and Seven), a few students also sought to utilize legal options. Their pursuit of the right to asylum through the Australian legal system is outlined in Chapter Five.

CHAPTER FIVE

UTILIZING LEGAL OPTIONS

It did not take long for the PRC students in Australia to understand and make use of another powerful tactic in their asylum seeking campaign, namely the option of utilizing legal channels to challenge the Australian government. In early 1991, five PRC students brought a case against the minister for DILGEA in the Federal Court in the ACT (Australian Capital Territory) and four of them won. This case, known as *Re Wei Jianxin; Zhao Shiji; Hong Lijian; Shi Xuehua and Liu Zhibin v The Minister For Immigration, Local Government and Ethnic Affairs (1991) FCA 207; 29 FCR 455*, set a landmark precedent for handling the student protection issue through the legal system.

As noted in earlier chapters, the Australian government made a range of major changes to its onshore humanitarian and refugee immigration programs in the late 1980s and early 1990s with the intent of controlling the increasing numbers of overstayers and onshore residency claimants. Eleven changes were made to the *Migration Act 1958* between 1989 and 1992, and 58 amendments were also made to the regulations governing Australia's immigration programs (Cronin, 1993; Gao, 2010, 2011), with more than six major changes also being made to the humanitarian and refugee immigration programs. These changes restricted the allowable residence period for all asylum claimants: under the new rules, asylum seekers would receive a four-year temporary permit instead of immediate permanent residence. This was the environment in which the students—both individually and collectively—were engaged in dealing with and, ideally, influencing the changing stance of the Australian government towards onshore asylum seekers. In the end, they would achieve their goal: residency not only for those who had arrived in Australia before June 4, but also for thousands of others who had arrived subsequently. The court case of 1991 was an important factor in this success.

In a ruling by the High Court of Australia in 1989, shortly after June 4, the court found in favor of an individual named Chan Yee Kin in his quest for residency in Australia. Chan came from China, but he was not part of the PRC student group. Nonetheless, his successful case was the 'starting point' (Crock et al., 2006: 86) for the students' actions through the court system. Encouraged by Chan's success, several students sought to replicate it. Both Chan's case and the Federal Court challenge to the Australian government, precisely the DILGEA, brought by several students were part of what has been called the 'tide of immigration litigation,' in the words of John McMillan, Australia's longest serving Commonwealth Ombudsman (2002b: 16). These cases were also part of the 'excessive' use of the court system by people who had been unsuccessful in seeking asylum by other means in Australia (Fonteyne, 1994: 258). This tide was only possible because of two changes to the Australian legal system in the 1970s. The first was the establishment of the Federal Court in 1976; the second was the enactment of the *Administrative Decisions (Judicial Review) Act 1977*, brought into use in 1980 (Douglas, 2006: 60), which created new avenues through which individuals could bring challenges against the government in court.

This chapter elaborates the utilization of legal action in the Chinese students' campaign for residence in Australia. The first section briefly examines the context for immigration litigation in Australia in the late 1980s and 1990s, outlining disputes against the state logic of controlling immigration and the shaping and implementation of 'migrant logic' for negotiating with the state's changing position. The second section looks specifically at the case of Chan Yee Kin. The third section discusses the case of five PRC students studying at the Australian National University (ANU) who took DILGEA to the Federal Court in the ACT, the victory by four of them laying the legal foundation for the resolution of the student protection issue through a blanket approach. The chapter seeks to convey a picture of the social experiences of Chinese activism at a high level, and to show how these Chinese students turned the seemingly impossible into the possible.

The Tide of Immigration Litigation

The 1970s was a transforming decade for Australian society, thanks to a wide range of radical sociocultural and sociopolitical protest movements in the 1960s. In the 1970s, Australian perspectives on war, immigration, the role of women, labor rights, and the rights of indigenous people were undergoing sweeping changes (Betts, 1988; Andrews and Curtis, 1998). The early 1970s were characterized by strong and widespread opposition to the Vietnam War (Kraus, 1994; Viviani, 1996; Firth, 2011) and when the Whitlam Labor government was elected in late 1972, after 23 years of conservative Liberal rule, it promptly decided to pull Australian troops out of Vietnam while introducing various radical sociopolitical changes domestically in the fields of health, education, immigration, industrial relations, and indigenous rights (Anderson and Ashton, 2004). One of the most significant changes that Gough Whitlam's Labor government made to Australian society and its history, however, was its abolition of the White Australia policy. This was a policy that was established in 1901, when Australia became a federation, by two pieces of federal legislation, namely the *Immigration Restriction Act 1901* and the *Pacific Island Labourers Act*, passed by the very first Federal Parliament in 1902 after Australian Federation (Willard, 1967; Lake and Reynolds, 2008). The central points of the policy had been the prevention of migration to Australia by non-white people and the forced deportation of the Pacific Islanders who had been recruited in the nineteenth century as contract migrant workers for the sugar and cotton industries in Australia (Hodge and Whitehurst, 1967; Willard, 1967).[1]

Upon the official abolition of the White Australia policy in 1974, tens of thousands of people from Asia and the Middle East were admitted into Australia in the second half of the 1970s and the 1980s (Meredith and Dyster, 1999), including many refugees from Vietnam (Betts, 1988). At the same time, multiculturalism was introduced as an official policy in Australia (Jupp, 2001). This not only provided new immigrants with a cultural space in which they were able to keep their cultural identity, but also meant that potential immigrants were now to be selected on the basis of relevant eligibility criteria (e.g. relationship to an Australian citizen or permanent resident, skills, qualifications, or humanitarian cases) rather than on the basis of their ethnic background. Multiculturalism as a state policy was further endorsed by the *Racial Discrimination Act 1975*

[1] The White Australia Policy notwithstanding, Chinese migrants and residency seekers from China and from Chinese communities elsewhere have been part of immigration litigation in Australia since the Gold Rush period of the 1850s (Rolls, 1992; Fitzgerald, 2007). The first very large scale Chinese immigration to Australia occurred in the nineteenth century, with about 100,000 Chinese arriving between the 1840s and 1901 (Willard, 1967: 59; Fitzgerald, 2007: 13). During this time, some Chinese migrants claimed the right to migrate and settle in Australia, and the validity of the government's actions against Chinese coolie workers also came under challenge in the colonial courts (Lake and Reynolds, 2008: 24, 40). *Toy v Musgrove* is regarded as the leading example (Bennett, 2007: 190). After Australia became a federation, and because of the impact of the White Australia policy, there was a large decrease in the number of Chinese in Australia, but there were also more court cases involving people of Chinese background (Rivett, 1975; Harris and Ryan, 1998).

(also introduced by the Whitlam government) and was accepted by the major political parties (Jupp, 1995).

Even after the White Australia policy was officially abandoned, and non-discriminatory selection for immigration was officially implemented, the decisions regarding who was allowed to enter Australia and who was not, or who should be deported from the country were in effect still at the discretion of immigration officials and the Immigration Minister under the *Migration Act 1958*.[2] This *Act* had been designed to provide the legal framework for the efficient enforcement of immigration policies and to add safeguards for the rights of the individuals,[3] but in practice it essentially continued the legislative approach endorsed by *the Immigration Restriction Act 1901* (Cronin, 1993) and continued to entail a certain level of discretionary power (Ozdowski, 1985). For most of the 1970s, these discretionary powers and executive decisions on entry and deportation had remained largely unchallenged at an administrative level (Cooney, 1995: 14–15; McMillan, 2002a). However, there was a growing consensus among immigrant advocates and legal professionals regarding the role that a judicial review might play in reviewing and assessing the legality of a range of immigration decisions (McMillan, 2002a); in other words, administrative decisions on entry and deportation needed to be judicially scrutinized and properly reviewed to secure fairness and justice for people in dispute.

The idea of a judicial review of immigration decisions, specifically, the utilization of legal channels to challenge the validity of unfavorable immigration decisions, was not completely new; it had been tried many times even well before Australia became a federation in 1901 and continued to an option or possibility afterwards (Palfreeman, 1967; Cronin, 1993; McMillan, 2002a; Lake and Reynolds, 2008). However, before the late 1970s, there were only two legal avenues available to migrants who wished

---

[2] The *Migration Act 1958* specifies four levels of discretionary power (the minister; 'authorised officers' who are authorized by the minister to exercise power; officers of the Australian police force, customs, and any other persons authorized by the minister to exercise power; and 'prescribed authorities' such as judges in a State Supreme Court and solicitors of five years standing appointed by the minister) (Ozdowski, 1985: 538). In the case of the onshore Chinese students, officials of the immigration department were the main authorities concerned.

[3] The *Migration Act 1958* abolished the notorious dictation test, which was made difficult for non-Europeans to pass and therefore was regarded as the basis of exclusion. The *Migration Act 1958* introduced an easily understood system of entry permits to manage admissions. The *Act* also required that all persons arrested as illegal immigrants or as deportees be given opportunities to obtain legal advice to avoid unfairness in migration controls (Opperman, 1966: 5).

to challenge an undesirable decision made by immigration officials or the Minister for Immigration (ARC, 1986: 30). At the time, they could take legal action against the decision in the High Court under the constitutional writs in Section 75(v) of the Constitution and the High Court's power to review the legality of a government action (McMillan, 2002a: 17). They could also challenge the decision in a State Supreme Court according to federal jurisdiction (McMillan, 2002a: 17). Of course, these legal avenues had not often been tried before the late 1970s and early 1980s, because they were commonly considered 'legally technical and expensive remedies to pursue' (O'Neil, 2003: 198).[4]

The establishment of the Federal Court in 1976 (as an outcome of the *Federal Court of Australia Act 1976*) and the subsequent enactment of the *Administrative Decisions (Judicial Review) Act 1977* reshaped the legal landscape in Australia, and made possible the 'unabated expansion of immigration litigation' in the words of John McMillan (2002b: 17). The establishment of the Federal Court of Australia made additional, and new

[4] Although a judicial review of immigration decisions in Australia was difficult to use before the late 1970s, Chinese migrants have never shied away from taking legal actions. In addition to those mentioned in the first footnote of this chapter, the online databases published by the Australasian Legal Information Institute (AustLII) records the very first ethnic Chinese litigant in the post-White Australia period, a student from Hong Kong. The litigant applied to the AAT in 1977 for review of the immigration minister's decision to deport him even though he had been granted residency (see *Chan and Minister [1977] AATA 19*). Also according to the AustLII, the AAT reviewed 12 immigration-related cases in 1978, and one of the litigants was singled out as having been born in New Zealand of Chinese parents (see *Gin and Minister [1978] AATA 47*). The immigration-related AAT cases in 1978 indicate that not only were the Chinese litigants not the first group of people to take legal action against unfavorable decisions, they also did not account for a large proportion of litigation cases in the late 1970s. In 1980, the AAT only reviewed two appeals from ethnic Chinese; one was from a Singaporean citizen of Chinese ethnic origin, with his wife and son (see *Ang and Minister [1980] AATA 15*), while the other was from a litigant of Chinese origin who was fearful of being imprisoned if returned to Indonesia (see *Kuswardana and Minister [1980] AATA 63*). During the years of the White Australia policy, however, there were more court cases involving people of Chinese background even though the numbers of Chinese immigrants had fallen sharply (Rivett, 1975; Harris and Ryan, 1998). The *Immigration Restriction Act 1901* was found to contain a number of loopholes, and even the then Prime Minister, Alfred Deakin, had to admit that the Chinese in Australia had taken advantage of them (Palfreeman, 1967: 5–6), a fact that led not only to the relatively large number of court cases filed by people from Chinese communities, but also the small increase in the number of these after 1901. Among the approximately 30,000 Chinese immigrants in post-Federation Australia, there were no less than 25 cases filed in 1902 by Chinese in New South Wales (Stacker and Steward, 2004: 22–23), and many other legal cases, such as *Chia Gee v Martin* (1905), *Attorney-General v Ah Sheung* (1906), and *Ah Yin v Christie* (1907). All of these have been well known and documented for decades (Cronin, 1993; Crock, 1998b; McMillan, 2002a; Gao, 2011).

legal, avenues available to immigrants who wished to test adverse decisions; and the *Administrative Decisions (Judicial Review) Act 1977* brought new opportunities for judicial review of such adverse decisions. Administrative procedures constitute the third most important component of Australia's immigration control system (in addition to policy making at Cabinet level and departmental level) (Ozdowski, 1985; ARC, 1986). At operational administrative level, procedural rules are developed, and departmental manuals and instructions are produced, in order to guide the implementation of immigration policies (ARC, 1986). These manuals and instructions have changed from time to time; they have moved from one departmental branch to another; they have not been subject to public scrutiny; and they are not consistent with some provisions or objects of the *Migration Act 1958* (Ozdowski, 1985). Because of many changes to Australia's migration laws, these materials did not necessarily provide comprehensible or complete instructions. In fact, these internal manuals and instructions could allow administrators a measure of discretionary power in any particular claim or personal circumstance (Crock, 1998a; Vrachnas et al., 2005).

The existence of these wide-ranging discretionary powers, and the way in which managerial powers were practically deployed, led to frequent dissatisfaction among immigrants in relation to decisions made by administrators or executives (Ozdowski, 1985; ARC, 1986). In the mid-1980s, Sev Ozdowski, the Commonwealth Human Rights Commissioner from 2000 to 2005, remarked that the smoothness that had characterized the operation and procedure of the immigration decision-making system in Australia had eroded since the early 1970s. He added that:

> Conflicts have arisen over the character of immigrant intake, treatment of undocumented immigrants, and certain aspects of settlement policies. Accusations, for example, have been made that the policies and their administration are not even-handed, but that they are racially or politically motivated, that the system is corrupt and favors those who have better access to power, and that decisions are made in an arbitrary manner and are often enforced with a disregard for human rights. In fact, almost no week passes in Australia without mass media reporting on or criticizing a particular immigration decision or policy (1985: 545).

The *Administrative Decisions (Judicial Review) Act 1977* was enacted on the basis that many Australians believed that there was a need for a system of external review with regard to immigration decisions (ARC, 1986: 9). This was also a response to changing community attitudes and interests, new socioeconomic conditions, and the multicultural nature of Australian society (Price, 1975, 1991). The *Act* simplified the course of action for judicial review; it set out, in the form of a list, the grounds on which the legality of decisions could be challenged; and it also provided immigrants who were not happy with decisions with the right to obtain, in writing, the reasons for an executive decision (Aronson and Dyer, 2000: 11–12; McMillan, 2002a: 17). From the late 1970s, a very wide range of mechanisms for administrative and judicial review were developed and brought into use (Crock, 2006). More than half a dozen review bodies became available to immigrants in their cases. They included the Federal Court or High Court of Australia, the Administrative Appeals Tribunal (AAT), the Immigration Review Panel, the Security Appeals Tribunal (SAT), the Determination of Refugee Status (DORS), the Human Rights Commission, the Commonwealth Ombudsman set up by the *Ombudsman Act 1976*, and Ministerial Representatives (Ozdowski, 1985: 543–544).

In Australia these changes resulted in an intensified debate from the early 1980s about the country's immigration and refugee programs (Betts, 1988; Jupp, 2007). As mentioned in earlier chapters, the changes and the debate also polarized opinions among ordinary Australians, who tended to become either very supportive of, or very unsympathetic toward, new immigrants (Betts, 1988). Consequently, the issue of whether or not the government was able to maintain effective controls became an important consideration in public opinion. At the same time, the 1980s also saw a significant upsurge of discussions about judicial reviews of immigration decision making and disputes over whether or not immigration-related rules were being properly implemented; so much so, indeed, that Roger Douglas (2006: 653) went so far as to conclude that 'judicial review is about migration decisions and little else.' The Federal Court of Australia (which was legitimately established in 1976, and began to exercise its jurisdiction in February 1977) received only two applications for review of immigration-related decisions in 1980, when the new *Administrative Decisions (Judicial Review) Act 1977* was brought into operation. Eleven applications were received in 1981, and there was then a steady increase in the following years. The number of review applications reached 30 in 1985 then increased to more than 84 in 1987–1988 (McMillan, 2002a, 2002b). From the late 1980s, there was an even more striking rise in the number of applications to challenge immigration decisions: 320 in 1993–1994, 673 in 1997–1998, and 914 in 1999–2000. In the first half of 2002, new applications for judicial review had abruptly risen to about 30 per week, including 287 applications before the High Court of Australia in the year of 2002 (McMillan, 2002a, 2002b).

A concomitant increase occurred in the caseload of the High Court of Australia. In 1988–1989, according to the online databases published by the Australasian Legal Information Institute (AustLII), there were only 65 migration-related cases before the High Court. By August 2002, the court had received 407 applications in relation to immigration matters, which was equivalent to an average of 17 new appeal applications per week (see AustLII; Gao, 2011). Philip Ruddock, the then minister for immigration (1996–2003) of the Howard Coalition Government (1996–2007) stated publicly that there were 1,340 cases before the Federal and High Courts in 2000–2001, and that litigation costs for his department had soared from $5.8 million in 1995–96 to about $15 million five years later in 2000–2001 (Ruddock, 2002). During the same period, a large number of applications were also submitted to the Immigration Review Panels, which received 463 cases in 1981–1982, 4,227 in 1982–1983, and 3,729 in 1983–1984 (ARC, 1986: 38).

Of these review applications, a large proportion was lodged by people of ethnic Chinese background. Chinese migrants in Australia have a long history of exclusion and discrimination, but they also have a long history of challenges to discriminatory migration legislation. They have even set a number of precedents in the Australian legal system (Cronin, 1993). Perhaps the most famous incident, and the one that is very relevant for this research, is the case of Chan Yee Kin in 1989, which even 'set the boundaries for refugee determinations in Australia by establishing the "real chance" test' (Crock et al., 2006: 86) and laid the legal foundation for resolving the PRC student issue in the students' favor.

The Chan Yee Kin Case

Born in China in 1951, two years after the Communist revolution, Chan Yee Kin belonged to the first generation that was previously described as being 'born in New China, growing up under the red flag' (*shengzai xin Zhongguo, zhangzai hongqixia*) (Barabantseva, 2005: 19). This was also the generation, who in their youth experienced the turbulent years of the Maoist Cultural Revolution, from mid 1966 to late 1976.[5] Although

[5] The Cultural Revolution (originally, it was called the Great Proletarian Cultural Revolution) was publicly launched by Mao Zedong in May 1966, and lasted for ten years until 1976, when Mao died that September, and his wife and her supporters were arrested the following month. From Mao's perspective, it was intended to 'touch the heart and

his High Court case is famous in Australia, knowledge about his personal background remains very patchy. Australian court records (see *Chan and Department [1985] AATA 119*; *Chan and Department [1985] AATA 149*; *Chan v Minister (1987) 14 ALD 172*; *Minister v Chan (1988) ALD 751*; *Chan v Minister [1989] HCA 62*) note that his background was in rural South China. It would seem that he did not grow up there, as these records also show that he not only joined the Red Guards, but was also involved in factional activities within a team of the Red Guards. These were activities that would only have been possible in an urban area. Of course, it is difficult to imagine how he could have become a Red Guard if, as is also recorded in the court records, his father had been identified as a member of the GMD (Guomindang, Chinese Nationalist Party, also known as KMT, Kuomintang), and had left China in 1950. What was also puzzling was that his father was able to return to China occasionally to visit his family. This would clearly not have been possible under PRC policies of that time, unless he came from a large urban center where his 'anti-revolutionary' family background could be considered negligible.

Australian immigration officers, lawyers and judges recorded that he had become a Red Guard member after leaving school in 1965, an obvious contradiction to known facts, as Red Guard teams were school-based and emerged after June and July 1966. A higher level of political awareness of the time also prevented school leavers from being involved in school-based activities, let alone a person who did not go to university nor have a job. The court documents also recorded that he had been detained in 1968 and listed in his local area as a person opposed to the Chinese government's policies and ideas. However, no court apparently had ever asked for any information as to the grounds for this detention and blacklisting. Despite the mystification as far as his background is concerned, it seems evident

soul of each person' (Feng, 1996: 145) or, more formally, 'aimed at primarily opposing and preventing revisionism' (Andrew and Rapp, 2000: 298). Since the late 1970s, it has been called the 'decade of disaster' (*shinian haojie*) or the 'decade of turmoil' (*shinian dongluan*) (Dillon, 2012: 325). From the perspective of party politics, it is regarded as 'an attempt by Mao to hold on to power and to defeat his opponents' (Glover, 2001: 284). According to Barmé (2005), the Cultural Revolution 'remains one of the most ill-understood and controversial periods in modern Chinese history' (2005: 170). Some outside the field of China studies, for example, consider it 'to be a mass movement of the people that would expose corruption and rid the government of unnecessary bureaucracy' (Cockerham and Cockerham, 2010: 99) or as 'an attempt to preserve revolutionary purity' (Banham, 2000: 208) while others regard it as the political movement that 'paralyse[d] Chinese society and the economy' (Johnson and Turner, 2003: 134). Overall, it had a significant and long-lasting impact on young Chinese (Chan, 1985; Schoenhals, 1996; Langley, 2008).

that Chan was a so-called sent-down 'educated youth' (*zhishi qingnian* or *zhiqing* for short)—an urban person with secondary education who was sent to the countryside to work among the laboring peasants. This was a result of the Maoist policy of 'going up the mountains and down to the villages' (*shangshan xiaxiang*) (Pan, 2003; Yang, 2003). This would be an explanation of why the court documents all refer to his experiences in rural rather than urban China.

It is also on record that Chan escaped to Macau from China in 1974, and that his father, who lived in Hong Kong then, helped him to obtain a Macau ID document with the status of temporary resident, after which Chan went to Hong Kong and stayed there unlawfully for several years (*Chan v Minister (1987) 14 ALD 172*). Having failed to apply for legal residence in Hong Kong, he was deported back to Macau, where he was also detained for more than two weeks. He then returned to Hong Kong illegally to seek an opportunity to board a ship to Australia. He entered Australia successfully, but unlawfully, in August 1980 (according to the High Court document *Chan v Minister [1989] HCA 62*) or November 1980 (according to a Federal Court judge, Mr Keely, *Chan v Minister (1987) 14 ALD 172*).

Again, according to the Federal Court record of the case of *Chan Yee Kin v Minister for DILGEA [1991] FCA 358*, Chan was also detained in Australia after living there unlawfully for more than one and a half years (*Chan v Minister [1991] FCA 358*). He was then held at Maribyrnong Detention Centre in Melbourne for about ten months from 15 April 1982 to 21 February 1983. After this, Chan started his long legal journey to seek residence in Australia in November 1982 by lodging an application for refugee status (*Chan and Department [1985] AATA 119*). He was subsequently interviewed by case officers on 15 December 1982. The Determination of Refugee Status (DORS) Committee considered his application on 22 July 1983, and decided not to grant him refugee status (*Chan and Department [1985] AATA 119*).

His case then went through a review process, and in late November 1983, the immigration minister's representative decided that the DORS recommendation was acceptable, and Chan Yee Kin was not a refugee (*Chan and Department [1985] AATA 149*). However, as noted above, because the *Administrative Decisions Act 1977* had made judicial review available to an immigrant who wanted to challenge an adverse executive decision, Chan's case was reconsidered in 1985. On 16 October 1985, officials from the Department of Immigration and Ethnic Affairs (DIEA), like the DORS tribunal before it, concluded that Chan was not a refugee, whereupon

Chan decided to apply for yet another internal review (*Chan and Department [1985] AATA 149*). He was interviewed again in June 1986 by a DIEA official, and his application for refugee status was once again re-examined by the DORS in August 1986. The committee also once again unanimously recommended that he should not be recognized as a refugee, as his case contained no any evidence to suggest any 'well-founded' fears of persecution (*Chan v Minister (1987) 14 ALD 172*).

As a series of above-mentioned case reviews was taking place, Chan formed a de facto relationship in 1984 with a woman from Malaysia who held a temporary entry permit (*Minister v Chan (1988) ALD 751*). The birth of their child in April 1985 made his case even more complicated. From that time, Chan and his de facto partner not only lodged individual applications for entry permits allowing an indefinite stay in Australia, but their Australian-born child was now also included in both applications (*Minister v Chan (1988) ALD 751*). He could cite his new partner and their child in his 1985 and 1986 applications, seeking a stay on compassionate and humanitarian grounds. His application for refugee status also dragged on. Finally, in late 1986, it went to the Federal Court. There, after a long wait, he received a positive ruling from the Federal Court judge, Mr Keely. In the ruling on *Chan v Minister for DIEA (1987) 14 ALD 172*, Mr Keely overturned the judgment of a DIEA delegate by expressing his belief that Chan was entitled to refugee status.

Soon afterwards, the DIEA appealed to the Full Court of the Federal Court against the ruling by Mr Keely, and the Full Court of the Federal Court reversed Mr Keely's judgment in its ruling *Minister for DIEA v Chan (1988) 12 ALD 751* in July 1988. This court process was the fifth time in over five years that Chan's application for refugee status had been rejected. The only possible option he had left was to take his case to the High Court of Australia, the highest court in the land.

At the time when Chan's case was being re-prepared and taken to the High Court, the phenomenon of onshore asylum seekers was still rather new in Australia (Crock, 2004; DIMIA, 2001), or had just started emerging (Gao, 2011). Mary Crock, a law professor at the University of Sydney and a leading researcher in Australian immigration and refugee law, has found that there were fewer than 500 onshore applications for refugee status per year before mid-1989. Consequently, the legal system in Australia did not have a great deal of experience, at that time, in dealing with refugee appeals, let alone a detailed knowledge of some countries from which numerous asylum seekers had come or the political situations of those countries (Crock, 2004).

More importantly, when the Cold War came toward an end or, more precisely, reached a turning point in the late 1980s, significant changes had taken place in international politics. What emerged was a political atmosphere in which Western democracy, liberalism and ideology, and capitalism and Western culture as well, appeared to emerge triumphant. For several years, Western liberalism came to be not only the prevailing order in Europe and Asia, but also as a blueprint for a new global order (Miall and McKinlay, 2002: 245). In practice, this atmosphere appeared to have made asylum seeking much easier for people from certain types of countries, including China.

As Chan's appeal was being prepared and heard by Australian judges in both the Federal and High Courts, a very significant political change was taking place in relations between Western countries and the Soviet-led Eastern European socialist bloc, the latter of which was coming to a dramatic end. Internationally, a decade-long fight led by the Polish trade union Solidarity was still continuing, and the massive and ongoing Polish strikes in 1988 severely destabilized and weakened the foundations of the socialist bloc (Lévesque, 1997; Ash, 2002). In 1989, the same radical changes were sweeping through more Eastern European countries. The Berlin Wall symbolically dividing the West and the communist East was first forced to open a few checkpoints then, soon after, was dismantled (Engel, 2009). The fall of the Berlin Wall was followed by the executions of the then communist Romanian dictator Nicolae Ceausescu and his wife (Laughland, 2008). Though the Soviet Union was still two years away from its ultimate collapse, 1989 was the year of the political showdown between the capitalist West and the communist East, which some even called the 'revolution of 1989' (Joppke, 1995; Tismăneanu, 1999; Siani-Davies, 2005; Dale, 2006). All these significant changes in international politics made the definition of 'refugee' (which in itself can oversimplify issues of religion, membership of a particular social group or political opinion) more easily applicable to people from the so-called communist-controlled countries.

Chan Yee Kin benefited greatly from persisting with his asylum case for so many years and dragging it on into 1989, when June 4 in Beijing brought strong and widespread sympathy in the international community for its victims. This sympathy included the famous tearful speech by the then Australian Prime Minister, Bob Hawke.[6] Chan's appeal had already

[6] As noted in Chapter One, Bob Hawke had announced in his televised speech, with tears in his eyes, that no PRC student would be forced to return to China (*The Age*, 10 June

been heard in the High Court of Australia before June 4 took place, but the judgment was not delivered until September 1989. In other words, the judgment was being made precisely during a period that began around June 4. It was evident that the personnel of the entire Australian legal system (just as with professionals in other areas) were influenced by what had taken place in China and in international politics generally. Explaining the circumstances in which the case of Chan was decided by the High Court of Australia, Mary Crock has described 1989, and its significance in the Asia Pacific region, in the following way:

> 1989 was a watershed year in the development of an Australian jurisprudence on the definition of refugee. It was also a year that put refugees on the map of political and public consciousness in a way that had not been experienced previously. The year was dominated by stories of conflict and drama in the Asia Pacific Region. Cambodia was in turmoil with the defeat of the Khmer Rouge and the withdrawal of the Vietnamese under the auspices of a United Nations peace plan. In June, after months of euphoric reporting about the imminent demise of communism in China to the forces of the Pro-Democracy movement, the Chinese government instituted a brutal and comprehensive crackdown on its citizenry. In September the High Court delivered its ruling in *Chan Yee Kin*, confirming that this particular fugitive from China did, indeed, meet the definition of refugee. Then, in November, the boats began to arrive—carrying fugitives first from Cambodia and later from China.... It is at this point that the political orientation of Australia's refugee determination system became both apparent and problematic (2004: 57–58).

It was precisely this 'definition of refugee' that was significant for the PRC students in Australia. The High Court reconsidered this definition in its deliberations and decision in the Chan case, and it made its ruling on the basis that the definition of refugee should be not determined ad hoc by immigration officials, but rather with reference to an international convention (Neumann, 2004: 79). The original decision by Mr Keely of the Federal Court was reinstated. The High Court ruling believed that the refusals by the DILGEA (formerly the DIEA) and the Full Federal Court to grant refugee status to Chan were made partly because 'the decision-maker must have misconstrued the proper test' and partly because 'his disbelief of the applicant's claims was grossly unreasonable' (Aronson and Dyer, 2000: 281).

1989). He delivered the speech on 6 June 1989 at the very emotional memorial service held in Canberra for the victims of June 4. For more information, please read Dodkin (2003: 31) and Jupp (2003: 191).

Significantly, the High Court decision led to a new understanding of 'well-founded fear' in determining precisely what constituted a refugee. Fear, as a state of mind, is a subjective condition of the person seeking recognition as a asylum seeker. Since fear is subjective, according to the *Handbook on Procedure and Criteria for Determining Refugee Status* produced by the United Nations High Commissioner for Refugees, the process to determine refugee status primarily requires an evaluation of the *applicant's statements* rather than a judgment on the situation in his or her country of origin (UNHCR, 1988: 9, my emphasis). Although the High Court decision in the Chan case mentioned both the subjective and the objective components of the phrase 'well-founded fear,' it in effect rejected the suggestion that objective assessment requires proof that the applicant would, in fact, be persecuted if one returned to his or her home country.

Up to the late 1980s, Australian politicians and bureaucrats had been reluctant to consider the subjective element of any refugee claim, even though this element was undoubtedly one of the international standards included in the UNHCR handbook. What the High Court of Australia did in the case of Chan was essentially to emphasize this clause from the UNHCR handbook as the basis for their ruling. For that reason, refugee application materials that focused on 'well-founded' fears of persecution became the critical factor in asylum seeking in Australia. This also meant that asylum seeking, to a great extent, became a process that was in the hands of the claimant. The *feeling* of the asylum seeker (i.e. his or her fear of persecution) was now as much a determining factor as—or indeed an even greater one than—the actual facts of the situation. This may have been the most vital element in the High Court decision on Chan's case. Of course, it is certainly the one that has generated the most controversy over the past 20 years (McMaster, 2001; Bagaric et al., 2006). It meant that more asylum seekers or refugee applicants could potentially be accorded refugee status (Cooney, 1995: 17).[7]

According to common law principles, the case of Chan Yee Kin set legal precedents by establishing three things. First, the definition of what

[7] It also emboldened Chan to seek a large sum of money from the immigration department in compensation for losses and suffering as a result of his detention, which he did in August 1991 (*Chan Yee Kin v Minister for DILGEA [1991] FCA 358*). His attempt was unsuccessful as the Federal Court judge found 'no tort or other legal basis exists for the award,' but the government was pushed to pass legislation in 1992 'to cap any compensation payment to an asylum seeker detained unlawfully at one dollar a day' in *Migration Amendment Act (No. 4) 1992 (Cth).* (Crock, 2004: 7).

constitutes a refugee was now to involve both subjective and objective criteria. Second, the definition of 'refugee' could now be satisfied if the person's fear of persecution has a reasonable basis, i.e. if there is a 'real chance' that the person could be in danger of persecution upon return to their country of origin (Crock, 1998a: 54; Crock et al., 2006: 86). Third, the High Court had sought to interpret the nature or the meaning of the persecution feared by asylum seekers. In doing so, the High Court in fact broadened the scope of 'persecution' to include any harm that would be regarded as offensive by ordinary people in Australia. Consideration of the actual circumstances of people and places now seemed relegated to secondary importance.

The inclusion of subjective elements in the refugee definition was excellent news for the PRC students who were, at that time, busy collecting various forms of evidence for their refugee claims (discussed in Chapter Three). Previously, they had all thought that the granting of refugee status would be determined by the factual situation, not by the feeling of the asylum seeker. Yet now the High Court judgment seemed to be suggesting to asylum seekers that they should, first and foremost, demonstrate their own subjective fear of persecution upon return to their country of origin, before substantiating their claimed fear of persecution with any evidence.

At a number of meetings, several Chinese student activists repeatedly exhorted that 'you have to show immigration officers your fear. Unless you clearly express it, no one will like to invite you to stay as a refugee' (Student activist meeting, early January 1990). While this kind of public appeal and any possible consequent actions made many students worried about competing with each other, student leaders and activists directly and openly warned that the real worry was that too many students would be 'fearless' and would not submit refugee applications. Failure to do so would mean that the student community as a whole would have no case to argue for having 'well-founded' fears of persecution. A former student who attended one of the above meetings summarized it in this way:

> Several student leaders appeared to believe that it would be a real problem if many [students] did not tell their fear clearly. For that reason, there were several meetings [to discuses this]. The most useful message [from the meetings] was that the refugee definition was practically explained as the 'well-expressed' fears of returning to China.... We were told not to worry about whether case officers believed our case. The [Western] media already told them the lot, and what we needed was to say [that] all those bad things happened to us (Interviewee 11, 14 February 1998).

These accounts showed that through their own reading and information, many PRC activists already understood what Australian legal specialists clearly became aware of only after the Chan Yee Kin case: that '"well-founded fear" is central to the definition of refugee,' as Justice McHugh of the High Court of Australia stated in his announcement of the court's decision (*Chan v Minister [1989] HCA 62*). This was why the student leaders and activists were now, genuinely and repeatedly, telling their fellow students that their fate was in their own hands, and that the key to their asylum seeking was to tell immigration officials and refugee case officers that they feared to return to China (*ACD*, 14 September 1989; *STN*, 31 October 1989).

Under the influence of June 4 and the speculative English-language media coverage that followed the incident—especially the predictions of serious large-scale persecution and even a civil war in China—(*The Age*, 5 June 1989; *The Australian*, 6 June 1989), the High Court Justices articulated the phrase 'well-founded fear' by offering the now famous 'real chance' test. The objective element in the UN's definition of refugee requires that subjective fear be well founded; but in terms of what actually constitutes a 'well-founded fear,' the High Court of Australia denied any distinction between 'real possibility,' 'good reason [for fearing]' and 'reasonable likelihood' of persecution. Instead, the High Court established that 'it is enough that persecution is a reasonable possibility' (*Chan v Minister [1989] HCA 62*). Anthony Mason, then Chief Justice of the High Court, stated that there does not need to be a 50 percent, or greater chance of persecution in order for a person's fear of persecution to be well-founded (*Chan v Minister [1989] HCA 62*). Justice McHugh took this particular point further by saying that a real chance of persecution excluded 'a far-fetched possibility of persecution,' but that even as little as a 10 percent likelihood of persecution could still amount to a 'well-founded fear' of persecution (*Chan v Minister [1989] HCA 62*). Justice Dawson in his part of the decision stated that a 'real chance' is one that is 'not remote,' regardless of whether it is less or more than 50 percent. As three of the five High Court Justices had all mentioned the phrase 'real chance,' the High Court's decision essentially ruled that the definition of 'refugee' would be satisfied provided there is a 'real chance' of persecution. This is now known as the 'real chance test.'

Along with their elaborations of the percentage possibility of being persecuted, the High Court ruling also briefly noted that the meaning of persecution includes various forms of penalty or punishment. According to three of these five High Court Justices, the meaning of 'persecution' ought to be interpreted as the way in which an 'ordinary Australian' would view the word: i.e., as 'harassment,' 'threatened harm' or 'other offensive behaviour' (Crock et al., 2006: 86). This definition was another controversial aspect of the case of Chan Yee Kin. Chief Justice Mason stated that the UN Refugee Convention considered serious punishment, penalty, major detriment or even disadvantage to be persecution. Justice Mason specifically defined 'harm or the threat of harm,' saying that harm or the threat of harm, as 'part of a course of selective harassment of a person, whether individually or as a member of a group subjected to such harassment by reason of membership of the group, amounts to persecution if done for a Convention reason' (*Chan v Minister [1989] HCA 62*).

The denial of fundamental rights or freedoms enjoyed by nationals of the country concerned was also construed as constituting persecution. In Justice McHugh's definition, persecution involved selective harassment (*Chan v Minister [1989] HCA 62*). He listed as many as nine points, called by Crock et al. (2006: 87) 'Justice McHugh's formulation,' to define what he considered to be persecution. First, it was not necessary that persecution be directed against a person as an individual, and it would be enough if an individual were a member of a group that was the subject of systematic harassment. Second, it was not a necessary element of 'persecution' that the person should be the victim of a series of acts. Third, a single act of oppression may suffice, as long as the individual was threatened with harm and that harm could be viewed as part of a course of systematic conduct directed against that person as an individual or as a member of a class for a reason cited under the UN Convention. Fourth, the threat did not need be the product of any policy of the government of the individual's country of nationality, and it might be enough to be considered persecution if the government had failed, or was unable, to protect the person from being persecuted. Fifth, to constitute 'persecution,' the harm need not be loss of life or liberty: other forms of harm short of interference with life or liberty may also amount to 'persecution,' including measures that are 'in disregard' of human dignity. Sixth, serious violations of human rights for a reason mentioned in the Convention would constitute persecution. Seventh, loss of employment as a result of political activities may be a form of persecution. Eighth, the denial of access to employment, to the professions, to opportunities for education, or the imposition of restrictions on the freedoms that are guaranteed in a democratic society (including those of speech, assembly, worship or movement) may constitute persecution. Ninth, being subjected to injurious action and oppression for reason of one's political opinion or membership of a social group opposed to the government constituted persecution (*Chan v Minister [1989] HCA 62*; Crock et al., 2006: 87).

Because of these detailed clarifications, the concept of 'persecution' became a simple phrase that could refer to any harm inflicted upon those who differ in race, religion or political opinion, in a way that would be consider being offensive by ordinary Australians. On the basis of these details, as noted, several student activists urged more students to clearly express their fear and show that they were very fearful of returning to China (Student activist meeting, early January 1990). This approach was once mocked by some students who paraphrased it as 'I am fearful and scared, therefore I stay.'[8]

The ANU Students v the Immigration Department

The Chan case was the touchstone for Australian acceptance of refugees from China. The highest court in the land had set legal boundaries for determining refugee cases and provided new guidance for immigration officials with regard to the process. Also, the Chan case had shown that Australian elites had very little understanding of Chinese politics and the political behavior of Chinese people and groups. Within the PRC student community itself, there were two widespread reactions to the case. Some believed that Chan was irrelevant to what had happened in 1989 or, in the words of the time, irrelevant to the Democratic Movement of 1989. Others pointed out that Chan was not from any of the clearly identified social groups (such as writers, artists, journalists and teachers) that had frequently been targeted by the successive campaigns, political purges and repressions in China. Student activists used these two viewpoints to argue that, if Chan was able to win, all students could succeed in seeking protection in Australia. That is, apart from forming a new understanding of 'well-expressed' fear in seeking asylum, the entire student community was making every effort to understand the implications of the Chan case for their own asylum seeking. The effort was so exemplary of the student

[8] Some readers may be familiar with this sentence pattern. It is based on the French philosopher Rene Descartes's famous phrase, 'I think, therefore I am' ('Cogito, ergo sum' in Latin; or 'Je pense, donc je suis' in French) (Pritchard, 2010: 37; Corballis, 2011: 1). This small example may help readers understand that some educated Chinese are not complete strangers to Western culture, and therefore the PRC students in this case were not only able to learn how to take legal action quickly, but were also able to identify new strategies for their campaign.

activism that it has left some with lasting memories. One former student recalled:

> The topic [of the Chan case] was brought up repeatedly whenever we met, with an intention to compare our own situation with that of the Chan case.... Overall, such discussions became very frequent and heated before mid December 1989 [the introduction of the new *Migration Act*], in mid 1990 [the four-year visa was granted], and then in mid and late 1993 [before the expiry of the four-year visa]. However, we all believed in one thing: Chan was not truly relevant to June 4, and his asylum case was not as strong as ours were. We had been encouraging each other to prepare ourselves to do what Chan did, if one day we were asked to leave [Australia] after the four-year protection (Interviewee 36, 30 May 1998).

In fact, such intense discussions about Chan's victory in the High Court generated strong internal pressure within the student community, which eventually caused several students to decide to take action earlier than other students. Of course, it was also logical that after Chan's victory, the next step was to test whether the principle that had been established in the Chan case would be applicable to the cases of the students. Chan had already been in Australia for many years and few students could have wished to put their lives and careers on hold for such a long period, or to persist in engaging in such lengthy legal battles with immigration officials as Chan had done. But many also wanted to see if the Australian legal system—their last possible resource to utilize—would find in their favor (Le, 2001). At the same time, the success of the Chan case in the High Court had created such an 'extraordinary furore within bureaucratic and political spheres' (Crock, 1998b: 134) that many Chinese students began to worry about the possible impact of the Chan controversy on their own refugee applications (*ACD*, 10–11 February 1990).

Five students studying at the Australian National University (ANU) in Canberra decided to take action: they took DILGEA, the department responsible for immigration, to the Federal Court in the Australian Capital Territory (ACT) on the grounds of DILGEA's 'bureaucratic delays' in making its decision on their applications for residence on strong humanitarian grounds. Interviews suggest that many other students felt that this move had to be taken quickly and at the opportune moment—at a time when many Australians still remained both sympathetic to the students and naïve in regard to what was then happening in China.[9] With the

[9] After June 4, there was speculation for a few years about a possible civil war or for long-term sociopolitical instability in China (Gittings, 2006). Such speculation was so

assistance of the lawyer Marion Le, who had been an active and prominent refugee advocate in Australia since the 1970s, four of the five ANU students eventually won their case. Their victory in the case known as *Re Wei Jianxin; Zhao Shiji; Hong Lijian; Shi Xuehua and Liu Zhibin v The Minister For Immigration, Local Government and Ethnic Affairs [1991] FCA 207; 29 FCR 455* (hereafter called *Wei v Minister [1991] FCA 207*) opened the door for the processing of some 20,000 other cases (Le, 2001).

According to the court records for the *Wei v Minister* case, all five applicants had come to Australia before 4 June 1989 in order to pursue their postgraduate studies or research at the ANU (*Wei v Minister [1991] FCA 207*). They had also arrived well in advance of the large cohorts of ELICOS students (see Chapter One). Dr Shi had arrived in Australia in January 1984; Messrs Wei, Zhao and Hong in December 1986; and Mr Liu in March 1987. The times of their arrivals, the fact that they had been accepted by the ANU, and the fact that they had all been officially sent by the Chinese government under its government sponsored student and scholar programs (Orleans, 1988) indicate without a doubt that they were all research students.

Each of the five applicants had applied for permanent residence on strong humanitarian grounds, the program of which was available before 19 December 1989. Among them, Shi and Liu applied in February 1989, Zhao in October 1989, Hong in November 1989, and Wei on 14 March 1990 (the last being later than 19 December 1989, the originally set cut-off date for onshore resident status claimants to apply to stay on strong humanitarian grounds) (*Wei v Minister [1991] FCA 207*). As introduced in Chapter Three, the new *Migration Legislation Amendment Act 1989* contained a series of provisions to firmly prevent what was called 'queue-jumping': as of 19 December 1989, it became no longer permissible for the people who had already arrived in Australia (whether lawfully and unlawfully) to apply to stay from within the country. In the case of the five ANU students, four of their applications (i.e. those of every student except Wei, the first applicant in the case) had been made to DILGEA under the old *Migration Act*. In order to get their applications considered under the old legislation, a resident status application had to have been submitted to DILGEA before 19 December 1989 for it to be accepted by

widespread in the Australian media and among PRC activist groups and their supporters that little attention was paid to fundamental changes taking place in China, especially the changes after Deng Xiaoping's southern inspection tour (Barmé, 2000).

the court for hearing. Wei's application was technically too late for this. The court records in the *Wei v Minister [1991] FCA 207* case show that the other four applicants had applied for refugee status as well as residency. This means that these PRC students were involved in two quite separate asylum-seeking processes: on strong humanitarian grounds, and through the refugee program.[10]

However, the court case brought by the five students did not relate to their refugee applications. The complaint of all five appellants was that no decision had yet been made regarding their submitted applications for permanent resident status on strong humanitarian grounds. All of them were seeking a court order of review under the *Administrative Decisions (Judicial Review) Act 1977* in respect of the failure to make a decision on their applications on the grounds of 'unreasonable delay in making the decision' within the meaning of several sections in the *Administrative Decisions (Judicial Review) Act 1977*.

Some PRC students thought that the five appellants' decision to seek a judicial review before taking any further legal action was a strategic move, believing that in the wake of Chan's High Court case, their chance of success would be greater if they took their case to court (*ACD*, 10–11 February 1990) (One-on-one interviews, 12 and 13 April 1998). In the Chan case, the High Court's decision had established the applicant's fear of being persecuted (on one of the several grounds specified in the UN Convention) as the standard to be applied in the so-called 'real chance' test. As mentioned, there was a widespread understanding among many PRC students at the time that Chan's case had no real relevance to June 4. And if Chan, who had no connection with June 4, could be granted refugee status, then all of them must easily meet the requirements to stay as refugees (One-on-one interviews, 12 and 13 April 1998).

Chan's victory was already established, thanks to the full bench of the highest court of the land, whose verdict was not reviewable and against whose decision there was no further appeal. However, Chan's residency was guaranteed; residency for other PRC students was not. Lawyers and a number of sympathetic bureaucrats advised the student activists that although the UN Refugee Convention prohibits the return of a refugee to a country where he or she may face persecution; there is no requirement to grant long-term or even short-term protection to such a person

10 This two-fold tactic was once known by the Chinese students as 'being double-locked' and it was widely used by the students.

(*STN*, 31 October 1989, Le, 2001). The students were also informed that there was another test, called the 'changed circumstances' test (*ACD*, 10–11 February 1990). Under the widely cited 1951 Convention, refugee status is not intended as a permanent category, and the 1952 Convention sets out circumstances in which it ceases to apply. These include a change in the circumstances in the country of origin that had led to recognition of refugee status (Milner, 2004). The clauses in the Convention that provide the framework within which refugee status may be lawfully withdrawn or 'ceased'—known as the cessation clauses—make it clear that refugee status may be transient where the situation in the country on which the refugee status application was originally based has so clearly changed that international protection is no longer needed.

The cessation clauses were a matter of concern to many PRC student leaders and activists (Student activist meeting, early January 1990; *ACD*, 10–11 February 1990; Crock, 1998b). Obviously, refugee status was not necessarily a guarantee of long-term residence in Australia; and because the cessation clauses had not been considered in any detail in the case of Chan Yee Kin, their precise effect was as yet unknown. In the Chan case, the High Court had explicitly recognized the force of political fear (the kind of fear that PRC students felt in the 1980s), regardless of whether or not it could be substantiated; but the court had not invoked the cessation clauses, and the students, therefore, had nothing to guide them as to how these clauses might be applied and whether there might be exemptions from them.

Two further factors added to the students' anxiety lest the Australian government invoke the cessation clauses. The first factor was the size of the student group. Shortly after June 4, the group totalled 20,000 or so (Jupp, 1991; Gao, 2001), but it increased to approximately 45,000 a few months after (Cronin, 1993; Birrell, 1994), and these increased figures did not include their spouses and children. In the Chan case, Chan as an illegal immigrant who had been living in Australia for more than eight years had not been able to bring other family members into Australia; the maximum number of people he could bring in being the three members of his new immediate family, and they were already resident in Australia. Because of their closer observation of Australian society, especially its politics, in the mid and late 1980s, these students were fully aware that Australia was not a country that welcomed Asians. They also knew that at the time when they were seeking to stay, many Australians held very negative attitudes toward Chinese and Chinese immigrants. Thus, what they were worried about was that the case of the Chinese student cohort as a whole could give rise to a very different scenario from that which had been there in the Chan case. That is, the enormous number of new Chinese immigrants that they could bring in under Australia's family reunification program could well have been an excuse or reason that the Australian government might invoke when applying the cessation clauses.[11]

The second factor that also worried many students at the time was the Australian government's decision to allow a further 25,000 students to come to Australia a few months after June 4. Many students interpreted this as a strong and clear signal that the Australian government did not intend to solve their issue (Student activist meeting, early January 1990); it was suspected that the government had deliberately increased the total number of PRC students so that they could make a strong case for not allowing them to stay.

These concerns were not groundless. These students knew as early as June 1989 that they could apply for permanent protection in Australia (*The Australian*, 7 June 1989), and since that time, the Chinese-language newspapers had been actively reporting on their quest for protection and permanent residency. However, at the very time when the students were considering applying for asylum and preparing their asylum applications, the Australian government had, as noted, suddenly removed the onshore humanitarian immigration program from its immigration system.[12] June 4 had drawn Australia into the international politics of the time, placing

---

[11] Their worries were not groundless at all. In fact, in 1992, Gerry Hand, the then Minister for Immigration (April 1990–March 1993, representing the left faction of the ALP) used the number against a blanket approach to the Chinese student issue (Easterbrook, 1992). Hand estimated that if the spouses and children of these 45,000 students were included, together with the effects of chain migration, 'the original 17,000 Chinese might increase to 300,000 by the turn of the century' (Jose, 1995: 58). Of course, Gerry Hand was 'dumped' or retired from the position soon after making the comment, which was said to be damaging to the Labor Party's ethnic support, and his estimate was quickly denied. As mentioned in Chapter One, especially in Footnote 16, there has been a significant increase in the Chinese-language speaking population in Australia since the mid 1990s. There were around 300,000 ethnic Chinese living in Australia in 1992, and the 2001 Census revealed that the number had increased to 401,357, with 555,560 claiming Chinese ancestry (Chan, 2005), proving that Gerry Hand was at least mathematically correct.

[12] This was part of the overhaul of the *Migration Act 1958* in the second half of 1989. To understand why the students had to act strategically, three changes should be taken into consideration: (1) the removal of the onshore humanitarian immigration program; (2) restricting onshore asylum seekers to applying for residency through a refugee program (Cronin, 1993); and (3) the introduction of mandatory deportation after a period of 28 days' grace if refugee status was not granted (DILGEA, 1989). The last policy alone created what many students described as a live-or-die situation, driving them into further politicization and taking more strategic action.

it in a position where it was compelled to join other Western countries in providing asylum for PRC nationals living within its borders. However, media coverage of the debates among Australian politicians about how, or whether, the PRC students should be protected (*The Sun*, 8 June 1990; *The Australian*, 28 June 1990) made it evident that June 4 could simply deliver protection or permanent residency if the students acted swiftly and strategically.

As mentioned, most of the Chinese students studying in Australia in the late 1980s had lived through the chaotic period of Chinese politics in the late 1960s and 1970s, and they all had many complex sociopolitical experiences and offered a wide range of skills. After many discussions about the risks that might be caused by the application of the cessation clauses to their asylum seeking, two different approaches emerged. The first one believed that the risk was not really caused by the cessation clauses, but by the 'June 4 victim mentality' and by those who simply wanted to wait for residency without contributing to the campaign. The students who believed in this idea advocated not only political action, but also organized action as a means to deal with any risks that may occur. One former overstayer explained his perspective:

> The [cessation clauses] talk sounded very scary at first, as not many [students] could find anything to read except a couple of Chinese newspapers. Later on, all my CAD friends said that the real danger was because many did not want to be a CAD or FDC member, and that if you were [a CAD or FDC member], Australia had to protect you forever.... These memberships would provide us with a better protection than going to the court (Interviewee 40, 13 April 1998).

At the same time, some postgraduate students, as exemplified by the five ANU students, tried to use their own connections and skills to take swift action. Accustomed to acquiring and interpreting clues from government policies, they were quick to find a way to argue to be permitted to stay permanently in Australia, even when there was only a slim chance via Australia's existing immigration policies or programs. Thus, the availability of a judicial review process for executive decisions under the *Administrative Decision Act 1977* was seen—and utilized—as a counter-balance to the Australian government's far-reaching effort to tighten its border controls. As the main vehicle for a judicial review, the above *Act* shifted attention away from specific remedies towards whether grounds for a judicial review could be established or 'whether a legal error could be shown' (Cane and McDonald, 2008: 53). Even if the changes to the immigration law and regulations in 1989 were a means of tightening controls of immigration, the numerous amendments had transformed the policy from a 'shell' that allowed broad discretion to a relatively detailed code of rules (Cooney, 1995). Therefore, a refusal or failure on the part of the immigration department to make a decision could be then brought under review. Since one of the most frequent complaints made against this department was related to its unnecessary delays (Aronson and Dyer, 2000: 274), this was a very real option.

Because of numerous amendments to the *Migration Act 1958*, which 'set out an exhaustive list of visas and entry permits and all of the criteria that needed to be met before any particular visa or entry permit could be successfully granted' (Vrachnas et al., 2005: 21), DILGEA was forced to set various priorities for processing the enormous number of applications it received (about 45,000 onshore applications from PRC nationals alone, including 20,000 from the 'pre-20 June group' and 25,000 in the 'post-20 June group'). This meant that there was a very long waiting period before applicants were informed of the results of their applications. Here the five ANU-based Chinese students saw their opportunity. If they took legal action against the bureaucratic delays, they would at least learn the results of their applications to stay on strong humanitarian grounds, and they could then make a decision on whether still to pursue residency by means of refugee status, and on how seriously they should pursue it. A number of Australian sympathizers and lawyers (Le, 2001) were behind their brave decision to take DILGEA to the Federal Court on the grounds of the 'bureaucratic delays' in making its decision on their applications. After a lengthy period of preparation, the five initiated their action (Le, 2001).

Though their applications were submitted individually, the five ANU student appellants agreed to have their cases heard together. This took place on 22 May 1991. The court ruled that in four cases (all except the case of Wei), the situation was not acceptable. It ordered that within a period of eight weeks from the date of hearing the case, the immigration department had to make a decision regarding the students' applications for residency on humanitarian grounds, or must ensure that an officer of the department had the authority to do so. Wei's application was a more complex case because it had been made after the two specified cut-off dates (the original cut-off date 19 December 1989 and the later, revised cut-off date 12 March 1990) for onshore claimants to apply for residency on strong humanitarian grounds. As mentioned, his application had been made on 14 March 1990. Approximately half of the court's judgment was devoted to Wei for this reason. His application was subsequently dismissed.

One aspect of the case that was particularly significant to the Chinese student community as a whole was the court ruling on the illegal status of Shi and Liu. The court believed that their illegal status resulted from DILGEA's delay in dealing with their asylum applications (one of which had been lodged as early as February 1989). The court was apparently upset by the fact that no decision, even a decision in principle, had been reached after a period of two years and three months. The court was also disturbed by the fact that no explanation had been offered as to why no steps had been taken by the department in relation to the two students' applications between February 1989 and December 1989 (i.e. prior to the striking increase in the number of onshore residency applications). The immigration department explained that the number of applications had strained its resources 'well over the limit' (*Wei v Minister [1991] FCA 207*), and this statement was supported by statistical material. However, the court found that the evidence failed to establish that DILGEA had taken any steps to consider the applications and make any decision. This was judged as an unreasonable delay.

The *Wei v Minister* case was part of the increase 'at an exponent rate' in the number of immigration litigation applications in Australia in the late 1980s and early 1990s (Crock, 1996: 288; also see McMillan, 2002a, 2002b; Gao, 2011). At the time, 44 percent of all appeals made by onshore asylum seekers to the Federal Court alone were subsequently determined in favor of the appellants (Crock, 1996: 290).[13] Whether or not a 44 percent success rate made judicial review into a helpful mechanism for redressing grievance, the Federal Court's decision on *Wei v Minister* was very significant for the Chinese student community in that it at least calmed the tense atmosphere generated by the administrative delays. It also significantly boosted the PRC students' confidence, especially when the case was taken in connection with the High Court's ruling on the Chan case.[14] The victory of the four ANU students in the Federal Court was, in the words of Marion Le, the moment when the door opened for the processing of many other onshore applications (Le, 2001). As a result of this Federal Court decision, out of the 4,300 or so humanitarian applicants who had registered before 31 March 1990, more than 2,000 PRC students were granted residence (DIEA, 1994: 6).

[13] The same analysis also revealed that in 1989–1990, and 1991–1992, 46 percent and 42 percent of the court cases respectively went against the Immigration Department, which 'would seem to be more than sufficient to encourage disgruntled applicants to seek recourse through the courts' (Crock, 1996: 291).

[14] According to Fung (1996), this successful court case against the then Minister for Immigration, Gerry Hand, by five Chinese students was 'the most inspiring lesson for the students in learning about Western society and democracy' (1996: 140).

CHAPTER SIX

LOBBYING

In late 1992, news was circulating among the Chinese students living in Australia on four-year temporary permits. Prime Minister Paul Keating, in a meeting in Sydney with Li Lu, one of the leaders of the Tiananmen protest of 1989,[1] promised that he would honor the commitment made by his predecessor, Bob Hawke. As noted in Chapter Two, Hawke once promised that no Chinese nationals would be forced to return to China. Moreover, Paul Keating had also said that he planned to consider their protection or residency issue in terms of a 'long-term strategy' (*ACD*, 17 December 1992; *FDC Newsletter*, No. 1, 1993).

The Prime Minister's assurance held the real promise of permanent residency for the entire student group, although 'long-term strategy' had very different meanings for Keating and Li Lu. Li urged the Australian government to let the students stay permanently as a way of keeping the 'seeds of revolution' alive for the sake of a democratic future in China.[2] Paul Keating, on the other hand, seems likely to have been envisaging the students playing a bridging role between Australia and China. At the time, China's economic growth was once again accelerating after Deng Xiaoping's famous 'southern inspection tour' in the spring of 1992.[3] In his first

[1] Li Lu, a former student at Nanjing University, had been one of the student leaders of the Tiananmen Square protests. Afterwards he fled to France and then later in 1989 went to the USA, where he studied at Columbia University. After completing his studies he remained in the USA as a hedge-fund manager and investment banker (Li, 1990; Cunningham, 2009; Pulliam, 2010). His visit to Australia was for the purpose of rallying Australian supporters for his election at the first joint FDC and CAD convention, which was to be held in February 1993 (Chen and Lu, 1994; Kong, 1999; Fan, 2007).

[2] The expression 'seeds of revolution,' a typical Chinese communist term, was met with laughter when the Keating-Li meeting was reported at FDC and CAD meetings in Australia. It had been a big joke to many students, and for this reason, it was occasionally changed to 'seeds of Chinese democracy.' However, it was indeed thought by some to express a convincing political argument for the student lobby.

[3] As noted in Chapter Five, Deng's southern tour to the Special Economic Zone of Shenzhen in early 1992 is considered by many to be a turning point in post-1989 Chinese politics (Zhao, 1993; Barmé, 2000). It was on this tour that Deng ordered people to 'stop arguing as to whether the Reforming and Opening movement should be labeled "capitalism" or "socialism"' (Huang et al., 1997: 100), but to be 'more risky and more daring to make experiments in reform and opening' (cited in Chen, 2008: 51).

political term (from December 1991 to March 1993), Keating painted a 'big picture' of Australia's future. A key aspect of his vision of future Australia was 'engagement with Asia' by Australia as a republic that was no longer bound by old ties to Britain, but by new alliances and attitudes that would help the country to create a new economic, strategic and cultural future in its Asia-Pacific neighborhood (Burke, 2007; Kelly 2010).[4] At the time he met Li, Paul Keating was planning his first Prime Ministerial visit to China. That visit eventually took place in June 1993, three months after Keating had won his second term in the 'unwinnable' 1993 federal election.[5] His meeting with Li Lu, which took place just a few weeks before he called the election, may well have been a calculated strategy to win support from Chinese constituencies.[6]

Li Lu was not the only Chinese student leader to visit Australia and meet local political leaders in 1992–1993. No less than half a dozen high-profile Chinese dissidents, including Wan Runnan,[7] Zhu Jiaming[8] and Yu Dahai,[9] came to Australia from the USA or Europe (where they were

[4] According to Geoff Raby, an Australian former ambassador to China, Paul Keating had fully understood China's economic and strategic potential on his first visit there in early 1989 (Raby, 2012). Keating expressed 'great respect and admiration for Deng Xiaoping' and regarded him as the leader of the twentieth century who would be most influential on the coming century (Keating, 2000).

[5] Even though Australia's Labor government had been in power for ten years and economic recovery from the recession of the early 1990s was slow, Keating led the party to its fifth consecutive victory in the 1993 election against the Liberal/National coalition led by John Hewson (Gordon, 1993; Kelly, 2010).

[6] There is little evidence that Keating's meeting with Li actually helped Labor to win any votes from Chinese Australians in 1993. However, it is also true that many casual observations of this group of new Chinese settlers have indicated that many of them have been Labor voters in the past 20 or so years.

[7] Educated at Tsinghua University, Wan Runnan was the founder of the Beijing-based Stone Corporation, the first private Chinese high-tech company (Miles, 1996: 227). Wan and his company publicly supported the Tiananmen Square student protests. Afterwards he fled to France, where he played a key role in the formation of the FDC and was elected its Secretary-General at the inaugural conference in September 1989 (Goldman, 1994; Kennedy, 1997).

[8] Zhu Jiaming, a graduate of the Chinese Academy of Social Sciences, was one of Beijing's 'four princes' (Chen and Jin, 1997: 144) or 'four gentlemen' (Fewsmith, 2001: 59) who were actively involved in the early rural and enterprise reforms of the 1980s. As a member of Zhao Ziyang's young think tank (Cunningham, 2009), he supported the Tiananmen protests. He too fled to France. He acted as chair of both the FDC (1991–93) and the CAD (1993–94) (Sausmikat, 2003).

[9] Yu Dahai graduated from Peking University and received a doctorate from Princeton. While studying at Princeton he was involved in the formation of the Young Chinese Economists Society (Chow, 1994: 66). He was president of the CAD (1991–93) and headed the *China Spring* magazine before becoming chief editor of *Beijing Spring* (1993–96) (Chen and Lu, 1994; He, 1996).

living in exile) to meet both their Chinese supporters living in Australia and Australian politicians. All of these visits and meetings were in fact part of the lobbying activities of the Chinese activist groups in Australia, which had been intensifying since mid 1990 when they were given four-year temporary protection permits. Unlike their earlier lobbying, which had been loosely organized by independent student unions or the IFCSS (discussed in Chapter Four), these new, intensified activities (including the visits by prominent Chinese democracy activists) were organized by the Federation for Democratic China (FDC) and the Chinese Alliance for Democracy (CAD) as part of an integrated campaign. In interviews for this study, many students said that they perceived the meeting between Paul Keating and Li Lu as the most successful activity of their collective campaign (Group-focused interviews, 14 March 1998). This was because the meeting had elicited the explicit promise of a blanket approach to the Chinese student protection issue if the Labor Party won the 1993 federal election (*The Tide*, 15 December 1992).

This chapter deals with the fifth strategic approach in the students' lobbying campaign, namely the selective and intensive interactions with a range of local Australian institutions over a period of four or so years (from June 1989 to November 1993). As mentioned in Chapter One, the Chinese students' collective campaign for residency/asylum in Australia, and its eventual success, was shaped by the active involvement of several organizations and institutions. Interviewees for this study identified six of such organizations or institutions as significant, including: (1) Chinese community organizations, (2) Chinese community media, (3) mainstream English-language media, (4) community services and organizations, (5) the Australian government and its departments, and (6) other community groups or organizations.[10] More than 80 percent of interviewees thought that the first four agencies played the most important roles in initiating and launching the Chinese student protection issue, but that all six had been essential in terms of influencing the campaign as a whole.[11]

This chapter focuses on the PRC students' contacts and interactions with three most important institutions or organizations in Australia.

[10] It should be noted that this same information appears in a different context in Chapter Two. This discussion of the student campaign should be read together with the above-mentioned discussions.

[11] The students interviewed also named certain student groups as having played a direct role in organizing the campaign as a whole, but not in initiating the issue. These were the IFCSS, the CAD, the FCFFPS, the FDC, the CASHR, the CSSCD, and the CSWC (Li, 1990; Chen and Lu, 1994; He, 1997; Grier, 1998; Mann, 1999; Gao, 2001, 2006a, 2009).

They include (1) the government and politicians, (2) community organizations, and in particular one publicly-funded migrant service center, and (3) the Australian media, both Chinese-language and English-language, which the student leaders and activists regarded as 'the main battlefield' in their collective campaign (*China Spring* [*Australia Edition*], No. 1, 1990; *FDC Newsletter*, 34, 1991; *The Tide*, 15 December 1992).

Interactions with the Government

James Jupp, a British-Australian political scientist who has studied and published extensively on immigration policy and multicultural affairs in Australia, has generally defined an immigration lobby as 'an organized group bringing pressure to bear on various levels of government' (1993: 205). He also identifies the principal lobbying groups as the print media, community members, voters, and formalized groups (Jupp, 1993). In the case of the Chinese students in Australia, it was residency claimants or asylum seekers themselves who became a 'formalized group' to lobby for permanent residency. It has often been assumed that lobbying forces are local residents working on behalf of some other constituency, such as refugees or asylum seeking groups, and that the residency claimants or asylum seekers for whom the lobbying is undertaken are often passive or powerless (Betts, 1993; Jupp, 1993; Jones, 1995; Zappala, 1999; Lopez, 2000; Warhurst, 2008). In this case, as onshore asylum seekers, the PRC students, both individually and collectively, were lobbying the Australian government for favorable policy outcomes even as early as the time they were collecting evidence for meeting the government's asylum eligibility requirements.

Individually and in groups, many of the PRC postgraduate students had already established their contacts with government departments and agencies well in advance of June 4,[12] because of visa issues (noted in Chapter Two). Most of them, even though selected and sent by Chinese

[12] Please note that in line with the usage of the Chinese student community at the time, the term 'government' is used here with a broad range of referents, including government departments and agencies (such as the Department of Immigration, Local Government and Ethnic Affairs or DILGEA; government agencies such as the Overseas Students Office or OSO, and the Australian International Development Assistance Bureau or AIDAB); Parliament in general; Members of Parliament; and the Joint Standing Committees on Foreign Affairs and Immigration. Usage of the term does not distinguish between government, government subsidiary institutions and legislative bodies such as Parliament. However,

universities and research institutions, were subsidized by the Australian government and were required to leave Australia on completion of their studies. Around the time of June 4, many held student visas that had just expired or were about to expire. This became a uniting force for them, as well as a proper pretext for contacting Australian government officials. Those whose visas would soon expire, or whose spouses were back in China waiting for Australian visas, were often in quite regular contact with government officials (Mackerras, 1996; Holenbergh, 2004). Other students who had specific issues (such as renewing near-expired visas, bringing in other family members, or changing their student status from government-subsidized to full-fee-paying) (Forth, 1994; Fung and Chen, 1996) were also in regular, if not very frequent, contact with the liaison officers of government agencies. In the few days before and after June 4, the international offices of Australian universities and in some cases the liaison officers of AIDAB, OSO, and even DILGEA, made contact with Chinese students and visiting scholars to express their concern and to ask if any assistance was urgently required. All these contacts appeared to have been made by arrangement with the Department of Foreign Affairs (IFCSSA meeting notice, 7 June 1989). A former postgraduate student recalled the initial contact and said:

> On the first day after June 4, I was called in by an overseas student officer at... [the University] to see a senior [university] leader. After expressing his sympathy, he told me that the Department of Foreign Affairs asked each university to contact all students from China to see if any assistance was required. I was offered several options and was asked to make a decision within a day. I decided on the spot to ask for help in speeding up my wife's visa application to come to Australia. I was not sure whether all [Chinese] students were contacted, but many were introduced to liaison officers of the Department of Immigration.... We then kept in contact with each other until our problems were solved. This was how our contacts with the government department were started (Interviewee 23, 13 April 1998).

Although these official contacts had been in place for some time, some student activists who emerged in the later stages of the student protection campaign tended to believe that many postgraduate students had been organizing on their own to form small working groups to lobby for their own chance to stay (IFCSSA seminar notice, 7 September 1989). This

this does not reflect the level of knowledge the students, especially student activists, had at that time on this issue.

widespread suspicion was not entirely groundless, as lobbying activities in the earliest stages had focused on seeking exemptions from various DILGEA policies (IFCSSA seminar notice, 7 September 1989). Many postgraduate students were mainly lobbying to be allowed to seek jobs in Australia without first leaving the country, to apply for returning to the Australia or permanent residency onshore, and to change their course of study and not be restricted to one specified course. Their early focus on the waiver of qualification-related visa requirements deeply divided the student community.

Shortly before June 1990 (i.e. shortly before the PRC students were granted a special four-year visa), an activist group formed primarily by postgraduate, and some undergraduate, students, known as the Working Group for the Basic Human Rights of PRC Citizens in Australia, was still urging the Australian government to consider their special case and their concerns first.[13] In a widely distributed report, published in May 1990 and titled *Human rights abuses in China: A survey of Chinese citizens in Australia*, the 'Working Group' urged the government to 'take a more sympathetic attitude to the applications from Chinese nationals for change of status on the occupational ground' (Working Group for the Basic Human Rights of PRC Citizens in Australia, 1990: 19). It was through this report, as well as through Chinese community newspapers and information circulating through their own primary group networks, that many ELICOS students came to understand the role of postgraduate students in creating contacts with the Australian government. It was also because of these postgraduate students that the case of the PRC student group as a whole became evidently differentiated from those of the many other onshore asylum-seeker groups. The contacts already established between the Chinese postgraduate students and a range of government agencies enabled them to establish and maintain a strong, well-organized lobby in Australia. In addition to their English-language skills, another reason that these PRC postgraduate students could play an active role in contacting government agencies was that before June 1989, they were already a well-defined and organized group. Their organization made it easy for the immigration department to contact them. They were directly looked after by AIDAB or OSO, and these agencies helped to pass on their concerns and demands to the decision-makers in the government. Furthermore, since they had been specifically selected and sent by the Chinese gov-

---

[13] This group was called the 'Chinese Human Rights Investigation Working Group' as discussed in Chapter Two.

ernment for further training, their qualifications and skills already met Australia's migration criteria.

These postgraduate students knew the importance of contacts with government agencies, even if these contacts were not as extensive or as easy as those they had with community organizations and local media. They also tried very hard to maintain their contacts, and to make their meetings with government officials as frequent as possible (IFCSSA meeting notice, 7 June 1989; IFCSSA seminar notice, 7 September 1989; *FDC Newsletter*, 34, 1991). They invoked various reasons for seeking meetings. Interviewees for this study listed ten, including: (1) to express their fears; (2) to express their concerns over a particular government policy; (3) to report any new political developments in China; (4) to ask officials to explain the implications of a policy; (5) to make a suggestion about how their problems might be resolved; (6) to pass on student group publications; (7) to inform officials about the formation of a new student group; (8) to invite the officials to meet other students, or to attend their meetings; (9) to make inquiries about special cases; and (10) to simply ask for regular contact (Group-focused interviews, 17, 24 and 31 January 1998). The key was to keep their contacts alive by raising a variety of issues.

After the Australian government's decision to amend the *Migration Act 1958* in December 1989, contacts between Chinese student activists and government officials (or, more often, their liaison officers) became even more frequent. As noted in Chapter One, the proposed amendments to the *Migration Act 1958* were aimed at controlling the rapidly growing numbers of visa overstayers and onshore asylum seekers by 1) removing the onshore humanitarian program from the immigration program, and 2) restricting all onshore applications for residency to the refugee program (Cronin, 1993; Crock, 1998b). A few months before the new *Act* came into effect, government officials had already informed the student leaders and some activists of these proposed policy changes before the news was reported in Chinese-language community newspapers in October 1989 (*ACD*, 13 October 1989). From this point, the student lobby underwent a rapid and fundamental change. Numerous student activists not only made even more contacts with many government agencies, such as those from MRC (Migrant Resource Centre), RACS (Refugee Advice and Casework Service), OSO, AIDAB and DILGEA, but also extended their contacts to politicians from both the Government and the Opposition—including the minister for DILGEA, the Prime Minister, and leading members of the Parliamentary Joint Standing Committees on Foreign Affairs and Immigration. These meetings were often reported—indeed over-reported—in the Chinese-language community media. In the *Australian Chinese Daily*, for example, in the 24 weeks from 13 October 1989 to 31 March 1990 (where 104 issues contained close to 200 news items on the student lobby, an average of about two items per day), there were approximately 200 news items covering 48 meetings held between student activists and politicians or government officials (see Table 6.1). That is, each meeting (with meetings averaging two per week) was reported, on average, about four times.

As noted, the close contacts with government agencies had been made and fostered by postgraduate students who constituted a small minority among the PRC student community. However, within a year of June 4, this 'elitist' small-scale lobbying by postgraduate students had then been expanded into a mass participation campaign. During that year, the newly independent student union and a few individual postgraduate students also established new contacts with the government. Gradually, more and more groups became involved in contacting government agencies (Group-focused interviews, 17, 24 and 31 January 1998) (see Table 6.2). Interviewees for this study stated explicitly that this was not a question of many individual students, including ELICOS students, seeking to turn the already-existing small-scale contact into mass participation. Importantly, however, the entire circumstances of asylum seeking at the time also required that the whole student community should become actively involved in order to maximize their opportunity for success (Group-

Table 6.1 Lobbying activities reported in the *ACD*. (13 October 1989–31 March 1990)

Community Leader and Student Activist Meetings	Number of Meetings	Average Number of Meetings Per Week	Number of Reports	Average Number of Reports Per Issue (104 Issues)
With senior DILGEA officials	24	1.00	99	0.95
With the Minister for DILGEA	15	0.62	63	0.60
With the Prime Minister	9	0.38	32	0.30
Total	48	2	194	1.85

Source: Australian Chinese Daily.

focused interviews, 17 January 1998). Of course, the Australian government was the chief target for lobbying, and the Chinese students did not miss an opportunity to lobby it. The students believed that the more groups that became involved in their collective efforts, the more likely it would be that their lobbying would be successful in the end (Group-focused interviews, 31 January 1998).

Table 6.2 below lists the significant meetings (group discussions and meetings) identified by students in terms of new events and new policy measures that were critical to the student campaign. As the table shows, in the first year of the campaign alone, there was a steady increase in the number of student groups and individuals becoming involved in lobbying the Australian government. By the end of the first year of the protection campaign, at least eight different categories of groups and individuals had joined forces to pursue lobbying activities.

Table 6.2 The expansion of student group involvement in lobbying the government.

Stages	Period	Participating Groups (in Order of Number of Mentions in Interviews)
1	04/06/89–01/07/89	1. Independent Federation of Chinese Students and Scholars in Australia (IFCSSA) 2. Individual postgraduate students
2	01/07/89–14/08/89	1. IFCSSA 2. Individual postgraduate students 3. Chinese Alliance for Democracy (CAD) 4. Federation of Chinese Full-Fee Paying Students (FCFFPS)
3	14/08/89–14/09/89	1. Australia Federation of Chinese Students (AFCS) 2. IFCSSA 3. Individual postgraduate students 4. Chinese Students Solidarity Campaign for Democracy (CSSCD) 5. Chinese Studies Group 6. Chinese Alliance for Democracy (CAD)
4	14/09/89–31/10/89	1. Federation for Democratic China (FDC) 2. CAD 3. IFCSSA 4. CSSCD 5. Chinese Association for Safeguarding Human Rights (CASHR) 6. Chinese Studies Group 7. Individual activists who emerged later

Table 6.2 (*cont.*)

Stages	Period	Participating Groups (in Order of Number of Mentions in Interviews)
5	31/10/89–19/12/89	1. FDC 2. CAD 3. CASHR 4. CSSCD 5. Chinese Student Welfare Committee (CSWC) 6. IFCSSA 7. Chinese Studies Group 8. Individual activists who emerged later
6	19/12/89–27/06/90	1. FDC 2. CAD 3. CASHR 4. CSSCD 5. CSWC 6. IFCSSA 7. Chinese Studies Group 8. Individual activists who emerged later

Source: Group-focused interviews, 17, 24 and 31 January 1998.

One key contact whose name was mentioned repeatedly by student activists in many interviews was Dr Andrew Theophanous, Chairman of the Parliamentary Joint Standing Committee on Immigration from 1989 to 1993. In this parliamentary capacity, Dr Theophanous was not only deeply involved in immigration matters, producing numerous reports on immigration policy, but was also directly and passionately involved in helping Chinese students gain protection and residency in Australia after June 4. About ten years after June 4, Dr Theophanous was to come under suspicion in 1998 for being involved in immigration fraud.[14] However, in 2011, he was still proudly claiming on his personal website that 'the historic decision on saving the 45,000 Chinese students' was one of his most signifi-

[14] Andrew Theophanous was investigated by the National Crime Authority (NCA), and he was charged, and jailed for a maximum six years in 2002 for bribery, conspiracy, and defrauding the Commonwealth. It was alleged that he had sought and obtained thousands of dollars to help Chinese nationals with their immigration visas and, in one case, sought sexual favors from a Chinese woman (Sheehan, 2002). Most PRC former students refused to believe the accusations, and many believed that his 'trouble' was a result of his involvement in the Chinese student issue (Group-focused interviews for a related study, 19 April 2003, see Gao, 2006b), though no one could explain why he should have been 'framed' by people of Chinese background.

cant contributions to Australian political and achievements in the Federal Parliament (http://www.andrewtheophanous.com/) (accessed May 2011).[15] As a Member of the Australian House of Representatives (Parliament) from the Socialist Left faction of the Australian Labor Party (ALP), representing Calwell constituency from 1980 to 2000 (then as an independent member from 2000 to 2001), and as a migrant himself (born in Cyprus) and having himself studied abroad (at Oxford University), Dr Theophanous was sympathetic to the Chinese students. During the student campaign, he had met student leaders and activists many times and had forged close relationships with many of them. One former student who only met him once still felt grateful to him and said:

> We simply called him Andrew, and he was Australia's Pelosi, the best supporter of the Chinese [students]. Yes, we had Uncle Hawke [see Footnote 13, Chapter One], but he was Prime Minister, and we could not contact him [easily]. Although I only met Andrew once with a group of students, I knew that many student leaders could contact him whenever they needed his help. Like [Nancy] Pelosi in America, Andrew was a key person in solving the student issue in Australia (Interviewee 19, 8 June 1998).

Over the course of the PRC student campaign, which lasted from 1989 to 1993, the ALP governments of Bob Hawke and Paul Keating had three ministers for immigration: Robert Ray (September 1988–April 1990), Gerry Hand (April 1990–March 1993) and Nick Bolkus (March 1993–March 1996). However, Andrew Theophanous was the chairperson of the Parliamentary Joint Standing Committee on Immigration of the Federal Parliament over the entire four-year period of the student campaign. As mentioned, many Chinese student leaders and activists regarded him as 'a person from the top in Canberra' (Group-focused interviews, 17 January 1998; also see Birrell, 1996; Fung and Chen, 1996).

For this reason, many PRC student groups based in both Sydney and Melbourne were keen to contact him. Because of his parliamentary post and his academic background, many students believed that he would have an influence on Prime Ministers Bob Hawke and Paul Keating

[15] One theory about the investigation into his activities was that he had 'so much trouble with the immigration department' (in the words of his parliamentary colleague Martin Ferguson, President of the ACTU from 1990 to 1996, and Minister for Resources and Energy from 2007 to 2013), precisely because of the Chinese student protection issue. Specifically, because he engaged in continuous battles with the immigration department and even criticized them for having allegedly discriminated against applicants from China and other countries (Berry, 2002).

(Group-focused interviews, 17 January 1998; also see Melleuish, 1998; Blewett, 1999; Betts, 2003). They also regarded it as vital that he be contacted on a regular basis and provided with updated information about what was happening in China and what the students wanted. It is also true to say that many student leaders and activists found Andrew Theophanous to be more approachable than other politicians, and that they regarded him as an easy-going person (One-on-one interviews, 11 and 25 April 1998, and 8 June 1998). For example, on one occasion, a closed meeting was arranged between him and several student activists, but more than 50 students turned up, and the meeting ended, in the words of the organizer, 'in something of a rally' (One-on-one interview, 25 April 1998) and twice had to be moved to larger rooms. The student community wanted to field a large team in order to increase the pressure on Theophanous and the ALP government. Theophanous was very supportive of a blanket approach to the Chinese student protection issue, which was ultimately adopted in June 1993 (Birrell, 1996; Fung and Chen, 1996). However, this also unfortunately sowed the seeds of later troubles in his personal life and in his political and professional career as a member of the Australian Parliament.

Lobbying Community Organizations

Even as they lobbied key politicians, the student activists were learning about Australian politics through their local contacts and gaining practical knowledge of how politics worked in Australia. This enabled them to make their protection campaign much more strategic than it had previously been. In fact, the student campaign had already become very well organized (as will be discussed in Chapter Seven) and very flexible, developing and adopting a series of new strategies to respond to the government's continually changing approach to the student issue. To make the most of their influence on the policy process, many student activists turned their attention to community organizations, lobbying them hard with an aim of influencing the government's decision-making. According to Jupp, some community organizations, although they were funded by the government and were therefore loosely part of the government system, could also act as lobby groups (Jupp, 1993: 205).[16] Several interviewees for this research

[16] As Jupp has pointed out, agencies such as the Migrant Resource Centre (MRC), grant-in-aid workers (workers funded by the Federal Government to offer settlement-related

also remarked that the government had appeared to have no idea how to deal with their claims other than repeatedly changing its approach. As noted, there was a gradual retreat on the government's part as it found itself under pressure to give in to the Chinese student lobby and faced a strong community outcry over June 4 and the issue of student protection. Here, publicly funded community services and agencies played an important mediating role.

The government's gradual retreat from its initial stringent stance on onshore seekers of residency took place in four stages.[17] First, when it decided to amend the *Migration Act 1958* and various regulations, the government urged PRC students as early as October 1989 to apply for permanent residency on humanitarian grounds, or for refugee status, before 19 December 1989 (*ACD*, 14 October 1989). Second, because many students had not submitted their applications,[18] the government announced on 8 December 1989 that all PRC students could have their visas extended to 31 January 1991. At the same time, they would all be allowed to apply for residency through the refugee program during this period if they had been unable to apply before the original cut-off date (*ACD*, 9 December 1989). Third, and even before the second policy measure had actually been implemented, the Minister for DILGEA again urged all the PRC students to apply for residency as refugees before July 1990. This minor change gave the individual students more time to prepare their refugee applications and provided the activists with more time to organize their campaign (*ACD*, 23 December 1989). Fourth, in February 1990, *Regulation 142A* was introduced, allowing PRC students to apply to stay on grounds similar to 'strong humanitarian grounds.' Only a month later, newspaper reports indicated that still more changes to the government's approach to

---

services to specific migrant groups or refugees as part of the community-based welfare system in Australia) and employees with the responsibility for ethnic issues or migrants were regarded by Australians as lobby groups (Jupp, 1993).

[17] The most obvious early change was the concessionary arrangement that was introduced for those who had been illegal before the 1989 amendments to the *Migration Act 1958*. Further modifications to many immigration control measures were made in 1990 (Cronin, 1993: 93).

[18] Poor English language skills were the primary reason for students being unable to fill in application forms and submit them. At that time, few migration agents provided assistance in this; in fact, most students did not initially want to spend money on migration agents anyway. More significantly, the Australian government had what students called a 'no-return policy': it required unsuccessful applicants to leave Australia if their application was rejected, thus precluding them from re-applying for a student visa to continue their stay in Australia.

dealing with the student issue were under way (*The Australian*, 15 March 1990; *STN*, 17–18 March 1990; *The Tide*, No. 3, March 1990).

From these policy changes, it seemed to the student activists that the Australian government did not have any predetermined or detailed policy for dealing with their protection issue and asylum claims (Group-focused interviews, 14 March 1998), and they felt that it would be relatively easy to influence the government to change its policies, and that they had to do it as early as possible (One-on-one interviews, 11 and 25 April 1998). They believed that this would be much easier (especially in the case of a Labor government) if demands were made on their behalf by already established groups and organizations (One-on-one interviews, 25 April 1998). The possibilities therefore included both existing ethnic Chinese community groups and various other organizations (discussed below).

Many PRC student activists knew that the influence of ethnic Chinese organizations on the Australian government's decision-making was very limited (Group-focused interviews, 21 March 1998). They were aware that the Chinese communities in Australia did not form a united group, and that some Chinese community leaders were not very supportive of their demand to stay in Australia anyway (Campbell, 1992; Cragg, 1995; York, 2003).[19] Ethnic Chinese community organizations in Australia were divided according to country or place of origin, and over whether or not to align themselves with China and its ruling political force, the Chinese Communist Party (since 1949) (Liu, 1989). This was the legacy of the historical divisions between supporters of the Communist and Nationalist parties and their governments in the early part of the twentieth century (Wang, 1970; Suryadinata, 1978, 2005; Frolic, 1980; Yen, 2006).[20] In addition, some segments of the Chinese community then believed that there

[19] The classic example (discussed later in the text) was Dr Wellington Lee, the then chairman of the Asian-Australian Consultative Council. Dr Barry York recorded the following in Parliamentary Library's Chronologies Online: 'Opposition Leader, Hon. John Hewson MP, and Opposition Immigration Spokesman, Hon. Philip Ruddock MP, condemn Prime Minister Hawke's decision to allow PRC nationals to remain in Australia. They argue that the decision sets dangerous precedents and pre-empts the established processes for dealing with refugees. Wellington Lee, chair of the Asian-Australian Consultative Council, accuses the PRC students of "duping" the Australian authorities and "living off the blood" of the Tiananmen massacre' (York, 2003). Controversial former federal MP Graeme Campbell once wrote that 'a prominent member of the Chinese community in Melbourne, Wellington Lee, accused the bulk of these students of trading "on the blood" of the victims of the Tiananmen Square massacre' (Campbell, 1992).

[20] As Marketa Moore has pointed out, 'attempts to gain influence over Chinese communities are known from the history of overseas Chinese, and so is the rivalry between pro-Chinese and pro-Taiwan associations that goes back to 1949' (2006: 281).

were some 'bad elements' among the PRC students (Group-focused interviews, 21 March 1998; *The Tide*, No. 3, March 1990). At the very least, some students were regarded as 'queue-jumpers,' as some English-language media portrayed them—in other words, foreigners unwilling to seek asylum through the appropriate channels that were believed to be readily available in their home country (*SMH*, 8 June 1990; *The Sun*, 8 June 1990; *The Age*, 15 June 1990; *The Australian*, 28 June 1990).[21] One prominent member of the Chinese community in Australia who put forward this negative view was Dr Wellington Lee, the former deputy Lord Mayor of Melbourne. Dr Lee then publicly opposed the four-year temporary residency visa that the Labor government offered to the PRC students in June 1990. At the time, he was chair of the Asian-Australian Consultative Council, accusing the students of 'duping' the Australian authorities and 'living off the blood' of the Tiananmen massacre (*The Sun*, 8 June 1990; *The Age*, 8 June 1990; *The Australian*, 28 June 1990).[22] This was another reason for the student lobby's concentration on government agencies rather than ethnic Chinese organizations in its search for support.[23]

The students focused their efforts on publicly funded organizations, such as MRC and RACS. Neither of these organizations had any special connection with the Chinese student groups before June 1989, but their services were recommended to them by other government agencies.

[21] In a statement to the House of Representatives on 16 March 1982, Minister Ian Macphee announced the Fraser Government's plan to tighten refugee policy, emphasising that the aim was 'to ensure that our limited program places are reserved for the genuine refugees.' This was the first use of the term 'queue-jumping' by a Government Minister (York: 2003). There has been intense debate in Australia about its immigration and refugee programs since the early 1980s, which has tended to make the local people either very supportive of or unsympathetic to migrants (Betts, 1988). The government's policies towards asylum seekers have developed into the most contentious issue in Australian politics (Brown, 2006), and the term 'queue jumpers' is frequently used by those who support tighter border controls, Philip Ruddock, for example, the immigration minister of the Howard government (1996–2007), repeatedly argued that asylum seekers arriving by boat were 'queue jumpers' (Brown, 2006: 8).

[22] On the occasion of the Olympic Torch Relay in Australia before the Beijing Olympics of 2008, Wellington Lee, 'a self-described "ABC"—Australian-Born Chinese, and fourth generation at that' said that he recalled 'a meeker era when asserting a Chinese identity was the road to nowhere' (*The Age*, 25 April 2008).

[23] The ethnic Chinese organizations from which students did seek support were organizations such as the Federation of Chinese Associations and the Chinese Community Social Service Centre that were partly publicly funded and had already been helping them. However, the students focused their efforts on MRC and RACS because of their closer links with the government than the ethnic Chinese organizations, and their worries about the details of their asylum cases to be leaked to the Chinese community, or through which to be leaked to other people.

A large number of Chinese students found the MRC and RACS people very keen to help them (*STN*, 31 October 1989; *ACD*, 9 December 1989; *China Spring* [*Australia Edition*], No. 1, 1990). One MRC in an inner suburb of Melbourne was being frequently mentioned in interviews for this study.[24] This particular MRC initially helped hundreds of students, especially those with relatively poor English language skills, with their applications for residency as refugees or on humanitarian grounds. The center even hired a couple of staff members who had reasonably strong Chinese language skills but who were not of Chinese background and had no prior connection to any ethnic Chinese community members. The presence of these staff members was reassuring to the students on two counts. First, it allayed their fears about their asylum seeking intentions or their case details being leaked to their fellow students. Second, it freed many students from concern about the sceptical attitude that some non-PRC Chinese people had expressed toward their asylum and their cases (Group-focused interviews, 21 March 1998). The case officers were all very sympathetic to the students' predicament. Unlike some members of Australia's ethnic Chinese communities, they never questioned and were never suspicious about the nature of the June 4 events and their relevance to the students living in Australia.

It was not just the MRC's services but also the apparent anger of its staff members over June 4 and their absolute belief in the students' political claims that led many students to regard this organization as 'the best local contact we had,' in the words of a number of former students (IFCSSA seminar, 10 September 1989). Through its highly professional services, the center quickly established a very good reputation among the Chinese students, and became the main, if not the only, community organization that many wanted to deal with. It then became even more popular when its staff members started participating in meetings, rallies and information sessions organized by the student groups. Although a small number of students actually suspected that the center was spying on the students' activities (One-on-one interviews, 25 April 1998), this direct involvement on the part of its personnel cemented the relationship between the center and the student activists.

[24] This MRC provided assistance to many PRC nationals, especially overstayers, to prepare their refugee applications for several months after June 4. For this reason, and also according to research ethics, this study has chosen not to identify the center.

Several debates took place among student leaders and activists about the involvement of the center's case officers in their activities. For some weeks, the students wondered if the Australian government was going to set quotas for the number of permanent residencies they were willing to offer. For this reason, some students urged their colleagues to 'adopt a unified approach' (*tongyi koujing*) and present the center case officers with exactly the same account, in accordance with their common goal of seeking asylum in Australia (IFCSSA seminar, 10 September 1989). This unified approach was called for in explicit opposition to the practice of 'exposing' (*jiefa*)—a term used extensively in China during the Cultural Revolution to refer to revealing a person's secrets and reporting their wrongdoing to the authorities for personal gain. In this case, 'exposing' also included the practice of attacking other PRC students as not being genuine refugees. Many activists realized that it would harm their cause if many individual students kept their intentions to themselves and dealt with case officers without taking the opportunity for direct contact with the government (Group-focused interviews, 21 March 1998). Arguments emerged: should the students make use of the case officers' services for their own ends regardless of the case officers' intentions? Should they adopt a 'participationist' approach in dealing with the case officers, who could approach their organizations and the government on the students' behalf? The issue was discussed repeatedly among activists and in CAD and FDC meetings (One-on-one interviews, 11 April 1998).

A consensus was reached, covering a range of key issues that ranged from how to comment on June 4, to whether temporary visa extension or permanent residency should be preferred, and to who was to represent whom (IFCSSA seminar, 10 September 1989). The activists had learned that the MRC had a crucial consultative role in the government's decision-making process, and also that it was the 'front desk' for organizations such as the Determination of Refugee Status (DORS) Committee and the Refugee Status Review Committee (RSRC). In addition, the importance of a 'participationist' approach was also supported by the fact that some case officers seemed very committed, and even militant, in the students' cause, involving themselves in most of the students' larger meetings and apparently prepared to fight for them. This also provided some activists with a chance to learn about how to pursue active politics in Australia as one interviewee described:

> A couple of people at the center were good in many aspects, and they were so passionate about political freedom, human rights and racial equality. They

> told us that the government was not the only decision maker [in Australia] and that we needed to tell them what we wanted to have clearly.... They told us how powerful some organizations and groups were, and who should be approached and how to do it. The most useful help from them [to the students], as far as I could see, was to organize some students to do surveys, giving them hand-on experience in organizing activities in Australia (Interviewee 8, 27 February 1998).

In the first year after June 4, the students' efforts to lobby community services and agencies went through three stages. The initial relationship began with individual cases. Second, when both students and MRC were pushing for an exemption for the Chinese students to the new *Migration Legislation Amendment Act 1989*, the relationship evolved into one of close cooperation between the center and student groups. Third, when the new *Migration Legislation Amendment Act 1989* took effect first in December 1989, and then in March 1990, the two sides joined forces to lobby for a blanket approach to the PRC students' residency issue (*The Australian*, 15 March 1990). Of course, these three stags overlapped, in particular in terms of the tasks performed. During the first stage, while individual students were taking their applications or cases to the center, a number of postgraduate students were (as noted above) also making frequent contact to lobby for exemptions to their visa restrictions (see Chapter Four). In the second and third stages, many individual students continued to make their own approaches to the center to seek advice on their applications.

As a reflection of the newly developed strategy of joint participation, and as a way of strengthening the relationship between the center and a few student groups, the Melbourne-based MRC mentioned above guided, or in the first instance assisted, a number of student groups in conducting three large-scale surveys among the PRC students. These surveys were organized by three Chinese student groups: (1) the Chinese Association for Safeguarding Human Rights (*ACD*, 14 October 1989); (2) the Chinese Students Solidarity Campaign for Democracy Inc. (*The Tide*, 16 November 1989); and (3) the Working Group for the Basic Human Rights of PRC Citizens in Australia (*ACD*, 21 February 1990).

The three surveys were very similar.[25] All were questionnaire-based and all were published in Chinese-language community newspapers. In

---

[25] The only major difference was that the survey by the 'Student Working Group for the Human Rights of PRC Citizens in Australia' asked detailed questions about the kinds of persecutions and risks that students might face if they were forced to return to China (see Chapter Three) and if other students did not.

terms of contents, they all expressed outrage about, and condemnation of, the events of June 4. All contained questions in relation to students' worries about instability in China and in their own lives if they were to return there; students' active participation in protest activities against June 4 and against Communist rule in China; and students' support for various overseas Chinese democratic movements and organizations. In other words, all these survey questions appeared to have been closely, if not accurately, based upon the application requirements for Australia's onshore humanitarian immigration program (which was still applicable at the time) and its refugee program. The subtle differences between the three surveys, which were not easy to detect, reflected the fact that the campaign organizers were gaining a better understanding of the onshore humanitarian immigration and refugee programs. Each successive survey showed a very clear focus on the selection criteria for granting refugee status, which required a more political emphasis and the provision of evidence.[26] This shift reflected the students' awareness of, and their new strategy for dealing with, the Australian government's determination to put to an end to its onshore humanitarian immigration program.

The reiteration of the surveys and their high degree of similarity (in regard to both the survey questions and the methods in which they were conducted) were also in accordance with the needs of everyone involved in the lobbying effort, including the politicians and decision-makers who were being lobbied. The duplication of information served a number of functions. Student activists wanted evidence of their own leadership roles in the PRC student community; community services and organizations wanted to use survey-based data to report to the government; and the MRC relied on this ongoing student issue to receive more funding from the government. Of course, Chinese community newspaper owners, for their part, wanted to boost sales of their newspapers (Bilic, 1989; *SMH*, 14 June 1989).

More importantly than the above functions, the surveys all played a very important role in educating the Chinese students about, or turning their attention to, two crucial elements that they were continually

---

[26] As noted in Chapter Three, many students understood the need to collect evidence for their asylum applications. However, it was only through these surveys that they were given the idea of including such things as receiving a letter from their former employer that seemingly deprived them of their right to work or a place to live, suspended their employment in their work unit in China, or informed them that their activities were under investigation (*ACD*, 21 February 1990).

being urged to adopt—this urging coming from several community organizations, and also by some politicians and senior DILGEA bureaucrats. First, if they wanted to seek protection in Australia, the students had to clearly articulate their fears about the events of June 4 and their concerns about returning to China. Without this expression, the Australian public would be unsympathetic to any government decision to grant them asylum, and no government would risk granting it, especially since the Australian political cycle is rather short and a general election is held every three years.

Second, in their dealings with publicly funded community agencies and government departments, the student community needed to be better organized in terms of representation and communication. For example, the activists needed to use the right kind of language when speaking in public. To provide the government with sufficient evidence on which to make its decision—evidence of reasonable, if not well-founded, fears of persecution if they were to return to China—they needed to emphasize their connections with democracy and their loyalty to democratic values, if not Western ideas. The publishing of multiple questionnaires in several community newspapers helped to focus the students' attention on the matters that community organizations and the government wanted them to discuss. The survey results were used in several reports to the MRC and to the government, and the students' answers were interpreted as a consensus of the entire student community.

Some students and their sympathizers believed that the relationship between the center and PRC student activists was not that of one side lobbying and the other side being lobbied, but rather of each side using the other for its own purposes (One-on-one interviews, 11 and 25 April 1998). The students who were deeply involved in the lobby believed that this symbiotic cooperation or teamwork was the direct result of their own lobbying and persistence, without which the center would not have become so active or creative in terms of their advice to the PRC student activists (One-on-one interviews, 11 and 25 April 1998).

The most notable success gained by lobbying the Melbourne MRC under study was a lengthy report that this center made to the Australian government. Written as early as 1990 and based upon the results of the three surveys, the report called for a 'blanket approach' to the Chinese student protection issue, recommending clearly that 'either refugee status or permanent residency be granted to all PRC [the People's Republic of China] refugee applicants' (RACS, 1990: 18). This stance formed the foundation for their further cooperation throughout the remainder of the students' four-year temporary residency visas.

Between June 1990 and 1993, Chinese student organizations made at least two more major efforts to lobby community organizations in order to put more pressure on the Australian government to adopt a blanket approach to the student issue and to apply that pressure in a more direct way.

The first of these lobbying initiatives focused on the fact that there were a high proportion of trained and skilled professionals among these PRC students. This was related to a lengthy debate in which a number of Australian politicians, policy advisers and bureaucrats strongly opposed acceptance of the students because their skill and education levels were lower than those of the Chinese students in the USA (*ACD*, 14 October 1989; *The Australian*, 28 June 1990; Fung and Chen, 1996). Some FDC activists believed this issue to be important to their quest for permanent residency, and the last of the three above-mentioned surveys was in some way designed to address it.[27] Student activists produced several reports within just a couple of years. These reports became more proactive than the students had ever been before, as they directly pointed out that the then minister for immigration, Gerry Hand (April 1990–March 1993) did not acknowledge that students were well educated and skilled. Because of this highly focused lobbying, Gerry Hand's successor, Nick Bolkus (March 1993–March 1996), publicly praised the Chinese students as 'an enormously highly talented group of people' based on his department's research (Banham, 2003).[28]

The second key lobbying initiative called attention to the substantial savings that many Chinese students had accumulated during their four-year temporary residency in Australia (let alone what they had already earned before being granted four years of temporary residency). This made a strong immediate impact in recession-stricken Australia in

---

[27] Several questions invited students to indicate the relevance of their professional training and expertise to Australia and enquired about their educational qualifications, the length of their work experience, and their previous positions in China (*ACD*, 21 February 1990). This reflected the concerns of thousands of ELICOS students and their organizations, namely the Federation of Chinese Full-Fee Paying Students (FCFFPS) and the CAD (One-on-one interviews, 11 and 25 April 1998).

[28] Later, Nick Bolkus recalled that his department carefully 'went through the profile of the students, and discovered that we had within our shores some of the crème of young China' (Bourke, 2009).

early 1990s. A few mathematically-minded student activists put forward the persuasive idea that permanent residency for the PRC students was an issue worth billions of dollars. Sending the students back to China, they argued, would result in the withdrawal from Australia of huge sums of money that could otherwise have been spent in the Australian housing market. The message was loud and clear: by 1993, each student family would have saved up to AU$40,000 or even AU$50,000, and there were 45,000 PRC student families living in the country (FDC meeting, late July 1992; *The Tide*, 15 December 1992; one-on-one interviews, 8 June 1998). The precise figure may have been inaccurate and even purposely exaggerated, but no one could deny its significance and persuasiveness of the argument at the time.

Student groups and some community agencies, including the MRC, spread the message widely. It finally caught the attention of a number of heavyweight national institutions. These included the ACCI (Australian Chamber of Commerce and Industry), the ACTU (Australian Council of Trade Unions), and the HIA (Housing Industry Association) that had not hitherto been involved in the PRC student issue (One-on-one interviews, 8 June 1998; also see Healy 1994, 1997; Newman, 2002; Betts, 2003; Guo, 2005). As the leading body representing the residential building, renovating and land development industries, the HIA took this issue very seriously and publicly expressed its support for granting residency to all Chinese students. At the time, Australia was in a very severe recession, characterized by high interest rates, high unemployment, and a slowing economy. In the 1991–1992 'recession that we had to have,' in the well-known words of the then-Treasurer Paul Keating, the housing market in Australia had been hit hard. Any withdrawal of money could have been fatal to the industry. Never before, in the students' campaign had there been such a strong and persuasive argument. Consequently, it not only attracted attention from new constituencies, but also immediately gained equal support from both sides of the political debate (One-on-one interviews, 8 June 1998; East Asia Analytical Unit, 1995; Jupp, 1995, 2002; *SMH*, 26 December 2003).

The housing industry in Australia was particularly sensitive to any cut in migration intake, and its response to the media suggested that the Chinese student issue was worth not only a couple of billion dollars, but even multiple billions if mortgages were taken into account. An internal research paper submitted to Australia's Productivity Commission in the early 2000s confirms that while immigration intake fell significantly in Australia in 1992 and 1993 because of Gerry Hand's recession-related immigration cutback, the Australian housing industry not only recovered in 1993, but went on to ever greater production, reaching its highest peak ever in 1994 (Newman, 2003: 63–64).

The Media as the Main Battleground

Both the Chinese-language community newspapers and the mainstream English-language print media played a very important role in shaping the student protection issue (see Chapter Two). As noted, the relationship was interactive; the media paid attention to, or took advantage of, this sensitive political issue while the student activists relied on the media for information and for expressing their demands. A number of student activists stated in interviews that their relationship with the media in the first three months or so after June 4 was their 'main battleground' (Group-focused interviews, 17, 24 and 31 January 1998), where student organizations and their leaders sought to influence public opinion and change the way in which their concerns could be discussed. In mid-October 1989, the media turned their attention to the vigorous debate and the lobbying by various institutions and groups over proposed amendments to the *Migration Act 1958* that were to take effect on 19 December 1989. This was to be the turning point in the students' relationship with the media.

The idea of the media as a 'battleground' was related to the formation of the FDC worldwide and its branches in Australia (Group-focused interviews, 17, 24 and 31 January 1998). The FDC (discussed in the following chapter) was established in Paris in late September 1989 by Chinese activists who had fled China after June 4 and a group of PRC postgraduate and visiting scholars in several Western countries. In order to increase its membership, it set itself two interconnected strategic tasks: to pursue the Chinese democratic movement outside China, and to work for its members' welfare (see Chapter Four).

Even before its first Australian branch was established in late October 1989, the FDC's preparatory committee had conducted several rounds of meetings and consultations with already-existing political groups, such as CAD, to explore how it might pursue its aims. Committee members also held a series of meetings, large and small, with Australian activists from several organizations, including Amnesty International Australia, the World League for Freedom and Democracy (WLFD), Trades Hall Councils in Victoria and New South Wales, the International Socialist Organization (ISO) in Australia, and the Young Liberal Movement. As indicated by the short list, these organizations ranged from those on the far right of the political spectrum (e.g. the WLFD) to those on the far left (e.g. the ISO).

These meetings were purposely aimed at learning how to run a public campaign in Australia. The student activists quickly discovered that not all organizations were useful examples. Some groups were judged to be too 'high-society' and 'too snobbish to be associated with' (One-on-one interviews, 25 April 1998). As partly shown in the previous discussion, even though the ideological or political beliefs of many PRC students in 1989 tended toward the right (opposing Marxism, Communism and even socialism), they found themselves in coalition with moderate left-wing groups and people. The FDC activists favored groups with experience in street politics and with political skills in dealing with the media; however, the most practical message they learned from local activist groups was that although street politics were very important, a far more effective strategy would be to use the media. A couple of activist groups[29] told the FDC activists how to feed the media with useful stories, information, updates and even fully prepared texts; importantly, they also introduced the FDC to some of their contacts in the media (One-on-one interviews, 25 April 1998).

Within the student community there was a strong awareness of the media's importance in influencing Australian politicians and government (IFCSSA seminar notice, 7 September 1989; *FDC Newsletter*, 34, 1991), and this made possible the FDC-led, media-focused approach.

Through their own regular and often personal contacts with different politicians, bureaucrats, community organizations and activist groups, many students had already realized how different the media in Australia were from the media in China. Journalists were not required to follow the government's line, and instead actively sought out voices that differed from the government in order to serve and attract more audiences. The media's commercial interests appeared to dominate news coverage, and therefore the media were particularly interested in things that were new, unique or bizarre. Overall, Australia seemed to student activists to be a loosely organized society in which the media were more powerful than the government and its leaders (Group-focused interviews, 17 January 1998). On the other hand, ordinary people in Australia did not appear to

[29] Interviewees specifically asked not to name these activist groups because of an unhappy episode in the relationship with one of their contacts in the latter stages of their campaign.

be as sceptical about the media in their country as many people in China tended to be in the late 1980s and early 1990s. Before June 4 and before the students started their protection campaign, many students had heard the term 'freedom of the press' but had no practical knowledge of what this freedom might look like. After a couple of months, during which the students became the focus of the media, they gradually learned that the Australian public were unsophisticated in their attitudes to the media and placed undue trust and confidence in them (Group-focused interviews, 14 March 1998; One-on-one interviews, 11 April, 8 June 1998).[30] These practical understandings that they competently obtained, not a blind faith in the media, laid a solid foundation for both the formation and the direction of their lobbying strategies.

More specifically, through their meetings with other political groups in Australia, the students gained a new understanding of the role of the media in shaping sociopolitical attitudes, and this equipped them well to pursue their lobby. They understood that it was not meaningless to hold events that were aimed at drawing the attention of the media, and they regarded participation in such events as a very important aspect of their collective campaign (One-on-one interviews, 11 April 1998 and 8 June 1998). Many other constructive ideas for action were put forward, such as organizing a series of events attractive to the media by a number of different student groups in turn, and changing the theme of the events in order to feed the media with stories that would be of use to the student campaign.

More and more PRC students (and activists in particular) were now in a position to make use of three features of the Australian media. First, and perhaps the most obvious aspect that differentiated the Australian media from the media in China at the time, was its commercial nature. In the late 1980s, the PRC media were state-owned and controlled, serving as the mouthpiece of the CCP and the government. In Australia, on the

30 The suspicion that many people in China had of the media in the 1980s and other periods—an assumption that 'if the authorities say that something was bad, they think it might be good' and vice versa (He, 2001: 289)—has been termed *nifan xinli* ('negative mentality; reverse mentality; rebellious psyche'). While the students relied on, and did not doubt, the media's coverage of June 4 for some months after the events, they tended to be suspicious from the very beginning of the overwhelming sympathy that Australians expressed for a few students living in Australia who untruthfully claimed in the media to have relatives who were killed in Beijing and family members who were detained a few days after June 4 (Group-focused interviews, 14 March 1998; One-on-one interviews, 11 April, 8 June 1998).

other hand, the media's reliance on advertising for much of its income determined its limitations in not only the content, but also the process of gathering information (Errington and Miragliotta, 2007). This opened up the possibility for the media to be used by the students for their lobby. One media avenue had already proved useful: very early on, numerous students had published written statements of opposition to June 4 and the CCP to serve as evidence to support their refugee claims (see Chapter Three). Through this, the students had come to understand the commercial nature of the Australian media and the extent to which they could make use of their purchasing power to keep their issue visible.[31] Many more initiatives of this kind were made over the entire four-year period of the student protection campaign. Hundreds of statements were published by the students, who were desperate for evidence for their applications. These statements then generated fear in the student community about the political situation in China and this 'fear' was subsequently interpreted as the shared view about the political risks in China and used by a number of activist groups in their lobbying activities.

In another media-related initiative, PRC activist groups (in particular the FDC) attempted to prompt newspapers—especially English-language ones, which periodically tended to lose interest in the Chinese student issue—in their coverage by using a range of approaches. These included placing political advertisements on the anniversaries of June 4, telling shocking stories about what happened in China, and reporting whenever a prominent Chinese dissident came to Australia and so on.[32] Student activists wanted to maintain a high level of media attention on their issue, with which they could further lobby policy-makers, or at least have more reasons to meet decision-makers. In fact, their political advertisements succeeding in drawing the attention of some journalists (Bilic, 1989; Ma, 1989; Chen and Lu, 1994; York, 2003) and several journalists contacted

[31] These published statements helped the student community towards their goals in several areas: collecting evidence for their applications (see Chapter Three), drawing attention from journalists, and influencing government agencies and politicians (*ACT Hansard*, 21 November 1989; *The Age*, June 15, 1990; *Australian Financial Review*, June 14, 1990).

[32] As discussed below, it was the students' media-related activities that provided the then-new *Xinbao* (*Australian Chinese Daily*) with an emerging market that helped it not only to survive as a new newspaper but also to thrive as the most popular Chinese-language newspaper in Australia during the recession of the early 1990s. According to the then chief editor of the *Xinbao*, the reason behind its success was its focus on the thousands of PRC students and the residency issue (Zhu, 2003; Shi, 2007). The twenty or thirty cents that each student paid per issue per week helped the *Xinbao* to become a major player in Australia's Chinese community media market.

the FDC and the CAD for that reason. The contacts that were very useful to both sides were maintained until the late stages of the student campaign (One-on-one interviews, 11 April 1998 and 8 June 1998).

The second feature of the English-language print media that student activists identified and tried to bring into play was the fixed, predictability of the themes and the predetermined understandings that tended to characterize the reporting of particular newspapers (such as the *Sydney Morning Herald, The Age* and *The Australian*) about China and Chinese politics. Indeed, in interviews a few years later, some students described the newspaper journalists as 'a bunch of narrow-minded, hard-core ideologues' (Group-focused interviews, 14 March 1998). It seemed to many students that the Australian print media were, to a greater or lesser extent, biased against almost everything associated with China on the basis of its one-party rule and Communist ideology (Group-focused interviews, 14 March 1998), and that the media relied on a small set of negative terms when reporting or commenting on China-related issues. These key expressions included 'torture,' 'purge,' 'persecution,' 'detention' and 'imprisonment' (Group-focused interviews, 14 March 1998). The students understood that these terms shaped public opinion in Australia regarding China. One student who was contacted by journalists several times recalled his experience and said:

> A few journalists often contacted us, and asked a few questions that were not relevant to our situation. When [Nicolae] Ceausescu [the former Romanian president] was executed, they asked us when we would be able to execute... [the then Chinese leaders]; when the Berlin Wall was destroyed, they turned up to ask us when the same thing would be possible in China. After June 4, we were all mainly worried about our own future, but they kept asking us questions, such as a coup in China, power struggle, Chinese democracy, and human rights.... I always wanted to ask them a rhetorical question: 'what about our human rights in your country?'... These were very much a learning exercise, and very soon, many of us realized that they wanted to 'put their words into our mouths,' and that we also needed to take advantage of them and to 'put our words into their mouths' (Interviewee 22, 12 April 1998).

In fact, the Chinese student lobby benefited a great deal from the abovementioned set of key words.[33] All the student activists needed to do was

---

[33] These terms, apparently based on a generalization about communist regimes, were routinely used to describe the lives of ordinary Chinese people. Christopher J. Smith has pointed out that the generalization resulted from a widespread attempt in the 1980s in the Western media 'to document the bankruptcy of Communist ideology in contemporary

provide the media with more evidence that would further reinforce the prevailing negative view of China in order to show that China was not a safe place to return to. This strategy worked very well. It could even be used to answer the big, difficult questions, such as what political power struggles were going on within the CCP, or whether a military coup in China was looming (*ACD*, 7 June 1989; *The Age*, 8 June 1989; *ACD*, 14 June 1989; *China Spring*, 15 July 1989; Nathan, 1989). Of course, at the start, the students could simply give the media answers that would indirectly help their own cases for protection. Slowly but surely, as the above quote suggests, the students included their protection issue in their discussions with the media.

This proactive media strategy enabled the Chinese student campaign to overcome two significant hurdles. The first of these was a debate in the mainstream English-language media in late 1989 in which a number of leading journalists argued that there had been no massacre in Beijing (*The Australian*, 6 September 1989). The second was a lengthy debate in the media, which lasted until 1993, over their motives for staying in Australia. This occurred while student activists were finding responses to deal with the new and unfavorable political situation that had resulted from Deng Xiaoping's inspection tour to south China in 1992, on which Deng had advocated further economic reforms and accelerated growth. As noted above, Deng Xiaoping's inspection tour revived the idea in Australia of engagement with Asia. Student activists became worried that Australia might sacrifice protection of the students in favor of trade with China, especially under the Keating Labor government (Raby, 2012). Though some activists (including Li Lu, whose visit to Australia was cited at the start of this chapter) were quietly taking up the role envisaged for them in the future relationship between Australia and China, and lobbying to be permitted to stay for that purpose, the student groups as a whole were still mainly relying on politics. Their campaign was pursued based on—and reinforced by—the widespread and oversimplified understanding of China and anti-Communist sentiment that prevailed in Australia. In fact,

China' (1991: 67). Wanning Sun has noted that 'American media—and the media in the Western world in general—tirelessly devote their attention to a repertoire of "Chinese problems," including China's abuse of human rights, ... This tendency to focus on the dark side of China is often a source of embarrassment and indignation for former Chinese nationals now living in Western countries' (2002: 99). The dominance of the Western media in covering China from the perspective of the West 'became a flashpoint' in the Beijing Olympics of 2008, when the Chinese worldwide challenged how China was portrayed by the Western media (Reese and Dai, 2009: 224).

the strategic utilization of these sentiments was one of the keys to their success in obtaining residency.

In addition to the accessibility of advertising space and the media's apparently entrenched, negative views of China, the third aspect of the media that the PRC students were able to make use of in their lobbying activities was the media's steady need of 'something newsworthy.' The Chinese students had grown up in a country where newspapers did not need to be newsworthy. At the time, newspapers in China were entirely subsidized by the state (Zhao, 1998: 53) and were 'basically to be used as propaganda instruments' (Gerdes, 1982: 41). The student activists had observed that the English-language print media in Australia either copied from each other, especially when there was a newsworthy piece or topic, or tried to 'put their words into our mouths' (Group-focused interviews, 14 March 1998) so for that reason they turned to the Chinese-language media. The Chinese-language newspaper with which they chose to collaborate was the newly established, Sydney-based *Xinbao* (also known in English as *The Australian Chinese Daily*, or *ACD*). Between mid 1989 and late 1993, while the students were carrying out their lobbying campaign in Australia, there were four main Chinese-language newspapers all over Australia: two Sydney-based dailies, namely *Xingdao Ribao* (*Sing Tao Newspaper*) and *Xinbao* and two Melbourne-based weeklies, namely *The Tide* (*Haichao Bao*) and *Chinese Herald* (*Huasheng Bao*). There were also two main Chinese-language monthly magazines, *Haiwaifeng Zazhi* (*Overseas Chinese Magazine*), and *Hansheng Zazhi* (*Chinese Culture Monthly*) (Gao, 2006c).

A statistical comparison of the four Chinese newspapers shows that *Xinbao*'s coverage of June 4 and the PRC student protection issue was significantly greater than that of the other three community newspapers. More precisely, its coverage was on average one and a half times longer (in centimeters per column) than that of any of the other three Chinese newspapers over the 24-week period from 13 October 1989 to 31 March 1990 (for an example see Table 6.1 above).

In interviews for this study, former students praised the *Xinbao* for being 'of great help' in their collective campaign while also noting that it had 'made a fortune from the student issue' (Group-focused interviews, 17, 24 and 31 January 1998). To be precise, *Xinbao*'s 'fortune' began with its publication of hundreds of political statements placed by many students shortly after June 4 (discussed in Chapter Three). Having found a new market among the Chinese mainland students, the *Xinbao*—which was under financial pressure after two years of competing with the other three newspapers in the then relatively small Chinese-language media market—developed and applied some new measures to expand its market share. It lowered its advertising fee to attract more statements from the students who were definitely in need of published political statements, and it hired salespeople who had no arrogant 'old overseas Chinese' attitudes toward the PRC students[34] to promote the newspaper and its advertising space.

The *Xinbao*'s editors were fully aware that the *Sing Tao Newspaper* and the *Chinese Herald* were all focused on the older, more established Chinese communities, while *The Tide* was mainly for the Vietnamese-Chinese community. The PRC student community and their protection issue presented it with a new opportunity. It became the only Chinese-language newspaper to send its staff to student rallies and organizational meetings. Its editors became convinced that the priority of the so-called Chinese democratic movement was not the promotion of democracy in China, but the students' permanent residency in Australia. Unlike some members of the Chinese migrant community, the *Xinbao*'s editors—who were new migrants from Hong Kong and China—did not hate the idea of having more Chinese to settle down in Australia. Also unlike the people who worked for the other Chinese community newspapers, the *Xinbao*'s editors were not strangers at all to the world of PRC politics and political culture. To attract the large constituency of PRC student readers, and to compete against its counterparts in the market, the *Xinbao* soon decided not only to focus on reporting the PRC student protection issue and the government's decision-making, but also to take on an active mediating role in the issue. The latter role involved liaison between the students and the 'highest authorities' who were the target of their lobbying campaign.

The *Xinbao* did this in a number of ways. As mentioned, it provided intensive coverage of meetings between politicians, government officials and student activists (see Table 6.1). For example, in the lead-up to the meeting on 21 July 1989 between several Sydney-based ethnic Chinese community leaders and Robert Ray, the immigration minister, the *Xinbao* ran reports on the meeting every day for more than ten days. On some days, the meeting was even mentioned in several different news items.

To demonstrate its connection to the government and its influence on national leaders, the *Xinbao*'s chief editor joined a small group of ethnic

---

[34] This was an issue in many Chinese migrant communities in the 1980s and early 1990s worldwide (Tian, 1999; Ember et al., 2005). Because China was poor at the time, some people in the so-called 'old overseas Chinese' groups regarded new migrants from China as poor cousins and looked down on them.

Chinese community leaders to meet Bob Hawke, the Prime Minister, to discuss the impending changes to the *Migration Act 1958*. Reporting the meeting, the *Xinbao* not only tried to give readers the impression that it was private and had taken place solely between the Prime Minister and the chief editor (a large-sized photo of whom appeared on its front page), but also emphasized that the chief editor had passed a letter from some student groups on to the Prime Minister. At the same time, the *Xinbao* was astute in its use of language. It surprised many readers by using the headline 'Chinese students seek political asylum, PM Hawke promises to consider' a few days after June 4. This particular issue of the newspaper quickly sold out (*ACD*, 7 June 1989). The newspaper sold out again on 12 December 1989 when it published an exclusive piece in which Bob Hawke, the Prime Minister, was reported as promising that 'no student would be forcefully deported after the new Migration regulations.' This was well in advance of the similar, well-known promise that Bob Hawke made to the mainstream English media in June 1990 (*The Sun*, 8 June 1990; *The Age*, 15 June 1990).

While the *Xinbao* was positioning itself in relation to its competitors, some student activists were also trying very hard to place the newspaper in such a position that it would be part of their lobby, seeking to push it to make more contacts with politicians or senior government officials to obtain information and express their concerns. They continually fed the *Xinbao* with 'newsworthy stuff,' which in turn helped to consolidate its position as the leading newspaper in the Chinese student community in Australia. Table 6.3 lists six types of initiatives by the students to use the *Xinbao* in their collective protection campaign. These six were the most-often mentioned in interviews, and they are listed in order of frequency of mention.

Table 6.3 Approaches used by student activists in their relationship with the *Xinbao*.

	Various Ways of Approaching the Relationship with the *Xinbao*
1.	To have more activities reported in the *Xinbao*
2.	To have articles published regularly in the *Xinbao*
3.	To establish accessible channels of contacting the *Xinbao*
4.	To make announcements in the *Xinbao*
5.	To provide the *Xinbao* with more 'newsworthy stuff'
6.	To publish student organizational newsletters in the *Xinbao*

Source: Based on individual interviews (from 11 April 1998 to 8 June 1998).

These initiatives are not dissimilar to the student activists' initiatives for maintaining frequent regular contact with the government (as discussed above). However, in their dealings with the community-based media, the activists paid more attention to the media than they did to the government, on how to meet the media's need for 'something newsworthy' in order to sustain and expand an interactive relationship with the newspaper. As a number of students mentioned in interviews for this study, the student community as a whole needed reliable representation in the media (One-on-one interviews, 8 June 1998), so many student leaders and activists took the initiative to make one Chinese-language channel into a reliable partner. In time, the students became able to lead the media's need for newsworthy stories, not simply to respond to it. Therefore, they became able to use the media effectively as a tool to influence the government.

To feed the *Xinbao* with 'newsworthy stuff,' student activists could provide 'internationally circulating rumors' or 'self-made news,' or make the content as temptingly sensational as possible. For example, a range of shocking stories showed that China was politically unstable, or accounts indicated the deteriorating human rights situation in China, especially the suffering of dissidents who were well known in the West. Thanks to its especially intensive coverage of some unusual stories, the *Xinbao* had soon accumulated enough political capital to play an active part not only at community level but also at national level. The 'newsworthy stuff' in the *Xinbao* (and to a lesser extent, *Sing Tao Newspaper*), which ranged from comments made by leading Chinese community leaders to major developments in the student protection issue, was sometimes reprinted by English-language newspapers, usually one or two days after the original reports (Group-focused interviews, 14 March 1998).

On one occasion, *The Australian* was even 'misled' by reports in the *Xinbao*'s and ran the headline: '30,000 Chinese Students Can Stay' (*The Australian*, 15 March 1990). This took place only a few days before the federal election of 1990, at which the Australian Labor Party (ALP) led by Bob Hawke hoped to win its fourth successive victory and the promise had therefore reportedly been made in private by senior ALP figures to a few Chinese community leaders. The ALP leadership wanted to utilize this to win the hearts of many ethnic Chinese voters. The promise had appeared in the *Xinbao* first, but when *The Australian* picked up the story, it was quickly denied by the ALP. However, *The Australian* kept raising questions, and forcing the ALP to explain its policy on the PRC student issue (17 March 1990). Even after the 1990 election, *The Australian* carried an editorial entitled 'Hawke: why Chinese may stay, Cambodians must go' (7 June 1990) that disputed the 'blanket approach' to the student issue that seemed likely. This was the first time that the student issue was raised in the federal election and, significantly, it did not have any major negative impact on the ALP. This was taken by many Chinese student activists and their sympathizers, such as Dr Andrew Theophanous, as solid evidence upon which to lobby for the 'blanket approach' in next three or so years from 1990 to 1993.

The *Xinbao*'s intensive coverage of the PRC student issue facilitated a coordinated approach to the issue, if not a shared understanding of it. The FDC activists once commented that even if it was impracticable to unify the entire ethnic Chinese community behind the students, letting the newspaper editors deal with the divided Chinese community might win further support for their cause. Statistically, as much as one third of *Xinbao*'s news coverage and commentary relating to the student issue took the form of appeals to various sections of the Chinese community calling for unity on the issue.[35] Of course, the newspaper's aim was to attract readers and to sell more papers, but their messages were crucial for the student lobby. The *Xinbao* carried a large number of appeals by ethnic Chinese community leaders all through the student campaign (11 September 1989; 16 November 1989; 14 December 1989; 20 February 1990; 14 June 1990). Some of these reports, especially the appeals, were then translated by students into English and distributed widely among key institutions outside the ethnic Chinese community. Despite negative comments made by several Chinese community leaders, such as those by Dr Wellington Lee cited above (in the previous section of this chapter), the key to a favorable government decision was to achieve some positive media coverage and with its help, to obtain further support from ethnic Chinese community leaders in a form of 'mass mobilisation' (cf. Jupp, 1993: 213). The *Xinbao* was believed to have helped the students on both counts. Of course, though the students regarded the media as their 'main battlefield,' the media such as the *Xinbao* also needed marketable, if not popular and eye-catching, topics like the student issue. One participant in a group discussion stated:

[35] As with Table 6.1, this figure is based on the number of items of PRC student issue-related news and commentary published in the *Australian Chinese Daily* from 13 October 1989 to 31 March 1990.

> I agree that we [the media and the Chinese students] were all in the same boat. The only difference [between us] was that we wanted to fight for protection and they wanted to sell more newspapers, and that we wanted to stay in Australia and they wanted to stay in the media market.... Once we were well connected with the media, we then became more closely linked to the government [than before]. This was because the government and the media were also in the same boat.... That is what a free country is all about (Interviewee 8, 6 June 1998).

With such a clear awareness, the PRC students both as individuals and as groups had devoted a great deal of time, thought and effort to managing their relationship with the media. The student organizations, especially the FDC and the CAD, played a crucial role in rallying support through the *Xinbao*. The newspaper raised the PRC student issue with ethnic Chinese community leaders repeatedly, and then published their sympathetic responses. These were further invoked as strong evidence to show the government, and other non-government bodies as well, that the Chinese community as a whole supported these students, and this 'evidence' was then forwarded for publication in the mainstream English-language media. Therefore, even though many students used the 'battlefield' metaphor to describe their relations with the media, the Chinese-language media (and the *Xinbao* in particular) in fact played a coordinating role at community and national levels that the students themselves were unable to play properly at the time. As the above quotation illustrates, the logic was very simple: the students wanted to lobby for the opportunity to stay, and the newspaper wanted to survive and thrive. Each could help the other achieve its goals.

CHAPTER SEVEN

ORGANIZED POLITICAL ACTIONS

As the PRC students' protection lobby began to gather momentum, both English-language and Chinese-language media in Australia carried more reports, repeating that refugee status was only going to be granted to the students on a case-by-case basis (*ACD*, 16 June 1989; *The Australian*, 6 September 1989; see also Slattery, 1991; Bruer and Power, 1993). This possibility brought increasing tensions in the student community, and the groups as a whole became more politicized. As mentioned, the students' attention had already turned from June 4 towards how they themselves could be considered genuine refugees and allowed to stay permanently in Australia. Very soon, they also formed their shared goal, which was to lobby for a blanket approach that would ultimately allow them all to stay permanently in Australia. Many of these students were keen to organize more community-wide actions; however, they could not be certain that a collective approach would succeed.

This new stage of activism created a great challenge to the already established student groups, particularly to the Independent Federation of Chinese Students and Scholars in Australia (IFCSSA). In the early stages of the student campaign, the independent Chinese student unions had led the way: raising and pursuing the student protection issue; organizing a range of lobbying activities, and even internationalizing the issue. Now, two new political organizations, namely the newly founded Federation for Democratic China (FDC), and the Chinese Alliance for Democracy (CAD), began to take the lead in the drive for many students to collect evidence for their asylum-seeking applications, and began to provide the organizational structure for a more active lobbying campaign.

The reasons for the expansion of the CAD and the formation of the FDC, and for the way in which these organizations were able to maintain their relevance to the student community well into the 1990s, have been misunderstood by some observers. Early discussions of these Chinese student groups' lobbying activities tended to over-emphasize their role in the Chinese democratic movement in exile (Barmé, 1991; Nathan, 1992; Ma, 1993; Goldman, 1994; He, 1996, 1997; Wang, 1999). Thus, some observers overlooked the role of the student groups as political vehicles for asylum seeking. For example, when the FDC was being established, *The New York Times* defined it as 'a new opposition group that seeks to provide a democratic alternative to China's communist Party' (4 August 1989). By mid 1990, when the FDC's asylum seeking functions could be clearly identified, the organization was still regarded as a political force 'crusading from abroad for a change of rulers and a change of political direction in Beijing' (*The New York Times*, 27 May 1990).[1] Political sentiments of this kind soon also spread to academic circles (as noted in Chapter Four). Though this explanation soon fell out of favor, there has as yet been little examination of the role of these organizations in the students' community-based activities in their quest for asylum.[2]

This chapter discusses the lobbying activities (defined as organized group political actions) of the Chinese students in their campaign to stay permanently in Australia in the aftermath of June 4. To take an organized political approach was a logical continuation of the student campaign. In fact, organized action was the students' last resort in their campaign. The Australian government acted slowly in dealing with the student issue, which appeared very reluctant to provide the students with asylum for fear of an electoral backlash if it did so. Only a handful of student political groups pursued organized political action, but their actions affected the entire campaign and its outcome, and thus affected every member of the student community.

This chapter will look at the PRC students' organized political actions with reference to three main aspects: (1) the transition from the independent student unions to the FDC; (2) the ongoing politicization of the campaign; and (3) factionalism and reorganization of the CAD.

The Rationale behind the Transition

To some extent, the Chinese students living in Australia were organized before June 4 (as discussed in Chapter Four), thanks to their own primary social groups, the CAD (as a political opposition group among overseas Chinese), and the education officers at the Chinese consular posts. As the

[1] The article, entitled 'Telling the Truth, Taking the Punishment,' was by Emily MacFarquhar, a long time China watcher and contributor to several leading dailies and weeklies in the USA.

[2] As noted, however, a few researchers have used the student case as an example of cyber-politics (Li, 1990; Matloff, 1997; Grier, 1998; Walsh, 1999; Grier and Campbell, 2000).

protection issue dragged on, the student community became more and more organized and politicized. The formation of local FDC branches was a decisive moment. The FDC was an organization formed in Paris in late September 1989 by a number of Chinese nationals exiled from China after June 4 (see Chapter Six), including student demonstration leaders, intellectuals, policy advisers and even bureaucrats. They held a meeting with some Chinese postgraduate students and scholars studying in Western countries, and decided to join forces under the banner of the FDC.

The FDC, which was called *Minzhu Zhongguo Zhenxian* in Chinese and abbreviated to *Minzhen*, was known in English by handful of different translations. For example, *The New York Times* initially called them the 'Democratic Front of China' (4 August 1989), and then the 'Front for a Democratic China' (27 May 1990) before the present name 'Federation for Democratic China' became official and fixed in the organization's own publications. Unlike the CAD,[3] which had been established in late 1983 in New York and already had many branches in major Western cities by the time of June 4, the FDC was a new (and explicitly political) group. It was formed and led by activists who had been directly involved in the events of June 4, and significantly, it was defined by the Chinese government immediately after its formation as a reactionary clique (see *Beijing Review*, 1990 [33]: 110; Han and Hua, 1990: 382). This gave the FDC greater political relevance than the CAD for PRC nationals seeking asylum or residency abroad after June 4, though membership and active participation in both groups were regarded by refugee advocates and Chinese student activists as strong indicators of a 'well-founded fear' of persecution which was the crucial test, as defined by the UN (UNHCR, 1988; Black, 1991; Crock, 1998a; more explanations in Chinese could be found from *China Spring* [*Australia Edition*], No. 1, 1990; *FDC Newsletter*, 34, 1991).

In the intensifying organization and politicization process, the student lobby pursued four specific aims.

The first aim was to formalize channels of communication among the students, especially among the activist groups. Many students were then very concerned that they would not have access to complete information in their loosely formed primary social groups, and even those who were well informed were worried about whether the information that they had

[3] As noted, the CAD (Chinese Alliance for Democracy) was known as *Zhongguo Minzhu Tuanjie Lianmeng* in Chinese (abbreviated to *Minlian*) (for more information, please read Yan, 1992; Chen and Lu, 1994; Qian, 2003).

received was trustworthy. Anxieties about gathering full and dependable information regarding their asylum seeking created enormous pressure on individual students and on student activist groups. This occurred not only immediately after June 4, but also as the entire community turned its attention toward the residency issue—especially when a high proportion of the students were found to be rather selective about the information they passed on to others and at what stage of their decision making they passed it on. Naturally, they were all anxious to learn more about how to apply for protection or residency. For that reason, they all wanted a more organized way of accessing information (Group-focused interviews, 14 and 21 March 1998). I conducted a small-scale survey in 1999, which suggested that as many as 80 percent of these students believed that a greater level of group organization was the best solution to these worries about communication (Gao, 2002).

The second goal of the intensifying organization and politicization process in the Chinese student community was to regularize evidence-collecting activities. Pressed by changing government policies to provide more evidence, and particular kinds of evidence, to support their refugee applications (see Chapter Three), the entire Chinese student community was mobilized in search of this evidence. However, the criteria by which the government would judge the acceptability of the evidence were not clear at all. Initially, the students knew only that there were two possible categories of protection applicable to them in Australia, which were the humanitarian immigration program and the refugee program. However, there were no other explanations of those categories—an absence of information that let everyone's imagination run rampant. Subsequently, evidence-gathering activities intensified and escalated, dividing the entire community and introducing rivalry among many students. This competitiveness would re-intensify whenever government officials, or even some commentators, hinted at a toughening of the refugee screening process. One interviewee observed:

> Maybe it was not too difficult to meet the government's criteria for asylum. However, because they gave us no indication as to what we needed to present [in our applications], we all became very worried, and started collecting whatever we could find.... The vague term 'well-founded fear' was another big headache and almost drove us mad.... It was just because of these problems that many of us liked the idea of taking up a [FDC or CAD] membership. It actually set a benchmark for evidence collection, because no evidence could be more [politically] serious than the membership of overseas Chinese democratic organizations. This worked in some way

> and stopped irregular [evidence collection] activities.... Of course, our attention was then attracted to student groups themselves (Interviewee 15, 24 May 1998).

In addition, as noted, there were already significant divisions between certain categories of the students because of the government's separate consideration of the 'pre-20 June group' and the 'post-20 June group.' The students in the 'pre-20 June group' could argue that they had already been in Australia on June 4, and that those in the 'post-20 June group' must already have cleared the Chinese government's post-June 4 security checks in order to leave China. For their part, the 'post-20 June group' could argue that they were the true sufferers and survivors of June 4, and therefore the ones in real need of protection.[4] This division posed a real threat to the collective campaign, as each group was working on its own strategies and activities. More and more students consequently came to realize that they needed organized groups to regularize their evidence-collecting activities and 'standardize' the evidence that many students would separately collect (One-on-one interviews, 25 April 1998).[5] In addition, organized groups would not only provide the campaign with a better decision-making environment, but would also place more members of the community on an equal political footing. They could also enable more student groups to be more proactive in setting the agendas for the protection issue, to which the Australian government would need to respond.[6]

The third aim of the student groups' organization and politicization process was to coordinate lobbying activities and prevent any ill-advised behavior by individual student activists. Three-quarters of the students

---

[4] This approach was pursued right up to late 1993 when the Keating Labor government decided to allow all the students to stay permanently. As will be detailed in Chapter Eight, the immigration department still insisted on the approach when introducing the Keating government's '1 November [1993] decisions' by creating four new entry permit categories (e.g., category 815, category 816, category 817 and category 818) corresponding to the old divisions (DIEA, 1994; Birrell, 1994, 1996).

[5] Because of the case-by-case approach the Australian government had insisted on in order to identify the so-called genuine refugees, the students had been collecting a wide range of evidence for their refugee claims—a process that added to internal tensions. Many students felt that there was a need to guide students to collect similar evidence, or at least to not present anything extraordinary, which not only did not fit into the refugee definition, but could also jeopardize the community-wide campaign.

[6] Some student activists by then already realized that the very considerable suffering of some individuals appeared to refugee case officers and immigration bureaucrats as something insignificant, although they took the organized political groups, such as the CAD, and their membership, very seriously.

interviewed for this study regarded this third aim as a vital driving force behind the politicization and organization of the student lobby (Group-focused interviews, 17, 24 and 31 January 1998), and various specific cases were mentioned to show how seriously the student community had been in need of coordinated actions led by highly organized and politicized student groups.

Two cases were mentioned particularly often. The first involved an open split among independent student unionists at a national IFCSSA assembly in late August 1989 (*ACD*, 28 August 1989). At this meeting, student representatives had a very heated debate over whether the union should focus their activities on supporting the democratic movement in China or on taking care of the welfare of the students studying in Australia. Several students described the proponents of the dominant arguments as 'unrealistic' (Group-focused interviews, 21 March 1998),[7] but they all believed that the dissension at this IFCSS meeting sowed the seeds for the tighter organization of the Chinese student community. That is, the IFCSS was not an ideal organization to lead the student campaign, as a number of their activists—as will next be discussed—appeared to have other strategies for staying permanently in Australia.

The second case was the intention of certain postgraduate students to lobby separately for their own residency on occupational grounds (see Chapters Four and Six).[8] Although there was no evidence to prove that the government had any plan to deal with the student issue in this way, this intention worried the rest of the student community on two fronts. First, the ELICOS students were worried that the government would not be interested in them any more, if postgraduate students were all granted residency first, as postgraduate qualifications were acquiring more and more importance in the government's immigration criteria. Second, the ELICOS students were worried that they themselves would be unable to deal with Australian constituencies, such as bureaucrats and politicians, if the postgraduate students were allowed to stay first, and therefore had no interest in pursuing residency for the ELICOS students. To forestall

---

[7] The student lobby in August 1989 was in its early stage and led by the IFCSSA. At that particular gathering, a few IFCSSA leaders who insisted on focusing on the Chinese democratic movement appeared to be strong and in control, but tense discussions about how to replace them were also started immediately after the meeting.

[8] In the late 1980s and early 1990s, students wishing to apply for residency in Australia after finishing their degree courses were obliged to return to their own country to do so (Iredale, 1997; Vrachnas et al., 2005).

these worse case scenarios, a large number of ELICOS students became very active in seeking not only membership but also leadership positions in organized political groups (first in the already existing CAD, then in the newly established FDC). This community-wide reaction revealed very clearly the need that the students felt for an organized political group that would lead and coordinate their lobbying efforts and activities.

The fourth aim of making the student campaign highly organized and politicized was to develop community-wide strategies to identify the best solution to the residency issue and to prepare the community for a long-term struggle to obtain it. Around 65 percent of the students interviewed in this study thought that the students felt at the time that they were in desperate need of a good strategy for their campaign. This was because of both the government's repeated statements that it would not grant all Chinese national permanent residency and its long delays in processing a large number of applications from the Chinese students.[9]

At the same time, the smaller PRC student unions and groups were still developing their own tactics or strategies. For example, no less than 30 Chinese student unions nationwide (*ACD*, 28 August 1989) attended the first IFCSSA assembly held in Sydney in August 1989 (mentioned above). This in itself was indication enough that the student community needed to become more unified. If the CAD, as the oldest organization in the Chinese student community, had not been able to unite the smaller student unions in an effective way and lead the protection campaign, then perhaps the more recently established FDC might be able to fulfill this function. These two political organizations were both active in the Chinese student community in Australia for most of the four-year period (from 1989 to 1993), during which the students waged their campaign for permanent residency. As mentioned, both organizations had political capital in the form of strongly negative official reactions from the CCP and the then Chinese government, and both had been officially identified as 'counter-revolutionary' political organizations.

Compared with the more recently established FDC, the reputation of the CAD was hampered by two factors. First, it did not seem to have any relevance to the student protests—or the student democratic movement

[9] In fact, the Australian government was giving in to the students' demands little by little (as detailed in other chapters), although official statements were still becoming tougher and more rigid.

as it was called at the time—that had occurred inside or outside China since April 1989.[10] At the time, the PRC student communities in the Western countries in which it carried out its political activities were largely led by the IFCSS. Second, given that there was not a large number of Chinese postgraduate students studying in Australia, the CAD in Australia had recruited mainly ELICOS students, a very high proportion of whom were overstayers. From the time the protection issue arose, the immigration department (DILGEA) had consistently treated overstayers differently from legal visa holders. For this reason, many students wished to keep their distance from the CAD, which was widely considered as representing the overstayers (*ACD*, 14 October 1989; *The Tide*, 16 November 1989). At the very least, the CAD's obvious connection with many overstayers precluded a leading role for the CAD in pursuing the student campaign. The FDC, by contrast, was established by newly exiled student leaders and activists of what was then known as the Chinese student democratic movement, which had been suppressed by CCP hardliners with the help of the military. These individuals were, in their own words, 'survivors of June 4' (*FDC Newsletter*, 34, 1991; Goldman, 1994; Kennedy, 1997; Chai, 2011).

Soon after the establishment of the FDC in Paris in September 1989, the Chinese government stated clearly that it was a counter-revolutionary organization whose aim was to rebel against the socialist system in China and the leadership of the CCP (*ACD*, 27 September 1989). The Chinese government also issued a protest against France for allowing the FDC to hold its meetings in Paris and notified other Western governments of its official position regarding the organization. This strong reaction from the Chinese government not only defined the political nature of the FDC as 'counter revolutionary' from the outset and gave this new activist group a great deal of much-needed political publicity, but also constituted vital assistance for its members in seeking political asylum in several Western countries.

The first Australian branch of the FDC (in contrast to the CAD) was founded by students with high-level political skills who were studying in postgraduate courses. No overstayers were involved in its early stages. In

[10] As mentioned, the CAD was established in the US in 1983, and before June 4 it recruited members mainly from the Chinese students studying in American and some Western universities. They had no meaningful connections to the student activists involved in the student protests in China in the first half of 1989 (Chong, 1989; He, 1996; Qian, 2003).

the first few months of its existence (i.e. from the end of 1989 to early 1990), as the FDC activists were busy setting up their branch, a number of Chinese students complained that it was turning into an elite and exclusive group (One-on-one interviews, 11 and 25 April 1998, and 8 June 1998). Once the local branch was in place in late October 1989, however, and more particularly in early 1990, and once many of the leadership positions had been filled by highly determined, experienced activists, this newly established organization gradually incorporated students of all types. This inclusivity may have been what allowed the FDC to take over the leadership role from other independent Chinese student unions (such as the IFCSSA).

Once established, the first Australian branch of the FDC asserted its leadership by taking on four roles to perform the functions that students felt they needed from their coordinating organization.

First, it provided its members with open, organized channels through which to obtain and exchange information. Indeed, students described the FDC as initially seeming more like a news agency than a political group (Group-focused interviews, 17 January 1998). To meet the PRC students' need for clear and formalized ways of accessing information, the FDC made significant innovations in the way communications with students were actually handled. Table 7.1 lists seven of the observable changes. For many students, especially those who were not members, the FDC derived its influence predominantly from the structured channel for communication that it provided at the start (Group-focused interviews, 14 and 21 March 1998; *FDC Newsletter*, 34, 1991). Two features of its communication strategy played an important role in helping the FDC to establish its leadership in the community (see Table 7.1). The first was its policy of having all its general meetings, seminars and public lectures open to the public from the very beginning. The second was its practice of holding a briefing session after almost every general meeting, seminar or public lecture, at which it reported on various issues concerning the welfare of its members and the community as a whole. The FDC's stated policy was to be open and democratic. This policy was in sharp contrast to certain other groups formed by student unionists as closed circles to lobby the government separately, in an ad hoc way, to waive their own visa restrictions.

Table 7.1 New communication practices.

No.	Changes Made by the FDC
1.	Holding general members' meetings, seminars and public lectures on a very regular basis
2.	Opened its meetings, seminars and public lectures to all students from the very beginning
3.	Publishing all notices of its meetings in Chinese community newspapers
4.	Holding briefing sessions after most meetings, seminars and public lectures in the interests of the welfare of all its members
5.	Publishing a local newsletter called *FDC Forum*; members also received the *FDC Newsletter* and the *Journal of Democratic China* from the central committee in France
6.	Running working groups on specific issues; each group having to report regularly to members' meetings
7.	Regularly dealing with the media, which disseminated information widely and gave the FDC publicity

Source: Based on group-focused interviews, 14 and 21 March 1998 and one-on-one interviews, 11 and 25 April 1998, and 8 June 1998.

Second, the FDC facilitated and regularized the collection of evidence for asylum applications. Membership of the FDC constituted evidence in itself, because of the FDC's strong associations with June 4 and inherent opposition to the CCP, and the widespread belief among many PRC students that there was no stronger evidence of the need for asylum than the FDC membership (One-on-one interviews, 25 April and 8 June 1998). For this reason, its membership expanded very rapidly from the moment it was founded in late October 1989. By the time the Australian government enacted the *Migration Legislation Amendment Act 1989* and introduced a series of new immigration regulations restricting onshore residency seekers' claim for residency on 19 December 1989, there were an estimated 350 to 400 FDC members in Australia. Three months later, before the new deadline (31 March 1990) for students' applications for permanent residency on strong humanitarian grounds under the old regulations, the membership of the Australian FDC was conservatively estimated at 550 to 600 (*STN*, 19 December 1989; *FDC Newsletter*, No. 32, 1991; He 1997: 92). Several students suggested in interviews that the figure was as high as 700 (One-on-one interviews, 25 April and 8 June 1998). Ironically and significantly, in May 1990, more than one third of the FDC's worldwide membership was actually in Australia; the Sydney branch was the largest FDC branch in the world, and the Melbourne branch was the second largest (*ACD*, 23 December 1989; 1 May 1990; 7 May 1990).

Many PRC students, especially overstayers and those from the 'post-20 June group,' flocked to join the FDC because the refugee program was their only option for applying for residency as a result of the rapid and unexpected changes to Australia's onshore asylum seeking policy. They all needed to associate themselves with a certain type of politics in order to identify themselves as seekers of political asylum. For numerous Chinese students who were already inclined toward activism, the FDC provided an organizational framework for their political activities and made a range of leadership positions available, in working groups as well as in its central organizational hierarchy. Immediately after its founding, almost all the early FDC members were offered a position in either the central structure or a working group.[11] As noted, this arrangement would provide members with strong evidence of being a 'political leader,' to help their asylum applications to be recognized as bona fide. This new opportunity obviated the need for the endless, irregular and somewhat random evidence collection activities that had been actively pursued by many students until that point.

Third, the FDC, with its organizational structure and its international political connections, coordinated unified actions by the Chinese student community. The FDC dealt actively with the Australian government, the Australian media, the local Chinese community and community groups or organizations. After the working groups for specific issues and regular meetings to exchange information (the two coordinating activities most frequently cited as essential by former students in interviews), the third most frequently cited organizational measure was the FDC's formation of broad coalitions with various student union groups and the local CAD. Cooperation between the FDC and the CAD was significant for optimal coordination of lobbying activities in Australia and for strengthening the lobbying power of the PRC student community (*China Spring* [*Australia Edition*], No. 1, 1990; *FDC Newsletter*, 34, 1991).

In the early stages of their political cooperation, the two organizations carried out joint activities in Canberra and Brisbane as well as Sydney and Melbourne (*ACD*, 22 December 1989; *The Chinese Herald*, 26 January 1990) and developed their shared strategies (*The Chinese Herald*, 17 November 1989; *STN*, 21 February 1990). For example, the FDC allowed many CAD

11 One student noted that many in the community aimed for a 'trifecta': to join the FDC, to be a member of a working group, and to take a leadership position in the organization (One-on-one interviews, 8 June 1998).

members to join without having to give up their CAD membership. This dual membership policy was extremely popular among the ELICOS students, since it gave them a chance to collect more solid evidence for their asylum applications, or at least it offered the option of making their asylum cases very complicated (a tactic that many PRC students believed to be the key to a successful case, as noted in Chapter Five). One interviewee made a number of comments on this dual membership and said:

> This [dual membership] virtually merged CAD with FDC into one political organization. Although they still kept their separate names, what actually happened was that more CAD members took FDC membership, not the other direction. It seemed to many [students] that it was an issue about the CAD's identity, if not about keeping its name, but I believed it was a tactic [that some students had] prepared just in case one membership was not strong enough to make an asylum claim.... All these were influenced by the Chan case. These CAD-FDC members wanted to prepare themselves for going to the court one day and showing the court that they had a stronger asylum case than the Chan case (Interviewee 12, 29 March 1998).

From the organizational point of view, the FDC effectively brought the CAD under its control by drawing in a large number of its members, thus preventing them from acting on their own.

Later, the FDC also played the principal role in developing strategies for the student campaign. There were several reasons for this. First, the FDC attracted more politically-minded and experienced PRC students than any other student group. It was broadly accepted that all the most politically talented PRC students at that time were directly or indirectly associated with the FDC (Group-focused interviews, 14 and 21 March 1998). Its members and some associates (without membership) included former mid- and high-mid-ranking policy advisers and bureaucrats who had worked in China's state-party systems at central and provincial levels. It also included mid- and higher-ranking researchers, professors and other kinds of professionals such as journalists, from the top Chinese universities, research institutes and other prestigious institutions. There were also a number of individuals, who were not connected with big institutions in China, but had strong political skills, experience and confidence because of their family backgrounds or personal experience in China. They had all grown up in a China that had been exceedingly politicized and emotionally charged for several decades. Second, as part of an international network, the FDC had extensive contacts with overseas members. In particular, the similar, but more intense and politically skillful efforts of PRC students in the USA encouraged the Australian group to be more political than the CAD. Third, and more importantly, the FDC formed good connections with a number of Australian political parties, organizations and groups, ranging from the ultra-left to the ultra-right (see Chapter Six); in this way they were able to learn about local politics and to amass new skills and knowledge. After 1991, the local FDC even registered itself with a local interest group network called 'Collective of Self Help Groups' (COSHG, 1991: 53) as a crucial step in its strategy to integrate the students' pursuit of residency into local political contexts in preparation for *chijiuzhan* (a protracted war)—a phrase borrowed from Mao Zedong.

Further Politicization of the Campaign

When the issue of residency for the Chinese students in Australia arose in the late 1980s and early 1990s, the Cold War was ending globally and Western liberal democracy was prevailing over its rivals. Democracy was fashionable and anything related to communism was out of fashion; any efforts to pursue democratization in communist countries would then be encouraged one way or another by the liberal-capitalist Western world. This global political atmosphere gave the PRC students the opportunity to form, or adjust to, a new political identity in a strategic way and to collect new political evidence for their refugee claims, and these students did their best, both individually and collectively, to establish a credible link between themselves and the global politics of the time. For example, one well-known student leader described the Chinese students seeking to stay in Western countries as the 'seeds of China's democratic future' (cited at the beginning of Chapter Six). The student lobby needed to capitalize on such statements and act collectively to maximize their effectiveness.

For many PRC students, however, it was difficult to adjust to their new situation as asylum seekers. Although few would refuse the chance to seek permanent residency in the West, not all were prepared to obtain it through refugee status. For example, most of the postgraduate student group had benefited from the social changes in China after the end of the Maoist era in the late 1970s and early 1980s. In addition, they had even been sent to Australia officially by the Chinese government after going through a series of selection-training processes in China, through which their loyalty to the state was reinforced in one way or another. They were aware that they had been luckier than the hundreds of millions of poor peasants and urban workers in China. That is, they might have disliked the CCP and the government, but they did not necessarily hate them.

The ELICOS students, for their part, had also been quite lucky in a different way in that they could at least afford to pay for the opportunity to study overseas. Moreover, according to two surveys (Wang, 1987; Wang, and Lai, 1987), a high proportion of the ELICOS students were members of the CCP and the CCYL (the Chinese Communist Youth League); a quarter to a third of them were CCYL branch leaders, and some had held mid-ranking CCYL leadership positions, at regional and county levels, before leaving China. Also according to those surveys, many students had also held skilled professional positions, such as engineers, doctors and nurses, or had even held low- and middle-ranking government jobs. All these indicated that their family backgrounds were less vulnerable to the politics of Maoism than the professions of teacher, journalist, editor, artist or writer, which had been particular targets of those politics. At least, these students themselves were already part of China's state-part system or its bureaucracy.

In fact, a high proportion of the Chinese students, both postgraduate and ELICOS, were the sons and daughters of privileged Chinese social classes or groups, such as senior or high-ranking government officials or CCP members, or senior or high-ranking officers of the PLA (the People's Liberation Army). A higher than average percentage of them had spent years in the PLA, and many had become CCP members. Such people had no connections with Chinese oppositional politics. Personal situations and backgrounds such as these were believed to be the main reason for the individual lobbying efforts of some postgraduate students for changes to the terms of their student entry permits (One-on-one interviews, 25 April 1998); if their migration status could easily be changed on occupational grounds, they would have no need to identify themselves as seekers of political asylum.

Of course, because of the scope of this research project, the extent to which these backgrounds of many students had influenced their activism does not become clear since the project was partially restricted by the requirements of modern research ethics. However, it was very evident that the Chinese activism of this particular type was largely reactive. In addition to their reactions to various external conditions, such as policy changes, certain reactions of the students seemed to be related to their family and personal backgrounds, or related to their own credentials for seeking asylum. One interviewee pointed out:

> It was initially difficult to understand why some [students] whose backgrounds were as *gongdang* [a CCP member], *gongjun* [a PLA soldier], and *gonggan* [a communist cadre] became unbelievably active in protest-

> ing June 4 and involved in rallies and some group activities. It took many of us a few months to realize that they had to do more than other students did, because their backgrounds were too 'good' to apply for refugee [status]. . . . They needed to build a stronger [asylum] case than ours (Interviewee 36, 30 May 1998).

The above factors, however, were often eclipsed by evolving dynamics resulting from rapidly changing external circumstances. The victory in the *Wei v Minister for Immigration* case in May 1991 (see Chapter Five), after which around two thousand Chinese applications for residency on strong humanitarian grounds were processed according to the court ruling (Le, 2001), was the final triumph of the IFCSSA activists' lobby. Almost all of those two thousand applicants were granted residency without going through the complex and politically charged refugee claims process and without further committing themselves to politics. However, the IFCSSA activists' decision to focus their lobbying efforts on both the onshore humanitarian immigration program and the right to apply for residency on occupational grounds not only alienated the overstayer group, but also created a division between those who wished to apply under the onshore humanitarian program and those who did not or who were unable to. These divisions became even more apparent than before, and were impossible to avoid or reunify—first of all after 31 March 1990 and then after June 1990, when the new *Migration Legislation Amendment Act 1989* was in place. The newly passed amendment legislated the cancelation of the onshore humanitarian immigration program, after extending the (19 December 1989) deadline twice for the PRC students who were legal visa holders (discussed in Chapter Three).

All these effectively precluded the IFCSSA's further leadership of the residency lobby. Therefore, The FDC stepped in to fill the vacuum for the majority of the community (totalling more than 40,000), who had not taken the chance to seek permanent residency on humanitarian grounds or through the precedent of *Wei v Minister for Immigration*. The activists stepped up their efforts to align this big majority with the new asylum seeking politics and to minimize the influence of different priorities and positions on the residency lobby, particularly after the granting of four-year temporary protection visas in June 1990. There were demands that the IFCSSA leadership be thrown out, political extremists removed from the CAD,[12] and the student community repositioned as participants in

[12] In the early stages of the campaign, some foolish and impractical strategies were put forward. For example, several ELICOS students invoked the notion of 'armed struggle'

the new democratization of Chinese politics. Even though there were no longer many signs indicating such change, this new alignment was well under way after the four-year protection visas were given in mid 1990. More students felt that they missed a few good opportunities, and now they needed to prepare for their last battle. One interviewee remarked:

> As far as I knew, though the [Australian] government did not want to have such a big group of Chinese to stay and kept delaying [in making a decision about the issue], there were quite a lot of people who were given permanent residency before the four-year [special temporary residency visa] decision. At the time, some were given refugee status, some went to the United States or Canada to apply for protection there, and some, including a few men, were married to Australians. All in all, our impression was that our chance [to stay] was getting slimmer and slimmer.... Our desire to catch the *mobanche* [the last bus or train service] of seeking asylum drove us into what we then called the last battle (Interviewee 43, 12 April 1998).

Accordingly, the next phase of the PRC student protection campaign was characterized by various fundamental changes. The students' links with current international politics were re-established. Several catchphrases emerged to promote the politicization of the residency campaign; such catchphrases included 'Be a fighter for democracy, not a victim of June 4' (noted above) and 'Show that you are fighting for democracy before being granted asylum.' Other catchphrases were about what not to do: for example the phrase, 'the GMD can't grant you asylum in Australia' referred to the association of a number of CAD leaders and activists with pro-GMD local overseas Chinese community groups, which was seen as distracting students from engaging in 'the new Chinese democratic movement' (a politically encoded term for the residency campaign). Among the core

and appealed to participants at a rally in Melbourne to set up guerrilla forces and wage guerrilla warfare in Yunnan against the CCP and its government. These individuals were working closely with members of the local Chinese community who were associated with pro-GMD (Guomindang) interest groups (One-on-one interviews, 11 April 1998), and appeared to wish to run their campaign in Australia along the lines of the CCP-GMD conflict (which was not an important issue in China after the 1950s, but remained a divisive issue in overseas Chinese communities into the late 1980s). These ELICOS student activists used emotive expressions with clear revolutionary connections, such as instigating uprisings of armed forces, organizing shopkeeper strikes and worker strikes, smuggling weapons into China, establishing armed separatist regions in China, or even mentioning kidnapping or even assassinating Chinese leaders (One-on-one interviews, 11 April 1998). These extreme ideas may have been to do with their associations with elderly remnants of the CCP/GMD conflict. This short-lived aspect of the student campaign was guided by foolish ideas, or the old political rhetoric of revolutionary early twentieth-century China, rather than by any clear or consistent strategy.

student activists, discussions focused on what their fellow activists of the American IFCSS had then discussed at the Harvard meeting (see Chapter Four) and how to put their political thinking and strategies into practice in Australia. Although the PRC students had abandoned the leadership of the IFCSSA, the new FDC leaders and activists followed the American IFCSS closely. This was partially because the political understandings and strategies of the activists in the USA had in fact been developed in cooperation with a number of active American congresspersons, in with a congressional working group on China.

A number of key phrases from the Harvard meeting proved useful for the Chinese student activists in Australia—phrases such as 'economic sanctions against China's crackdown [of the democratic movement],' 'human rights issue,' 'promoting democracy' and 'political change.' With a strong awareness of Australia's commercial interests in China, the local activists made one small but significant change to the American approach by deciding not to include the idea of economic sanctions against China into their strategy. Phrases such as 'human rights issue,' 'the promotion of democracy in China' and 'political change' appeared to be more strategic than other phrases because they were vague and immeasurable, and therefore they could be used indefinitely.

It was not easy to get rid of the radicalism of the student campaign altogether, and repositioning the collective campaign as part of the new democratization in Chinese politics also did not forestall impractical or silly ideas—one of which was the attempt to portray the leadership of overseas student organizations, in particular the FDC leadership, as the Chinese government-in-exile. When the FDC's Vice-President, Wan Runnan, a high-profile intellectual-turned-entrepreneur of the 1980s, visited Australia in 1991, he was introduced as the 'Chinese Premier-in-exile.' When Li Lu visited Australia, he was portrayed not only as a leading figure of the Tiananmen protest of 1989, but also as the future national leader of China. However, even these extremes appeared to be more helpful to the protection campaign than to simply portray the students as victims of either June 4 or the old CCP-GMD conflict.

The strategy of dealing with residency as a human rights issue had been raised within weeks of June 4 (see Table 7.2), by an activist group called CASHR (Chinese Association for Safeguarding Human Rights) in Sydney; now, it became the key campaign strategy. The FDC and CAD published a joint statement on 21 February 1990 calling for the students' right to stay permanently in Australia to be considered as a human rights issue but the student community as a whole did not automatically identify with this as a key strategy (see Table 7.2), and a working group called the 'Chinese Students Human Rights Delegation' was formed jointly by all the student organizations in mid June 1990. It took one year for most students to come to terms with this highly politicized idea.

The human rights issue became the student community's core strategy for two key reasons. First, it rested on strong international criticism of China's human rights record, especially in the early 1990s. As noted, this notion was from America but, as introduced in Chapter Four, it seemed to be created partially by several Chinese students or scholars living in the USA (the case was often called 'made in USA, but by Chinese'). Of course, one of the important conditions was that Australia followed the US closely in international politics. Second, and more importantly, the ambiguity of the phrase 'human rights' had exceptional strategic value, because it seemed to the PRC student activists that there were hardly any objective criteria for accurately assessing and measuring whether one's human rights are respected or violated.[13] Playing the human rights card

Table 7.2 How the human rights issue became part of the lobbying strategies.

Date	Raised Human Rights Issue
30 July 1989	Establishment of 'Chinese Association for Safeguarding Human Rights' (CASHR) in Sydney
3 October 1989	FDC forms 'Human Rights Committee'
14 October 1989	First human rights survey organized by CASHR
6 February 1990	US Department of State accuses China of abusing the human rights of Chinese people
21 February 1990	FDC and CAD jointly publish a statement titled 'The students' problems should be solved as a human rights issue'
10 May 1990	In a meeting with a Chinese minister visiting Australia, the Foreign Affairs Minister, Senator Gareth Evans, protests against human rights abuses in China
Late May 1990	A report titled 'Human rights abuses in China—a survey of Chinese citizens in Australia' is distributed
13 June 1990	Working group called 'the Chinese students human rights delegation' formed jointly by all the student organizations

Source: Australian Chinese Daily, 30 July 1989 to 13 June 1990.

[13] The students' understanding of the ambiguity of the term 'human rights' has already been reflected in recent discussions on the concept, but the discussions have focused on aspects of the term different from what the students emphasized. For example, Parekh believes that the ambiguity is because of the term 'human' (2006: 19), and Griffin simply regards it as an incomplete idea (2008).

might have appeared to many activists to be more strategic than other, more easily achievable demands put forward by some students—such as the demand to remain in Australia until certain Chinese leaders stepped down or the Chinese government was overthrown. As the issue dragged on, a consensus emerged that the student campaign could not stake their own futures on short-term outcomes and goals, but should keep in mind what they actually wanted to achieve: to stay permanently in Australia. Thus, the student organizations had to search for a strategic and practical way in which this could be fulfilled.

Factionalism and Reorganization

While the FDC was quickly taking over the leadership role in organizing the student lobby, and while CAD members were seeking to get rid of more radical individuals from their groups and eliminate the influence of pro-GMD overseas Chinese groups on the student protection campaign, members of the CAD were struggling to keep their political identity as the first anti-CCP organization in Chinese politics. CAD members saw this identity as a crucial factor in terms of seeking political asylum. Their reactions to these changes were manifested in comments such as 'all our accumulated political capital would be wasted,' and 'our asylum cases would be groundless.' In order to keep its organizational structure and political identity, CAD's efforts to maintain its salience and perceptual prominence had predominantly taken the form of factional activities and reorganization within the organization itself.

Table 7.3 presents the case of one Australian CAD branch to show the broader factional struggles and subsequent reorganization, which was already taking place before June 1990. Yet Table 7.3 does not show the negative effects of factionalism and the demands for reorganization on the CAD before June 4, when some members had become aware of the imminent arrival of an opportunity to stage their political activism. Even before June 4, some CAD members already realized that there would be the need for individual students to collect evidence for their asylum cases. After June 4, of course, the community-wide demand to lobby for permanent residency became apparent and even more pressing. What Table 7.3 does show is that, according to the *Australian Chinese Daily*, the Australia-based CAD experienced three major disputes, over: (1) re-registration of CAD membership; (2) restructuring of the CAD leadership; and (3) the CAD's relationship with the FDC and the joint organization of activities.

Table 7.3 The CAD's factional activities and reorganization as reported in the *ACD*.

Date of the Report	Factional Activities within the CAD
27 November 1989	– Calling to re-register all CAD members
22 December 1989	– Calling to re-register membership – Meeting held jointly with FDC to discuss political changes in Eastern Europe
18 January 1990	– CAD Australia divided into two local branches, approved by headquarters in the US
26 January 1990	– Series of activities organized jointly with FDC during Chinese New Year period
21 February 1990	– Joint statement with FDC proposing that 'the student issue should be solved as a human rights issue'
28 February 1990	– CAD national conference – Calling to publish of Australian edition of *China Spring*, a US-based Chinese magazine
15 March 1990	– Participation in organizing an independent workers union
5 April 1990	– Announcement that there were three local CAD branches in Australia, and 'CAD Australia' no longer existed – Calling to re-register CAD membership
7 April 1990	– Announcement of establishment of CAD national headquarters in Australia – Disputing in Chinese community media over a report about a 'real' or 'fake' CAD
19 April 1990	– Newly exiled well-known student leader invited to be leader of CAD in Australia
7 May 1990	– Calling for merge with FDC to form new political party – Meeting held jointly with FDC to discuss collapse of Berlin Wall

Source: Australian Chinese Daily, 27 November 1989 to 7 May 1990.

After June 1990, the community print media was no longer so interested in covering the CAD's internal disputes and such reports as were published still focused on the same three issues.

What was actually taking place within the CAD branches, nationwide in Australia, was a little different from what was reported in the Chinese-language media. The actual conflicts occurred because more and more CAD members wanted to: (1) eliminate from the CAD leadership those incapable of helping them seek asylum (but with this criticism expressed as being 'unable to lead the democratic movement'); (2) clarify which CAD branch and its leadership, among a few branches, was legitimate;

and (3) address its political and organizational relationships with the FDC. Regardless of how these were expressed, all these factional activities were in essence intended to reinvent the CAD in response to the new political situation after June 1990 (when they were all granted a special four-year visa). In the aftermath of June 1990, all these were in fact intended to meet the community's demands for an organized and politicized organization to lead the student campaign and deal directly with the asylum issue. They are discussed in more detail below.

The removal of several CAD leaders from their leadership positions took place in a very direct way: they were named and asked to step down at general meetings, and their names were later published in the Chinese-language community newspapers. This confrontational approach, which was believed by some to be very 'un-Chinese,' indicated the seriousness with which CAD members regarded the leadership issue.[14] This took place before 27 November 1989 (see Table 7.3), when the Chinese-language print media first began to be used in the internal fighting. Once the students had all been given four-year temporary protection visas in June 1990, and especially after the *Wei v Minister for Immigration* court ruling, many CAD members became more anxious about the possibility of staying permanently. Bad memories of DILGEA's inflexible stance on overstayers and suspicions of the government's real intention to provide them with three more years of residency intensified their preparation for the period after June 1993.[15] This preparation was regarded as their last battle, the seriousness of which resulted in an open and ongoing power struggle in the CAD. In the Chinese-language community newspapers, members from both sides of the leadership dispute repeatedly called for the re-registration of

[14] The reason why it was considered 'un-Chinese' was because it happened in a very direct, aggressive and confrontational way, which was different from what was believed by many people (Gao and Ting-Toomey, 1998; Lu, 2006; Saxon, 2006). The Chinese people are normally held to be a prosaic people (Westcott, 1895), who are often dull (Goldsmith, 1850) and shy (Videbeck, 2010), but they are neither reticent (Clennell, 1917) nor bellicose (Bos, 1937). At least, in the late 1980s and early 1990s, it was strange to use the media in their internal fighting.

[15] Many students believed that Australia did not really want to have them stay permanently (the argument of which was supported by reference to Australia's anti-Chinese history since the 1850s), but it did not want to say it clearly because of its international reputation and its moral responsibility to protect the people who lived in the country. Even when the Prime Minister Bob Hawke was announcing the introduction of the four-year protection visa on 6 June 1990, he mentioned the possibility of reassessing the political situation in China after a couple years (*The Sun*, 8 June 1990; *The Australian*, 28 June 1990). Therefore, many believed that the government would ask some of them, if not all of them, to leave Australia after the term of their visa or entry permit expired.

CAD members. Each side hoped to attract enough members to win a vote on the leadership. According to a number of CAD members, the motivation behind the leadership challenge was to remove several individuals who had been elected before June 4. Those pre-June 4 leaders were considered irrelevant to the new political situation, and more CAD members wanted to choose new activists from the PRC who were in the same situation as the new majority within the CAD (*ACD*, 7 and 19 April 1990).

A strong commitment to the right of CAD members to be protected from political persecution by the CCP and its government became the key for selecting the new leaders. However, for several months after June 4, the CAD in Australia was still led by a person who was called Huang Fan, who was not only born outside China but was also believed to be unfamiliar with PRC or even Western sociopolitical cultures, for example.[16] Many members claimed that they did not know where he was educated, how he was making a living in Australia, and how he became an enthusiastic follower of Sun Yat-sen and other anti-Qing revolutionaries of the late 1890s and early 1900s. He embraced Sun Yat-sen's dictum that the overseas Chinese served as the mother of the Chinese revolution, and wanted to be part of another revolution after the fashion of the Tongmenghui (as mentioned in Chapter Four), an anti-Qing secret society of Chinese revolutionaries that played an important role in the overthrow of the monarchy in China in 1911. He was found to have no interest in assisting CAD members to seek asylum in Australia and it was purely because members wanted to avoid clashing with any agencies that they believed to be supporting, if not guiding, him that no CAD member was brave enough to challenge his leadership until early 1990.

When the expected leadership challenge finally occurred, it did not turn out quite as members would have wished. After several months of fighting for new leadership, the CAD finally had a new leader who was from the Chinese mainland, very familiar with Chinese politics and took the asylum seeking issue very seriously. He was believed to meet almost all the criteria that CAD members could then require, including the level of education and the ability to speak Cantonese in order to maintain the CAD's connection with the established overseas Chinese communities in Australia. This last point is one which evidently indicated that the CAD

[16] There are some memoirs by, or biographies about, the people who were involved in the CAD and its internal fighting (Chen and Lu, 1994; Qin, 2012). Qin in his recent book mentioned this particular person named Huang Fan (Qin, 2012).

was still considering how to prepare themselves for *chijiuzhan*, a protracted struggle for seeking political asylum in Australia. Only a few weeks after being elected, however, the newly elected CAD leader went to the USA to attend a CAD international conference and vanished there (One-on-one interviews, 11 and 25 April 1998, and 8 June 1998). As the chair of the CAD Australia, he sought and won political asylum in the US. This set off another leadership crisis in the Australian CAD, and the internal fighting continued. One former CAD member recalled what happened then:

> After the new CAD leader vanished with the strongest evidence for his asylum claim in the USA, several [CAD] members were very happy because they once again saw opportunities for themselves to grab a big [leadership] title. However, the majority of the members were stunned by what they heard.... They were worried about how other people would take it and how [Australian] immigration office people would judge the CAD as an organization after this incident. Actually, the CAD at the start tried very hard to hide it from other [Chinese] students, because this was after all about the credibility of the CAD.... Since then, the [CAD] members had to pay attention to not only how to select the right people to leadership positions, but also to the structure of the CAD. These two issues caused a lot of debates, finger pointing as to who was to blame, what should be done, and all that 'bla-bla-bla' (Interviewee 40, 29 May 1998).

The dispute about legitimacy (about which CAD branch in Australia was the legitimate one—or, as members put it, the 'real' one) was also a kind of leadership challenge and centered on the same crucial issue as the first dispute: the right of CAD members to be protected from persecution by the CCP and its government, and how the CAD leadership must deal with it. After the initial challenge to the leadership, a number of CAD leaders and activists left, taking with them strong evidence for their asylum cases (as noted). As several out-voted leaders did not step down, rival groups formed within CAD Australia and the CAD headquarters in the United States twice intervened in the internal fighting in Australia. The out-voted leaders maintained that the new leadership was not legitimate and so no government agency or institution would trust them;[17] thus, they argued, the new branch leaders were in no position to help CAD members and other Chinese students to obtain protection or permanent residency. The newly elected leaders argued that the former leaders had no interest

[17] The term 'legitimacy' was used in their argument in a number of senses, but mainly referring to whether the new leaders were properly voted in and whether they organized the election based on a normal procedure (Qin, 2012).

in the basic welfare of members, were not dependable, and were incapable of dealing with the asylum/residency issue. Interestingly, both sides of the leadership dispute (the legitimate and old branch, and the illegitimate and new branch) tried to make these internal debates public, and early versions of their arguments appeared in Chinese-language newspapers as early as April 1990 (*ACD*, 3 April 1990). To put an end to this endless internal dissension, the entire CAD organizational structure in Australia was then re-organized and three Australian branches were subsequently established (they were no longer named after two big cities: Sydney and Melbourne; but after three big states in Australia: New South Wales, Victoria and Queensland). In a public statement, the old leadership was characterized as a clique of fellow provincials without mass support; it was also criticized as being incompetent in terms of political knowledge and skills, and incapable of leading the Chinese democratic movement in Australia (*ACD*, 7 and 19 April 1990).

Though less conspicuous than the leadership and legitimacy disputes, the strife within the CAD over its relationship with the newly established FDC was in fact even more intense, with longer-lasting, divisive effects. On the surface, the two organizations worked in cooperation and seemed to have a smooth relationship (*China Spring* [*Australia Edition*], No. 1, 1990; *FDC Newsletter*, 34, 1991). However, a number of former CAD members pointed out that the question of how to deal with the emergence of the FDC had not only worried them personally but had sent the CAD into a crisis over its political identity and its organizational structure (Group-focused interviews, 17, 24 and 31 January 1998).

Some CAD members argued that the Australian CAD branch needed to work in full cooperation with the FDC in order to overcome its image of irrelevance to the new political circumstances after June 4; otherwise, its members might not be regarded as bona fide asylum seekers. Many CAD members took FDC membership as well, and organized a series of joint activities with the FDC. Those who preferred a CAD identity were concerned that if they simply relied on CAD's relationship with the FDC, they would be disadvantaged in competition with FDC members in seeking political asylum. However, they feared that if the CAD did not keep its own political identity as an independent political organization, as mentioned above, their longtime political efforts would be wasted, and the evidence they had collected for their asylum applications would be inadequate if not useless. This attitude was reinforced by the Australian government's stated preference for a case-by-case approach to the PRC student issue. Only a strong political identity would be considered in a case-by-case approach, and to maintain the CAD as an independent and dynamic pro-democracy organization would help preserve its members' political identity. For this reason the CAD was able to survive as a self-motivated force alongside the FDC to the end of the student protection campaign.

Thanks to these factional activities and reorganizations, the CAD in Australia eventually changed into a new political organization, at least a few new branches, providing more students with leadership positions in this Chinese democratic organization. The frequent leadership challenges also led to the election of new leaders who were interested in the student protection and residency issue. The endless internal power struggles and leadership challenges effectively helped to prepare the CAD as a whole for the changes to its organizational strategy that would be required to respond to the new circumstances. Through its cooperation and rivalry with the FDC, it slowly but surely lost its image of irrelevance to post-June 4 Chinese politics; indeed its political relevance to the post-June 4 political situation was reinforced by the efforts of many CAD activists to retain the political identity and image of the CAD as an older and independent democratic organization. Whether or not this was the wish of every member of the CAD, the endless factionalism and reorganization discussed above drove the CAD to the point where the students' residency stay in Australia was pursued solely in the name of the Chinese democratic movement.

CHAPTER EIGHT

THE FINALE OF THE CAMPAIGN

In the preceding chapters, this book has examined the strategic activism of the campaign for protection and permanent residency in Australia that was waged by 45,000 or so Chinese nationals, mostly students, in the late 1980s and early 1990s in the wake of June 4. The activist strategies and the skilful approaches of the Chinese students in their campaign to stay permanently in Australia constitute an unusually clear case to illustrate the political skills and approaches of the generations who were teenagers and young adults in the turbulent years of the Cultural Revolution of the late 1960s and 1970s and who are now leaders in China.

As introduced in Chapter One, no sufficient research work has focused on Chinese activism, and general awareness of Chinese activism is still under the influence of various shallow, oversimplified, and fractured views of the attitudes, behaviors, common practices and activism of Chinese people. Both the modern and the early contemporary periods of Chinese history have somehow given many people an impression of Chinese culture, society and its people that is at odds with the facts. The generalizations that have been repeated have made it seem to many readers, especially to outsiders, that the Chinese are often timid, introverted, reserved, inactive, and obedient. On the other hand, the Chinese people as a whole have been found to often opt for various radical or even revolutionary alternatives, such as the May Fourth Movement in the early part of the twentieth century or the Cultural Revolution in the late part. These oversimplified reviews have been reinforced by an incessant internal debate—within China for the last hundred or so years—over the causes of China's backwardness (Schwarcz, 1985; White, 1999), and particularly by a cultural or national nihilism caused by the debate (Barmé, 2000; He and Guo, 2000). An overemphasis on the authoritarianism in Chinese political culture and the totalitarianism in its sociopolitical system has further biased the general understanding of the Chinese culture, people and their behaviors, making it fairly shallow, narrow and one-sided. For that reason, it has long been a problem in the field of contemporary China studies that scholars have somehow ignored not only sociopolitical dynamics among ordinary Chinese, but also underlying sociopolitical processes driven by many different types of Chinese activism.

Earlier instances of Chinese activism tended to be closely related with nationalist-inflected radical or revolutionary activism, the most iconic case being the May Fourth Movement in 1919. Many still remember what happened in China when it was profoundly disturbed by Maoist activism first and then by anti-Maoist sentiment (Domes and Myers, 1995; Boren, 2001). The Chinese student campaign in Australia had rather a different nature. Oriented toward the prospect of permanent residency in Australia rather than toward any idealistic goals of 'saving the nation' as put forward during the May Fourth Movement (Schwarcz, 1985: 170) or of 'building socialism and achieving communism' as was used in post-1949 China (Joseph, 2010: 156), this particular campaign was waged tactically in response to, and by means of, the new social, cultural and political environment of Australia in which the students found themselves.

It has to be acknowledged that activism of various kinds within China has lately attracted some scholarly attention. Internet activism (Tai, 2006; Yang, 2009; Shen and Breslin, 2010), labor activism (Zhang and Smith, 2009; Lee, 2010), consumer activism (Hooper, 2000; Davis, 2006; Wang, 2008), environmental activism (Ho and Edmonds, 2007; Xie, 2009), grass-roots economic activism of various kinds (Zhou, 2009; Li, 2010; Lee and Hsing, 2010) have all been important foci of recent research. Activism in the defence of human rights has, in particular, attracted a great deal of public attention for decades (Copper and Lee, 1997; Goldman, 2005; Ching, 2008). All these new studies have brought with them an emphasis on the people-focused, grass-roots nature of these political activities. My study, with its concentration on the efforts of Chinese students abroad seeking to pursue a common goal, may be seen as part of this tendency. It shows the Chinese students actively pursuing the chance to gain permanent residency in Australia in an organized and strategic way, by drawing on a coherent and self-conscious cultural-political identity not only as Chinese nationals, but also as asylum seekers who faced the possibility or likelihood of political 'persecution' in China.

This final chapter recapitulates the main arguments and points the way for further research. It begins with a brief account of the Australian government's '1 November [1993] decisions,' which finally allowed all the PRC students to stay in Australia permanently—the largest intake of onshore asylum seekers in Australian history. It then summarizes the key features of the strategic identity formation process among these students. The final section touches on broader theoretical and policy implications and directions for further study.

The '1 November [1993] Decisions'

In addition to the Federal Court ruling in May 1991 on *Wei v Minister for Immigration* (by which, as discussed in Chapter Five, more than 2,000 PRC nationals out of the 4,300 or so humanitarian applicants who had registered before 31 March 1990 were granted the right to stay), the ultimate acceptance of the majority of these 45,000 or so PRC students as permanent residents resulted from the Keating Labor government's '1 November [1993] decisions.' This marked the official conclusion of the so-called Chinese student issue in Australia. Bob Birrell, one of the most prominent critics of Australia's lax immigration rules since the 1980s, described the decision as follows:

> On 1 November 1993 the Australian government announced a new set of measures intended to resolve the long-standing problem of People's Republic of China (PRC) nationals who have refused to return home after the expiry of their visas. Most of these nationals had originally entered Australia as English language students (Birrell, 1994: 39).

Also according to Birrell (1994), the above decisions affected three main categories of Chinese nationals and some others who were in a similar situation. The latter also included a number of smaller groups of people from Hong Kong, Taiwan, Malaysia, Indonesia, Bangladesh, Sri Lanka, former Yugoslavia and even a few from Japan and South Korea who were in Australia on temporary humanitarian visas (DIEA, 1994). In fact, the great majority of the Chinese students were granted permanent residency under four visa, or entry permit, categories that were newly introduced: categories 815, 816, 817 and 818.

As noted in Chapter One, approximately 20,000 Chinese students of the 'pre-20 June group' were in Australia on 4 June 1989, and they were all granted permanent residency under visa category 815, an onshore immigration intake category, without any restriction other than the requirement to have a medical check-up. This decision honored the commitment that had been made by Bob Hawke when he had been Prime Minister, and that had been endorsed by his successor, Paul Keating, that none of the students would be forced to return to China when their visas expired. The figures from the DIEA (the Department of Immigration and Ethnic Affairs) showed that by 1 November 1993, there were 28,650 people in Category 815, including 14,750 eligible principal applicants, 8,400 spouses and 5,500 dependents. Since they had all lived in Australia for more than four years, this intake was not counted in the annual immigration intake for

1993 and 1994. They also became eligible immediately to sponsor family members to migrate to Australia and to access Australian entitlements.

The 'post-20 June group' and other later arrivals, who had arrived in Australia before 12 March 1992 and applied for refugee status before 1 November 1993, were all allowed to stay permanently under three visa categories: a special onshore permanent residency visa (Category 816), refugee status (Category 817), and a highly qualified permanent permit (Category 818).

The Category 816 visa was specifically introduced to cope with the dilemma created by the government's decision in August 1989 to allow more Chinese students to come to Australia in order to help the ELICOS industry, but at the same time to raise the qualification requirement in its pre-visa evaluations in the post-August 1989 period. As mentioned, these students made up the 'post-20 June group,' and a high proportion of the group were tertiary educated, which was helpful in raising the profile of the Chinese student community, and it also made their asylum seeking highly political and strategic. Apart from the statistical data mentioned in Chapter One (such as how many of this group became illegal after arrival and how many applied for refugee status), Category 816 was created to solve the problem created by the large number of refugee applications from this group of asylum seekers. At one stage their number was well beyond the managerial capacities of both the DORS (Determination of Refugee Status) committee and the Department of Immigration.

According to Birrell, the DORS had received as many as 31,000 or so refugee applications between June 1989 and 1 November 1993. Among them, more than 18,200 were from Chinese nationals. Until 1 November 1993, only 1,102 applicants were granted refugee status, while 13,502 were still waiting for a preliminary assessment of their applications, and 6,082 of the rejected applicants were preparing their appeals to the Refugee Review Tribunal (Birrell, 1994: 40). Category 816 was a refugee-related immigration category, but it was rather similar to the abandoned onshore humanitarian immigration program. Of course, unlike the 'pre-20 June group,' the PRC students in this category had to have already applied for refugee status before 1 November 1993. They also had to satisfy a set of criteria. These criteria included (1) possession of a tertiary educational qualification; (2) being under the age of 45; (3) having passed a vocational English test or having enrolled in a vocational English course; (4) having passed the character test, which in practice meant being able to present a satisfactory police check result; and (5) having passed a health check. The Category 816 visa was granted to more than 13,200 Chinese nationals, and this policy significantly, and quickly, reduced the unexpectedly large number of refugee applicants on the DORS waiting list (DIEA, 1994). Around 5,000 PRC nationals did not qualify for the 816 category but stayed under Category 817 or because of the '13 June 1997 decisions.'

The Category 817 visa was a mystery to numerous people outside the refugee system and to certain sections of the immigration department. It even confused several immigration policy experts, such as Bob Birrell, who defined Category 816 as the asylum seeker category (Birrell, 1994: 40). In fact, one of the pre-conditions for applying for a Category 816 visa was the submission of a refugee status application, but successful applicants for refugee status were given a Category 817 visa. By August 1994, it was estimated that as few as 1,100 or so asylum claimants had actually been granted refugee status in Australia (DIEA, 1994). While the mystery of Australia's refugee claim assessment and review process has often been cited as evidence that the UN's definition of 'refugee' is problematic in that it is not only ambiguous but also highly politicized, the results of a community-based survey confirmed that although many Chinese students had applied for asylum, not many of them believed in the UN's refugee definition or the refugee system. According to many interviewees who observed the process, the Category 817 visa was given to many FDC and CAD activists, whom they regarded as opportunists. This was because these people neither possessed a tertiary qualification nor really believed in democracy, caring only for their own opportunity to stay permanently in Australia. Several interviewees stated the belief that it was because of these people's lower qualifications that they had become very active in FDC or CAD politics (Group-focused interviews, 17, 24 and 31 January 1998).

The Category 818 visa was introduced on 31 January 1994 in order to include a group of highly qualified people who had arrived in Australia before the time covered by the '1 November [1993] decisions' and who had been studying in postgraduate courses there. This Category 818 visa was also called the 'highly qualified' permanent visa, and the decisive factor was the possession of, or the study for, for a local postgraduate qualification. This category resulted from the extensive series of lobbying activities pursued by a group of Chinese postgraduate students who had missed out by Categories 815, 816 and 817. Leading Chinese activist groups, such as the FDC, again played a vital role in lobbying the government for this group of highly qualified students (One-on-one interviews, 8 June 1998). This was a rather small category, however, and was offered to only around

2,000 people, about a half of whom were Chinese nationals (Birrell, 1994; DIEA, 1994, 1995).

In addition to the Chinese students who were permitted to stay under the above four visa categories, there were approximately 4,000 from the 'post-20 June group' (more than 5,000 according to other reports) who did not meet all the criteria for residency (Birrell, 1994; Senate Hansard, 1996). Fortunately for them Australia was a very different place by 1996. After the Federal Election in March of that year, the newly elected Liberal-National Coalition government abandoned the tough stance on the Chinese student issue and adopted a more pragmatic approach to solving the problem left unsolved by the '1 November [1993] decisions.' The following passage is taken from the Senate Hansard record. Through the question-answer exchange between two senior Liberal Senators, one of whom was once regarded as a hardliner on immigration issues, it is evident that the new government had determined to solve the Chinese student issue to the satisfaction of itself and the students:

> Senator COLSTON—My question is directed to Senator Short in his capacity as the Minister representing the Minister for Immigration and Multicultural Affairs. Is it correct that, of the 50,000 Chinese students who came to Australia during the late 1980s and early 1990s, there remains a group of about 4,000 who were not granted permanent residency status and whose futures are still uncertain? If so, was the group of students given an assurance—either before the election in March or since then or both—that the coalition government would consider this matter with a view to satisfactorily resolving these students' long-term status? Further, I ask the Minister to advise the Senate what efforts have been made to resolve this situation. When can the Senate expect to be advised that a resolution has been reached which is satisfactory to the government and this group of students?
>
> Senator SHORT—I thank Senator Colston for his question. It is an important question and I thank him for giving me some advance notice of it so that I can give him the full facts.
>
> Senator Colston's questions relate to a number of people who have sought permanent residency in Australia and are referred to as the 1 November caseload. The majority of those cases are from the People's Republic of China. All but 500 to 600 of those people have had their cases finalized; 41,527 people—mainly from the PRC—have been granted permanent residency in Australia; and 2,641 applications covering 3,129 persons from the PRC have been refused. Those applicants who have been unsuccessful and who seek a review of their decision will take longer, of course, to have their cases finalized.
>
> The government is aware that many of those who have been unsuccessful have been in Australia for a considerable period of time. We are concerned, and have been for some time—including before we were in

> government—about the length of time taken to finalize their situation. During the recent election both major parties indicated that the situation of those PRC students who failed to benefit from the '1 November [1993] decisions' would be examined. The coalition stated that it would resolve the matter satisfactorily.
>
> Discussions have been held with representatives of the Chinese students and the Chinese community since the election in both May and July of this year on the students' situation. The government has not, as yet, come to a concluded view on the matter. When we have come to such a concluded view on a satisfactory basis—which I hope will be a view that we can communicate sooner rather than later—the people concerned will, of course, be advised (Senate Hansard, 1996: 3782–3784).

Several months after the above question-answer session in the Senate, the '13 June 1997 decision' was made by the Coalition government. This decision extended the 'post-20 June group' to include the PRC nationals who had arrived after 12 March 1992 but on or before 1 November 1993. To implement this, and to resolve the status of several groups of people who, for humanitarian reasons, had been allowed to remain in Australia as long-term temporary residents, the government created two new visa categories and three sub-classes on 1 October 1997 (DIMA. 1998). These were collectively called RoS (resolution of status) visas. The process for RoS applicants for obtaining permanent residency involved two stages. Eligible applicants were first granted further temporary residency, but with all employment and welfare rights, including the right to sponsor spouses and dependent children. Permanent residency would be given to eligible applicants 10 years after the date of their arrival in Australia. In the case of the remaining PRC students, the real end of the matter did not come until 2003, when many former student activists either had returned to, or had started making a living from re-identifying themselves with, China.

Summary of Findings

As discussed in Chapter One, this book utilizes a framework of strategic identity formation to examine the activism of a large group of Chinese students in their campaign to stay in Australia in the late 1980s and early 1990s. The book has addressed six distinctive features of this specific form of Chinese activism, documenting and theorizing the PRC students' collective efforts as they formed their new identity as asylum seekers and lobbied the Australian government to allow them to stay in Australia.

The students' efforts to seek asylum onshore were embedded in their contextualization of their own situation, which occurred as these PRC students sought to familiarize themselves with Australian society and local Australian agencies became involved in their asylum cause. As this contextualization process was taking place, these Chinese students were also expanding their primary social groups (see Chapter Two). The contextualization process was followed by what I have called strategic identity formation (see Chapter Three). In their new identity as asylum seekers, the students utilized existing international networks and formed new political organizations (see Chapter Four). They also utilized legal options (see Chapter Five), engaged in a range of lobbying activities (see Chapter Six), and took organized political actions (see Chapter Seven).

Two concurrent and intertwining processes were found to be involved in the contextualization of the students' collective campaign for asylum. First, in the wake of June 4, various segments of local Australian society became vigorously involved in the Chinese student issue. In particular, because the number of the Chinese students in Australia was significant, many local agencies became involved. This in turn enabled the majority of the students to become aware of their possible chance, and their right, to stay in Australia. Six local agencies or organizations were involved in the contextualization of their collective campaign: (1) the ethnic Chinese community media; (2) the mainstream English media; (3) community services and agencies; (4) the government and its departments; (5) ethnic Chinese community organizations; and (6) other community groups or organizations. The dominant feature of the contextualization process was its interactive nature. The involvement of so many local organizations and agencies significantly increased the chances for each agency to react to the student issue on its own and to interact with other agencies. This developed into a continuous and interactive process, and its momentum kept the student issue alive.

Second, to ensure that their collective campaign could be effective, the Chinese students went about familiarizing themselves with Australian society. Their original familiarization process consisted of four parallel sub-processes. The students needed to familiarize themselves with (1) local people's attitudes to June 4, and the extent to which local people sympathized with and welcomed the Chinese students; (2) Australia's humanitarian immigration and refugee programs, in order to find policy parameters for their opportunity; (3) all the possible differences between the approaches of different local agencies at an operational level; and (4) local people and their networks, so that the student campaign could be rooted in the local scene. By means of these familiarization initiatives, the student community as a whole was able to contextualize the issue of their own protection in Australia in a way that enabled them to deal with it strategically.

As the contextualization of their protection issue was occurring, the students' primary social groups—formed after arriving in Australia—were also rapidly expanding as part of their internal preparation for their collective campaign. In theory, these Chinese students being away from their families they had to make their asylum-seeking decisions in these newly formed primary social groups (rather than within their family, the most commonly defined and documented migration decision-making unit in migration studies). In practice, the formation and expansion of their primary social groups was a very important element in the development of the student issue in that it laid the structural foundation for the student activism. This was because their groups were initially formed through work, school or through sharing a house, but were not formed for the purpose of seeking political asylum in a foreign country. Therefore, the groups were unable to cope with the demands of the students' quest for asylum in the host country. The students had to adjust to their changing circumstances after June 4 and expand their groups. The groups changed in size, formation, and in the topics of daily discussion; and also in accordance with the level of each member's dependence on the group. The most visible changes were in group size and pattern, changes that can be explained as a way to compensate for the deficiencies of the existing groups. Thus, as the student issue was becoming contextualized and the students were familiarizing themselves with the host society, the organizational structure of the student community was also changing.

Chapter Three examined the ways in which the students constructed their new strategic identity. Collecting evidence for their refugee cases in line with the UN's definition of 'refugee' and meeting the criteria set by the DORS were basic, but crucial, requirements for seeking asylum, but the process was complicated by the changes in Australian government policy in relation to onshore residency claimants and asylum seekers in the late 1980s. The Australian government offered the Chinese students unconditional visa extensions four times within one year after June 4, at the same time as allowing the students to apply to stay on humanitarian grounds or through the refugee program but the government also insisted on dealing with asylum applications from legal student visa holders and overstayers separately. The amendment to the *Migration Act 1958* and the introduction of the new *Migration Legislation Amendment Act 1989*, which removed the humanitarian program from the country's onshore immigration program, further intensified the students' efforts to collect evidence for their asylum claims.

To transform themselves from international students into refugees or onshore asylum seekers required spending a great deal of time and effort on discussing and seeking to comprehend the Australian government's changing policies on onshore immigration. I have defined this stage of the asylum seeker's identity formation as the collective construction stage. It involved three smaller processes, including (1) information-gathering; (2) information-analyzing; and (3) task-forming. This collective identity construction was characterized by an exaggerated interpretation of the Australian government's criteria for granting political asylum. This was influenced by the students' determination to stay and their efforts to meet the eligibility requirements set by the government. It may also be a result of the incomplete information that students had in terms of polices and criteria. It could equally be regarded as another strategy in the reactions of activists to policy issues and policy changes.

The efforts by individual students to collect evidence for their asylum applications can clearly highlight the strategic aspect of their collective identity construction. In response to the Australian government's criteria for asylum seeker from within Australia, the student activists concluded their strategic identity construction with purposely formed tasks for each member in the community, calculated to utilize all possible methods of collecting evidence to form a new political identity. Three types of evidence were actively collected: (1) locally collected evidence, (2) evidence from family or friends and colleagues in China or elsewhere, and (3) evidence from the relevant authorities in China. In terms of asylum seeking, each type of evidence carried a different weight in the task of constructing an identity as an onshore refugee claimant. Collecting evidence locally was considered easier and less risky, and it was also more easily compared with the evidence collected by other students.

Interestingly, the evidence gathered from the relevant authorities in China appeared to suggest that an onshore refugee identity could in fact be formed by making careful use of the gaps between normal practices in China and the Australian understanding of those practices. A clear example of this in the fact that if a Chinese studying abroad in the late 1980s and early 1990s decided to stay overseas longer than the time allowed, his or her employment in a work unit would be suspended and he or she would be advised of this by the work unit management. In the context of asylum seeking, this new practice that China learned very much from

Western countries was then regarded as a type of persecution and could be presented as evidence of persecution (i.e. evidence that one's job had been terminated), and the written notification could be then used as a piece of strong evidence in a refugee claim.

The formation and utilization of organized international networks (as detailed in Chapter Four) is the third significant feature of this instance of Chinese activism. Earlier studies on the Chinese student issue and on other forms of international migration have usually been based on the cases of individual countries, and the contacts established between their (student or migrant) communities worldwide have often been overlooked. For the most part, Chinese student communities worldwide—all a by-product of the social changes taking place in China in the late 1970s and early 1980s—were organized before June 4, but such organization processes were neither independent nor fully networked. PRC student communities in foreign countries were organized in three ways. First, all the Chinese students at each university were organized in an officially controlled student union coordinated by the Chinese education consuls in each overseas country. This union was commonly called the Friendship Association of Chinese Students and Scholars (FACSS). Second, students formed social groups that helped them become not only organized but also partially networked. Third, the Chinese Alliance for Democracy (CAD) formed its branches in the major Western cities in which Chinese students lived, if not at every overseas university. All of these existing structures prepared the way for the students to transform their groups or communities into asylum seeker networks nationally and internationally. After June 4, the FACSS declared that it was terminating its associations with the Chinese education consuls, and renamed itself the IFCSS (the Independent Federation of Chinese Students and Scholars). In Australia, the Australian IFCSS (IFCSSA) was established on 27 August 1989. The IFCSS played an important role in internationalizing the Chinese student issue. In the United States, where the Chinese student community had formed earlier than the Australian one, the IFCSS worked jointly with several members of Congress on a number of bills as part of their effort to seek legalized changes that would protect the Chinese students from being asked to return to China after graduation. One such bill, the bill introduced by Nancy Pelosi, became the setting for a major confrontation between Congress and the Bush administration over China policy and a key factor in the IFCSS's campaign for protection.

The student protection campaign was carried out in the early years of the computer age, and computer-mediated communications were a very important part in the formation and maintenance of international student networks. The Chinese students in the USA were among the first small group of professors, researchers and postgraduate students to have access to computers when most of America had not heard of the Internet. Their technical expertise enabled them to communicate quickly and effectively with PRC student communities in other countries, and without it, the widely dispersed students could not have engaged in their highly organized and coordinated lobbying activities after June 1989. Indeed, the PRC student campaign has been identified as 'the first major network political activity' (Grier, 1998: 137).

The utilization of legal channels in the Chinese student campaign to stay in Australia (discussed in Chapter Five) is the fourth main feature of strategic action that this study has identified. To be part of the 'tide of immigration litigation' taking place in Australia in the late 1980s and 1990s required political skills, strategies, networks, and a great deal of knowledge relating to the state's logic of controlling immigration so as to develop a migrant logic to negotiate with the state. Two developments in the Australian legal system from the late 1970s prompted or resulted in the 'tide of immigration litigation.' The first one was the establishment of the Federal Court in 1976. This made new legal avenues available to an immigrant wishing to challenge an adverse decision. The second was the enactment of the *Administrative Decisions (Judicial Review) Act 1977*, which came into effect in 1980. This development has included a range of changes favorable to immigrants or asylum seekers (e.g. the fact that judicial review of undesirable immigration decisions became not only available, but also simplified) (Aronson and Dyer, 2000; McMillan, 2002a).

Of many immigration-related court cases in Australia from the late 1980s to early 2000s, a high proportion of them have been brought by people of Chinese background (Cronin, 1993; Crock, 1998b; McMillan, 2002a; Gao, 2011) and Chinese people in Australia have set precedents in the Australian legal system, the most famous case being the High Court case of Chan Yee Kin in 1989—a case that set the boundaries for refugee determinations in Australia and laid the legal basis for dealing with the PRC student issue in the early 1990s. Although Chan was not a student and hence not a part of the student issue, he benefited from the fact that he maintained his case for so many years and dragged it on to 1989. His appeal was heard in the High Court of Australia before June 4, but the court's decision was not delivered until September 1989. This was an earlier indicator of a possible influence of June 4 and a level of politicization in Australia's system of determining refugee claims.

Chan's case also showed other Chinese asylum seekers the degree to which Australian elites understood Chinese politics and the sociopolitical behavior of Chinese people and their groups. The next step in the student campaign was thus to test whether or not the rules established in the case of Chan would be applicable to others. Five research students studying at the ANU took on the Australian government in the Federal Court in a legal case called *Wei v Minister for Immigration*, the legal basis for their challenge to the government being the bureaucratic delay in processing their applications to stay on humanitarian grounds. The students won the case, and it set a legal precedent for solving the PRC student issue through the legal system; at the same time also restricting local politicians from using the issue for their own political benefit.

The fifth key feature of the student collective campaign, discussed in Chapter Six, is the lobbying activities of the students. The focal point of these activities was closer contact and interaction on the part of PRC student activists and their groups with the Australian government, community service organizations and the media. In Australia, immigration lobbies are normally defined as an organized group bringing pressure to bear on various levels of the government, where the lobbying forces are typically people working on behalf of asylum seekers or migrants, rather than the migrants themselves (Jupp, 1993). In the Chinese student case, however, the students themselves were involved—both vigorously and strategically—in lobbying the government for more sympathetic policy outcomes, while collecting more and more evidence to meet the requirements set by the government for granting asylum. The students had already established contact with a number of government agencies well before June 4; after June 4, they tried very hard to maintain these contacts and escalate them into regular meetings. To achieve this goal, student leaders and activists presented a number of reasons for needing to have more meetings with government officials (e.g. case officers, liaison officers, and ministers). A further strategy was to turn so-called elitist involvement in lobbying by a very small group of postgraduate students into a mass-participation activity that involved many student groups all lobbying the government and key politicians.

Through the lobbying process, the students acquired a great deal of practical knowledge of how politics works in Australia. They then turned their attention toward certain community organizations to harness their influence in dealing with the government. As many student activists were generally aware that the influence of ethnic Chinese group lobbies on the government was comparatively limited, they identified migrant service organizations as their second main target. The role of these organizations was to help onshore asylum seekers to prepare their asylum applications, but the students treated them as the 'front desk' of the government and as a part of the system determining refugee status. As a result, not only did many individual students try to establish contact with MRC and RACS, but student activists also made efforts to nurture mutual trust with these agencies, laying the foundation for cooperation in lobbying activities. A few student groups invited MRC staff members to participate in student rallies and other meetings and worked with them on several surveys in the student community, the results of which were subsequently used in MRC reports to the government. This particular lobbying strategy proved successful as both sides joined forces in the end to lobby the government for a 'blanket approach' to the student protection issue.

Throughout the lobbying process, the media was considered as 'the main battlefield.' Therefore, lobbying activities were carried out in both the ethnic Chinese community media and the mainstream English media. Relationships between the PRC students and the media were interactive. The media took advantage of the newsworthy student issue for their own publicity purposes. At the same time, the students relied on the media not only to express their demands, but also to influence public opinion with regard to their protection issue and to shape the way in which the issue was publicly discussed, which in turn could impact on the government's decision making. There was also a strong awareness among the student community of the value of the media for their lobby. The students started out using the media to create evidence for their refugee applications by self-publishing political statements; later in the collective campaign, their interactions with the media became far more organized. Student groups learned from local activists about how to purposely feed the media with useful stories, updates and even prepared texts. The commercial nature and ideological orientation of media outlets meant that it was easy for the students to have their own issues raised in the media. A new community newspaper, the *Australian Chinese Daily*, played a very active role in the student issue, which enabled it not only to survive as a community newspaper but also to thrive as the most popular one during the recession of the early 1990s.

The sixth and final key feature of the Chinese student campaign lay in highly organized political action (as discussed in Chapter Seven). This political action—a logical stage and conclusion of the campaign—resulted from the ongoing pressure on each individual student to collect more and more highly politicized evidence to meet the criteria for political asylum. The first stage of the organized political action consisted in a change in leadership: the existing student unions were replaced by the FDC. This made it possible for the student campaign to achieve four common aims. These aims included (1) the formalization of the channels of communication among the students; (2) the regularization of evidence-collection activities and the halting of irregular ones; (3) the coordination of the lobbying activities of the various student groups and the preventing of student activists from acting in any ill-advised way; and (4) the development of community-wide campaign strategies to find the best solution to the student issue and the preparing of the community for a long term struggle to achieve it. This study has presented the activities of one local FDC branch as a case study demonstrating how and why the organized political group came to take the lead in the student lobby.

To achieve its goals, the overall strategies of the student campaign were continually changing and developing. It became a priority for the students to find ways, in which their demands could be expressed and fulfilled through organizational process. The students put forward many different initiatives, both individually and collectively, to form credible links between themselves and the international politics of the time. All through these efforts, many student leaders and activists identified a set of crucial strategic phrases. Three of these, namely 'human rights issue,' 'the promotion of democracy' and 'political change' were particularly strategic and could be used for a long period of time. Once these three phrases had been identified, three concurrent changes also took place in the student group strategies. These were (1) a shift in the campaign focus from small arguments to bigger issues; (2) a focus on, and strategies for, seeking asylum that was no longer indirect or passive, but explicit and active; and (3) the continued expression of their demands specifically as a political issue. The most decisive step in politicizing the entire student campaign was to incorporate the concept of human rights and to present the quest for protection as a human rights issue. This was possible not simply because of strong international criticism of China's human rights record, but also because of the fluidity of the concept itself. The term of human rights could also be used strategically in a protracted fight for asylum.

To seek political asylum in a foreign country is a form of politics that not only involves special skills, but also creates rivalry between fellow asylum seekers. In this particular case, the CAD's role in politicizing the student protection campaign was very distinctive for its factionalism and continual reorganization. This resulted not only from the imperative for individuals to collect strong evidence and for the entire community to deal with the residency issue, but also from the struggle of many CAD members to keep their political identity as the first anti-CCP organization in Chinese politics. Identification as a CAD member—and hence as an opponent of the CCP—was regarded by many as an important factor in seeking asylum. Factional activities within the CAD took a number of forms, but all were aimed at removing from the CAD leadership those who were clearly uninterested or ineffective in dealing with the student protection issue. Through this reorganization and factional activity, the local CAD was able to reinvent itself, successfully changing its image from its former irrelevance to the post-June 4 politics of the community. Better organization in the CAD and the protection campaign enabled the entire student community in its turn to become better organized and to successfully politicize their protection campaign.

A Better Understanding of Chinese Activism

There are at least two important reasons for studying this unique case of Chinese activism. The first reason is that the salient social experiences or actions of this group of Chinese students deserve to be documented; the second is that their experiences can contribute to a wider understanding of Chinese activism. Analysis of this particular student lobby of the late 1980s and early 1990s in Australia can at least offer both empirical and theoretical contributions to our knowledge of Chinese activism, but there still remains a need for further research on forms of Chinese activism that have, until now, received relatively little attention from researchers and policy advisers. To have a better understanding of Chinese activism in general and in its various forms, it is crucial to identify where the gaps in current research literature and areas of future focus lie.

There appear to be five main directions for future research that promise to evaluate and extend the theoretical ideas and approach of this research, and these can be summarized as follows.

The first direction is to conduct studies similar to this present project. More research on the issues studied in this book might add more weight to the findings and ideas presented here. Furthermore, new findings will provide more information on, and a deeper analysis of, Chinese activism that can shed light on contemporary China as well as on the student asylum case. Of course, the historical case examined by the present study was a unique, large-scale event in which a large number of onshore Chinese asylum seekers living in Australia were collectively seeking asylum at the same time. One case that is potentially analogous to this PRC student issue of the late 1980s and early 1990s might be the Falun Gong issue or movement. The Falun Gong poses one of the most serious challenges that the Chinese state has faced since June 4; it has also been reorganized outside China and has been remarkably active in garnering support from a number of Western countries. Like the student issue in Australia, the Falun Gong issue has also resulted in large numbers of PRC nationals seeking political asylum in numerous Western countries. I am unaware, however, of any reasonably large-scale research project comparable to that in this book that has been carried out on the experiences of Falun Gong members and organizers outside China. In fact, it is highly likely that the student issue and the Falun Gong are interrelated both temporally and thematically. At the very least, they are very similar in a number of aspects (e.g. being active in some Western countries, and having many members who have sought asylum), though one significant difference is that the Falun Gong movement appears to include fewer Chinese people with post-secondary education than the student protection lobby in Australia. Findings from studies of the Falun Gong movement could be very useful and instructive for confirming, refining or modifying aspects of the present analysis; in particular if similar theoretical approaches were used. This will lead us toward a deeper and better understanding of Chinese activism.

The core concept I have drawn from the case of the Chinese student protection campaign in Australia is that of strategic identity formation. This concept considers an event or a social process from a perspective that pays attention both to the event or the process and the participation of individuals and their groups within them, combining behavioral analysis with motivation analysis at both individual and group levels. Similar, if not identical, theoretical approaches applied to different situations and scenarios (similar or different groups of people, and groups of different sizes) could shed more light on the concepts, issues, structures, activities and issues examined in this book. Here again the case of Falun Gong could prove a valuable comparison. Also comparable are several other smaller groups of Chinese nationals who have staged a range of smaller campaigns for protection and permanent residency since the early 1990s and 2000s in Australia and in other countries, basing their asylum claims on issues associated with China's one child policy, or related to ethnic conflicts, or the membership of house churches or underground churches (Gao, 2011).

Simple comparisons between the post-June 4 student groups, Falun Gong, and other smaller groups of Chinese asylum seekers suggest that a cautious approach should be taken when extending the present study to examine other cases. The scale of an event, the scale of a sociopolitical process and the size of a group could have significant influence on how people react and interact, and how their groups might behave. The PRC student campaign for residency in Australia was pursued by a sizeable community. As a result, strong group dynamics emerged from the very beginning and played a more obvious role in driving the campaign than has been observed in any other groups. For example, several groups of Chinese asylum seekers in Australia have since the mid 1990s based their asylum claims on several different reasons, ranging from the birth control and abortion policies, same-sex relationships, ethnic conflicts, house or underground churches to the Falun Gong. With regard to the sample size or the size of the research subject this is not simply a matter of whether or not enough data could be produced to generate strong conclusions; it could also influence what a research project is likely to find out. This caution notwithstanding, extending this research to other cases is still a fruitful direction. It would be useful to discover whether or not smaller groups of Chinese asylum seekers operate in the same manners and whether or not their political identity and activism are characterized by the same features.

The second new direction for research would be to extend research efforts into other related areas of the topic—in particular, into in-depth analysis of each of the features I have identified in the process of what I have called strategic identity formation. While the main features drawn from this particular Chinese student campaign warrant further study and examination, the present study has not examined or even touched on a number of aspects. For example, I have not examined issues of gender, despite the fact that the student community was male dominated. There were, of course, female activists in the student campaign; indeed the very first leading activist group—namely one Australian branch of the IFCSS—had a female leader at one stage. The serious gender imbalance among the students makes it difficult to consider the role of gender in any detail, but it would be a fruitful field of investigation for future researchers. Social class factors are also in need of examination. Class factors were mentioned at the beginning of the book and were also included into the background analysis, but my focus on strategic identity formation and on the unique features of their protection campaign has not left space for the thorough examination that the issue of social class deserves. I have repeatedly mentioned education and the political experience of the students as key factors that influenced a range of decisions of the student lobby. However, it is still not very evident, for example, how particular individuals' previous social and political affiliations influenced their role in the asylum seeking process. This was once (indirectly) questioned in public by Chen Yonglin, the former Chinese diplomat who defected from his post in Australia and openly claimed that there were more than 1,000 Chinese secret agents and informants living in Australia (Xiao and Zeng, 2005). Chen's claim is highly politicized and extremely problematic, but it is strategic because there is insufficient research and knowledge of the issue; no one knows much about it apart from what they have heard as gossip.

A third possible research direction would be to consider a longer time period. Activism, a type of social practice involving forceful action as a means to accomplish certain goals, is characterized by temporal changes. Some simple initial observations of this same group of Chinese students in the post-1993 years indicate at least four change in their interests and involvements in sociopolitical activities. Generally, while the majority of the students have turned their attention away from 'asylum politics' to business-related activities (part of which, ironically enough, means embracing opportunities brought about by China's economic development), two smaller groups among them have started to participate in two very different types of activities. One of these small groups, which include a few former FDC and CAD activists, has tried to restore their links with old friends, schoolmates or colleagues in China, and some of the group have even relocated themselves to China. The other, smaller group has kept an active interest in the so-called overseas Chinese democratic movement, but more lately has been involved in Falun Gong activities. To some extent, it makes sense that the majority of students should have abandoned their activism and that the small minority who are still politically active should have identified a new focus for it, as their earlier activism was clearly associated primarily with the campaign to stay in Australia. Once that goal was achieved, they would look for new directions and new inspirations and would take part in activities other than asylum-related actions. However, in the case of those who continue their activism, it is unclear to what extent their later choices relate to their earlier activism; it is also unclear what connections exist between their later choices and the strategic activism of their early protection campaign. All of these are in need of further exploration.

A fourth new direction would extend the use of the research methods of the present study to explore a wider area than has been examined here.

This study has tried to avoid a narrow selection of research methods by utilizing a multi-method approach, combining in-depth interviews (both individual and group), questionnaire surveys, participant observation and documentary sources. Documentary accounts from a number of Chinese-language community, and mainstream English, newspapers were used in order to take into consideration their influence on the students and their campaign, and official documents or figures provided empirical data. The bulk of the findings that underpin this research project, however, come from interviews, questionnaires and observations of PRC student groups. Further use of a wider range of documentary sources might provide more insight into what Australian decision makers (including politicians and bureaucrats) were thinking about this particular issue while the students were engaged in their active lobbying. The use of interview methods could be similarly extended. Throughout this research, the snowball method was used, perhaps without sufficient awareness of its limitations. It is always a risk that the selection of interviewees can be restricted to a narrow circle of activists and supporters. Though I believe the multi-method approach is the best one for bringing adequate depth, subtlety and accuracy to the findings, this study adjusted the use of the snowball method to include a number of former PRC students who were outside activist circles, and this helped to produce a clearer picture of the part that ordinary students took in the campaign. For example, it was clear from the interviews with ordinary students how extensive the strategic construction of the asylum seeker identity had been in the student community as part of the asylum seeking process.

Fifthly, and finally, deeper research on, and analysis of, the key features of the student activism would be a further important way to gain a better understanding of this particular instance of Chinese activism. I have in this book presented six features as central to the campaign (listed above). Each of these could be examined further to assess the general relevance of the findings presented here to other forms of activism. Among the six main features, for example, international networks were unique and very important to the student campaign (as discussed in Chapter Four), but a range of questions remain to be answered. During the interviews, several interviewees in this research project raised questions about whether any other international networks existed at the time the student groups were pursuing their campaign. Others questioned why the CAD, which was established earlier than the FDC, was unable to play a greater leadership role than the lately established FDC. In group-focused interviews, there was discussion about the use of the Australian legal system by student activists in their asylum seeking, and questions were raised about whether the utilization of legal channels simply reflected tensions between the executive and the judiciary, between the courts and lawyers, and between lawyers and bureaucrats in Australia at the time. This book has tried to answer all these questions according to the results obtained through the multi-method approach, but further empirical and theoretical studies are definitely required to look at these issues further and to refine our understanding of the major features of this unique type of Chinese activism.

Further study could also deepen our knowledge about what drove this Chinese activist campaign, and about the link between the motivations of individual activists and the process of activism. The students' efforts to seek asylum in Australia have largely been attributed to June 4 and the sociopolitical uncertainties caused by that shocking episode. This theory or explanation might not convince all readers. In fact, there are some facts and specifics about the motivations of some student activists, which are in contradiction to the above wisdom. Some interviewees pointed out a few unlikely alliances between people with different interests in the PRC student campaign, and they were somehow puzzled by the combination of anti-CCP activists with people who had what was called in China called a 'strong revolutionary family background' in the student lobby (Group-focused interviews, 24 January 1998). Many believed that there was an unusually large proportion of sons and daughters of CCP revolutionaries among this large group of Chinese asylum seekers. Several interviewees also admitted that to obtain residency in a Western country had been a dream for many young Chinese at the time. However, it is hard to use the student campaign and its achievements to prove how attractive Western democracy is, or perhaps more precisely how attractive foreign residency is to many young Chinese, as many of these asylum claimants returned to China after being granted residency in Australia; moreover, a strong pro-China sentiment has risen in the Australian Chinese community. As this book has emphasized, this group of Chinese nationals who fought for—and won—the right and the opportunity to stay permanently in Australia had excellent political skills. In the light of the numerous and drastic sociopolitical changes that have taken place in China since the beginning of the last century, many of them were very good at lobbying, political strategy development and organization. Significantly, this group of Chinese people grew up under a regime in which they learned to make frequent changes to both their political identities and their ideological identities. As well as acquiring skills through their family backgrounds, as this book has also mentioned, some were officially sponsored postgraduate students or even mid- and low-ranking leaders of CCP or CCLY branches. Further study could clarify whether or not the attributes of the entire campaign and the distinctive features identified based on this student group are universal for activist campaigns everywhere, and to what extent the PRC student activism was more driven by their particular generational characteristics and the political skills associated with them than by other factors. At the same time, variations in social class, generation and region—or more precisely sociocultural and sociopolitical differences—that characterized this activist group and Chinese activism in general could also be further identified.

Future studies might also delve into the influence of party politics and international politics on Chinese activism, as the changes taking place in international politics in the late 1980s were helpful to the PRC nationals who were seeking political asylum in the West. As noted, PRC student activists in the United States and their counterparts in Australia both had some contacts with politicians, to the extent that the student protection issue became part of the rise of Nancy Pelosi in American politics and the fall of former MP Andrew Theophanous in Australia. In America, the issue of Chinese student protection was used by the Democrats against the Republicans, or at least it provided the Democrats with new, powerful ammunition against Bush in 1989 and after. Conversely, in Australia, the Chinese student issue saw the Chair of the Parliament's Joint Standing Committee on Migration become enmeshed in a number of scandals. This book has identified the role of local politicians in making Chinese student protection and residency a political issue, but it is not as yet clear to what extent Australian party politics influenced this particular instance of Chinese activism and thereby affected the fate of the PRC students as onshore asylum claimants. The Chinese student issue garnered enormous international support in 1989 and 1990. On the one hand, these students were supported by tens of thousands of Chinese students living in other Western countries, and the PRC nationals struggling for the opportunity and the right to stay in America were the best international connections for those in Australia. On the other hand, the significant changes taking place in international politics in the late 1980s and early 1990s were of enormous help to them in that a shift in the focus of global politics from the collapsed Soviet Union and its Eastern socialist bloc to China created a favorable political climate for the Chinese students. It is unclear how this climate was actually translated into collective activism in the student community.

In conclusion, I would caution against drawing any causal connection between the findings presented here and current debates about the rise of Chinese power in the contemporary world; I would also caution against any oversimplified utilization of the findings of this study, especially for journalistic or overly politicized purposes. There is still a great need for further research on Chinese activism, and the directions suggested above could be fruitfully explored in future studies which would assess, extend and deepen the theoretical ideas and approaches presented in this book.

APPENDIX A

INTERVIEW SCHEDULE

Stage One

1 *The first round of interviews*

- Thematic category: fact-oriented interviews with former students
- Type of interview: one-on-one interview
- Time: to be scheduled after receiving the ethics approval
- Key questions: to be listed in Appendix B

2 *The second round of interviews*

- Thematic category: reactions toward June 4 and Australian government policies
- Type of interview: one-on-one interview
- Time: after the first round of interviews
- Key questions: to be listed in Appendix B

3 *The third round of interviews*

- Thematic category: networks or the formation of new primary social groups
- Type of interview: one-on-one interview
- Time: after the second round of interviews
- Key questions: to be listed in Appendix B

Stage Two

4 *The fourth round of interviews*

- Thematic category: structures of the post-4 June networks or primary social groups, interaction patterns, and their main activities
- Type of interview: group interview based on former residential groups
- Time: after the third round of interviews
- Key questions: to be formed after the first three rounds of interviews

5 *The fifth round of interviews*

- Thematic category: structures of the post-4 June networks or primary social groups, interaction patterns, and their main activities
- Type of interview: group interview based on former non-residential groups

- Time: after the third round of interviews
- Key questions: to be formed after the first three rounds of interviews

Stage Three

6 *The sixth round of interviews*

- Thematic category: influences of the media, Chinese student groups, and community groups or agencies
- Type of interview: one-on-one interview
- Time: to be formed after the previous interviews
- Key questions: to be based on earlier interviews

7 *The seventh round of interviews*

- Thematic category: influences of the media, Chinese student groups, community groups or agencies
- Type of interview: group interview based on former residential groups
- Time: to be formed after the previous interviews
- Key questions: to be based on earlier interviews

8 *The eighth round of interviews*

- Thematic category: influences of the media, Chinese student groups, community groups or agencies
- Type of interview: group interview based on based on former non-residential groups
- Time: to be formed after the previous interviews
- Key questions: to be based on earlier interviews

9 *The ninth round of interviews*

- Thematic category: roles of the media, Chinese student groups, community groups or agencies; and the impact of the Australian government's policies toward the PRC student issue
- Type of interview: one-on-one interview with members of former community groups and agencies
- Time: to be formed after the previous interviews
- Key questions: to be based on earlier interviews

10 *The tenth round of interviews*

- Thematic category: lobbying activities by student groups
- Type of interview: group interview based on former non-residential groups
- Time: to be formed after the previous interviews
- Key questions: to be based on earlier interviews

11 *The eleventh round of interviews*

- Thematic category: roles of the media, student groups and community groups or agencies; roles of primary social groups; and influences of personal background and experience
- Type of interview: one-on-one interview with former student activists
- Time: to be formed after the previous interviews
- Key questions: to be based on earlier interviews

Stage Four

12 *The twelfth round of interviews*

- Thematic category: asylum-seeking decision-making process
- Type of interview: focus group interview (geographical groups)
- Time: to be formed after the previous interviews
- Key questions: to be based on earlier interviews

13 *The thirteenth round of interviews*

- Thematic category: asylum-seeking decision-making process
- Type of interview: focus group interview (former 'language students')
- Time: to be formed after the previous interviews
- Key questions: to be based on earlier interviews

14 *The fourteenth round of interviews*

- Thematic category: asylum-seeking decision-making process
- Type of interview: focus group interview (former 'degree students')
- Time: to be formed after the previous interviews
- Key questions: to be based on earlier interviews

15 *The fifteenth round of interviews*

- Thematic category: asylum-seeking decision-making process
- Type of interview: focus group interview (former activists)
- Time: to be formed after the previous interviews
- Key questions: to be based on earlier interviews

APPENDIX B

KEY QUESTIONS FOR STAGE ONE

1. What was your personal situation in Australia in 1989 when June 4 happened?
2. Did you have an extensive group of friends in Australia before June 1989?
3. What new contacts did you have after June 1989? Were they your fellow students or workers?
4. Were your friends mainly from China? Which part of China were most of them from?
5. How and how frequently were you in contact with your friends who were living in Australia or elsewhere?
6. How did you feel about June 4? Did the event make you feel as if you were so far away?
7. Did you attend any allies or gatherings shortly before or after June 4?
8. What were your main worries and concerns at that time? What about your friends?
9. How did you feel about the report that many Chinese students rushed to local immigration offices a few days after June 4?
10. What did you do after you heard that many Chinese students rushed to local immigration offices? What did your housemates and fellow students or workers do after that?
11. How did you feel after the Australian government said that they would consider providing protection to the Chinese nationals?
12. When were you first aware that you would have the chance to apply for permanent residence on strong humanitarian grounds and refugee status?
13. How did you know that you would have such a chance to apply for permanent residence on strong humanitarian grounds and refugee status?
14. How did you and your friends help each other when considering putting an application in?
15. How was the potential protection discussed among your friends or fellow students or workers?
16. What were your friends' common conversation topics before and after 4 June 1989? What were they after 10 June 1989?
17. What were your main worries and concerns after 19 December 1989 when the new *Migration Act* was in effect?
18. How did you feel about the Australian government's decision to give the students a four-year protection visa in June 1990?
19. What action did you take to meet the deadline set by the government to apply for permanent residence on strong humanitarian grounds before 19 December 1989 first and then before 31 March 1990?

20. Were you a so-called 829 Visa holder, and how did you feel about being granted this type of visa?
21. In the months after April 1989, were there any other changes that you had observed in your group or among your friends or fellow students or workers?
22. What was your observation on the influences of the media, including the Chinese community media and the mainstream English media, on you, your friends and on the Chinese student community as a whole?
23. How was major news discussed among your friends?
24. What were your normal ways to get general information before and after June 1989?
25. Which newspaper did you read most often?
26. Where were you and what did you do in the years between 1990 and 1994?
27. Did you know of any Chinese student activist groups before or after June 1989?
28. What was your observation on the formation of new groups among your fellow students or worker?
29. What role do you think the Chinese student activist groups or some individual activists had played after June 1989?
30. What were other students' perceptions of the roles of some activist groups and individual activists in the student community?
31. What is your comment on the roles of some Chinese student leaders in leading the student protection campaign?
32. Did you observe any effort made by your friends to use or influence the media?
33. What was your observation on how the official Chinese message reached the students?
34. What is your comment on the roles of various community groups or agencies in the student protection issue?
35. Do you still remember any differences between a humanitarian application and a refugee claim?
36. Did you ever use the services offered by some community groups or organizations?
37. What was your observation on the influences of a person's main contacts on his/her general responses and final decision-making?
38. Had you and your main contacts experienced any changes in your own attitude toward the student activist groups and their leaders?
39. To what extent do you think that you also played a role in your circle of friends' communication, discussion and decision-making even if you were not an activist?
40. What was your observation on the influences of family members and relatives in China or elsewhere on every one's reactions and everyday activities?
41. Of your family members and relatives in China or elsewhere and your direct contacts in Australia, which one did you think to have a strong influence on your decision-making then?

42. What was your observation on the influence of the individuals' background, and their experiences as well, on their reactions to June 4 and the protection issue?
43. Did you observe any differences in the roles that 'language students' and 'degree students' played in the decision-making of their groups?
44. To what extent do you think a student's reactions and activities were decided by his/her residential status in Australia at the time?
45. What was your observation on the impact of the special visa that the Australia government offered to overstayers in June 1989 on the student protection campaign?
46. What is your recollection of the role that the FDC or the CAD played in the student community?
47. What is your comment on the impact of the government's frequently changed deadlines on the students' decision-making process?
48. Did you feel that the Australian government responded better to the Chinese student issue than other Western governments?
49. In the years between 1989 and 1994, did you meet any Australian politicians?
50. What was your plan if the Chinese students were not allowed to stay permanently in Australia?

BIBLIOGRAPHY

ABS (Australian Bureau of Statistics) (2001) *2001 Census—Basic Community Profiles and Census Snapshots*. http://abs.gov.au/websitedbs/D3310114.nsf/home/Census+data (Accessed in June 2010).

—— (2007) *2006 Census of Population and Housing: Media Releases and Fact Sheets, 2006*. http://www.abs.gov.au/ausstats/abs@.nsf/mf/2914.0.55.002/ (Accessed in July 2011).

—— (2012) *Cultural Diversity in Australia: Reflecting a Nation: Stories from the 2011 Census*. http://www.abs.gov.au/ausstats/abs@.nsf/Lookup/2071.0main+features902012-2013 (Accessed in December 2012).

ACT (Australian Capital Territory) *Hansard (1989) Debates of The Legislative Assembly*. http://www.hansard.act.gov.au/hansard/1989/pdfs/19891121.pdf (Accessed in December 2012).

Adas, Michael (2003) 'From Machines as the Measure of Men: Science, Technology, and Ideologies of Western Dominance,' in Kevin Reilly, Stephen Kaufman and Angela Bodino (eds.), *Racism: A Global Reader*. New York: M.E. Sharpe, pp. 180–193.

Addleton, Jonathan (1992) *Undermining the Centre: The Gulf Migration and Pakistan*. Karachi: Oxford University Press.

Agnew, Vijay (2009) 'Being White and thinking Black: An Interview with Frances Henry' in Vijay Agnew (ed.) *Racialized Migrant Women in Canada: Essays on Health, Violence and Equity*. Toronto: University of Toronto Press.

Alitto, Guy (1986) *The Last Confucian: Liang Shu-Ming and the Chinese Dilemma of Modernity*. Berkeley: University of California Press.

Allan, Kenneth (2011) *The Social Lens: An Invitation to Social and Sociological Theory*. London: Sage.

Anderson, Mark and Paul Ashton (2004) *Australia in the 20th Century: Working Historically*. Melbourne: Macmillan Education.

Andrew, Anita and John Rapp (2000) *Autocracy and China's Rebel Founding Emperors: Comparing Chairman Mao and Ming Taizu*. Lanham: Rowan & Littlefield.

Andrews, Kevin and Michelle Curtis (1998) *Changing Australia: Social, Cultural and Economic Trends Shaping the Nation*. Sydney: Federation Press.

Ang, Ien (1997) 'Racial/spatial Anxiety: "Asia" in the Pscyho-geography of Australian Whiteness,' in Ghassan Hage and Rowanne Couch (eds.), *The Future of Australian Multiculturalism*. Sydney: University of Sydney, pp. 189–204.

—— (2000) 'Transforming Chinese Identities in Australia,' in Ang-See, Teresita (ed.) *Intercultural Relations, Cultural Transformation, and Identity*. Manila: Kaisa Para Sa Kaunlaran, pp. 249–58.

ARC (Administrative Review Council) (1986) *Review of Migration Decisions*. Canberra: AGPS (Australian Government Publishing Service).

Arce, Hugh and Taylor, Christopher (1997) *The Effects of U.S. MFN Status on China*. Washington: U.S. International Trade Commission.

Argyle, Michael (1969) *Social Interaction*. London: Methuem and Co.

Aronson, Mark and Bruce Dyer (2000) *Judicial Review of Administrative Action*. Sydney: LBC Information Services.

Ash, Timothy Garton (2002) *The Polish Revolution: Solidarity*. New Haven: Yale University Press.

Bagaric, Mirko and Kim Boyd, Penny Dimopoulos, Sue Tongue, John Vrachnas (2006) *Migration and Refugee Law in Australia: Cases and Commentary*. Melbourne: Cambridge University Press.

Bailey, Paul (1988) 'The Chinese Work-Study Movement in France,' *The China Quarterly* 115: 441–461.

Banham, Cynthia (2003) 'Children of the Revolution,' *The Sydney Morning Herald* 26 December 2003. http://www.smh.com.au/articles/2003/12/25/1072308628745.html (Accessed in June 2010).

Banham, Martin (2000) *The Cambridge Guide to Theatre*. Cambridge: Cambridge University Press.

Barabantseva, Elena (2005) 'Trans-Nationalising Chineseness: Overseas Chinese Policies of the PRC's Central Government,' *ASIEN 96*: 7–28.

—— (2011) *Overseas Chinese, Ethnic Minorities and Nationalism: De-Centering China*. London: Routledge.

Barker, Michael J. (2008) 'Mediating a Polyarchal Public Sphere in China,' Australian Political Studies Association Conference. www.uq.edu.au/polsis/apsa2008/Refereed-papers/Barker-Asia.pdf (Accessed in June 2010).

Barmé, Geremie (1991) 'Travelling Heavy: The Intellectuals Baggage of the Chinese Diaspora,' *Problems of Communism* 40(1–2): 94–112.

—— (1996) *Shades of Mao: The Posthumous Cult of the Great Leader*. New York: M.E. Sharpe.

—— (2000) *In the Read: On Contemporary Chinese Culture*. New York: Columbia University Press.

—— (2005) 'Cultural Revolution' in Edward Davis (ed.), *Encyclopedia of Contemporary Chinese Culture*. Abingdon: Routledge, pp. 170–173.

Bennett, John Michael (2007) George Higinbotham: Third Chief Justice of Victoria 1886–1892. Sydney: Federation Press.

Benton, Gregor (2007) *Chinese Migrants and Internationalism: Forgotten Histories, 1917–1945*, London: Routledge.

Benton, Gregor and Edmund Terence Gomez (2001) *Chinatown and Transnationalism: Ethnic Chinese in Europe and Southeast Asia*. Canberra: Centre for the Study of the Southeast Chinese Diaspora, ANU.

Berg, Lawrence (1993) 'Between Modernism and Postmodernism.' *Progress in Human Geography* 17(4): 490–507.

Berry, Jamie (2002) 'Theophanous Tells of Ferguson Rage,' *The Age*, 2 May 2002, http://www.theage.com.au/articles/2002/05/01/1019441391421.html (Accessed in June 2010).

Betts, Katharine (1988) *Ideology and Immigration: Australia 1976 to 1987*. Melbourne: Melbourne University Press.

—— (1993) 'Public Discourse, Immigration and the New Class,' in James Jupp and Maria Kabala (eds.), *The Politics of Australian Immigration*. Canberra: AGPS, pp. 222–238.

—— (2003) 'Immigration Policy under the Howard Government,' *Australian Journal of Social Issues* 38(2): 169–192.

Bian, Yanjie (1994) *Work and Inequality in Urban China*. Albany: State University of New York Press.

Bianco, Lucien (2001) *Peasants without the Party: Grass-Roots Movements in Twentieth-Century China*. New York: M.E. Sharpe.

Bilic, John (1989) 'Ethnic Presses Run Hot,' *Sydney Morning Herald*, 14 June 1989.

Birrell, Bob (1994) 'The Outcome of the 1 November 1993 Decisions,' *People and Place* 2(3): 39–46.

—— (1996) 'Our Nation: The Vision and Practice of Multiculturalism under Labor,' *People and Place* 4(1): 19–27.

Black, Richard (1991) 'Refugees and Displaced Persons: Geographical Perspectives and Research Directions,' *Progress in Human Geography* 15(3): 281–298.

—— (1993) 'Geography and Refugees: Current Issues,' in Richard Black and Vaughan Robinson (eds.), *Geography and Refugees: Patterns and Processes of Change*. London: Belhaven, pp. 3–14.

Blecher, Marc (2010) *China against the Tides: Restructuring through Revolution, Radicalism and Reform*. New York: Continuum.

Blewett, Neal (1999) *A Cabinet Diary: A Personal Record of the First Keating Government*. Kent Town: Wakefield Press.

Block, Alice and Carl Levy (1999) 'Refugee and Social Policy,' in Alice Block and Carl Levy (eds.) *Refugees, Citizenship and Social Policy in Europe*. London: Macmillan, pp. 1–19.

Blythe, Wilfred (1969) *The Impact of Chinese Secret Societies in Malaya and Singapore: A Historical Study*. London: Oxford University Press.

Bonchek, Mark S. (1995) 'Grassroots in Cyberspace: Recruiting Members on the Internet or do Computer Networks Facilitate Collective Action? A Transaction Cost Approach,' paper presented at the 53rd Annual Meeting of the Midwest Political Science Association, Chicago.

Bondes, Maria (2011) 'Negotiating Political Spaces: Social and Environmental Activism in the Chinese Countryside,' *GIGA Working Paper No 173*, German Institute of Global and Area Studies (GIGA), http://papers.ssrn.com/sol3/papers.cfm?abstract_id=1894665 (Accessed in January 2012).

Boren, Mark Edelman (2001) *Student Resistance: A History of the Unruly Subject*. New York: Routledge.

Bos, Carlo (1937) 'My Friends, the Chinese.' *The Rotarian*, July 1937: 17–19.

Bourke, Emily (2009) 'Post-Tiananmen Migrants Leave Lasting Legacy,' ABC's PM Program, 4 June 2009. http://www.abc.net.au/pm/content/2008/s2589754.htm (Accessed in June 2010).

Bowen, Alister (2011) 'The Merchants: Chinese Social Organisation in Colonial Australia,' *Australian Historical Studies* 42(1): 25–44.

Brannen, Julia (2008) 'The Practice of a Mixed Methods Research Strategy: Personal, Professional and Project Considerations' in Manfred Bergman (ed.), *Advances in Mixed Methods Research*. London: Sage, pp. 53–64.

Brennan, Frank (2007) *Tampering with Asylum: A Universal Humanitarian Problem*. St Lucia: University of Queensland Press.

Brettell, Caroline and James Hollifield (2000) 'Migration Theory: *Talking Across Disciplines*,' in Caroline Brettell and James Hollifield (eds.), *Migration Theory: Talking Across Disciplines*. New York: Routledge, pp. 1–26.

Brown, Judith M. and Rosemary Foot (1994) 'Introduction: Migration—the Asian Experience,' in Judith Brown and Rosemary Foot (eds.), *Migration: The Asian Experience*. Oxford: St. Martin's Press, pp. 1–11.

Browne, Peter (2006) *The Longest Journey: Resettling Refugees from Africa*. Sydney: University of New South Wales Press.

Bruer, Jeremy and John Power (1993) 'The Changing Role of the Department of Immigration,' in James Jupp and Marie Kabala (eds.), *The Politics of Australian Immigration*. Canberra: AGPS, pp. 105–123.

Bullock, Mary (1993) 'the Effects of Tiananmen on China's International Scientific and Educational Cooperation,' in Joint Economic Committee, the U.S. Congress (ed.), *China's Economic Dilemmas in the 1990s: The Problem of Reforms, Modernization and Interdependence*. New York: M.E. Sharpe, pp. 611–628.

Burke, Anthony (2007) *Beyond Security, Ethics and Violence: War against the Other*. London: Routledge.

Butler, Judith P. (1993) *Bodies that Matter: On the Discursive Limits of 'Sex.'* New York: Routledge.

Cadwallader, Martin (1993) *Migration and Residential Mobility: Macro and Micro Approaches*. Madison: University of Wisconsin Press.

Campbell, Graeme (1992) 'Immigration and Consensus,' http://www.ironbarkresources.com/articles/campbell1992consensus.htm (Accessed in May 2011).

Cane, Peter and McDonald, Leighton (2008) *Principles of Administrative Law: Legal Regulation of Governance*. Melbourne: Oxford University Press.

Cartier, Carolyn (1998) 'Preserving Bukit China: The Cultural Politics of Landscape Interpretation in Melaka's Chinese Cemetery,' in Elizabeth Sinn (ed.), *The Last Half Century of Chinese Overseas*. Hong Kong: Hong Kong University Press, pp. 65–79.

Cartwright, Dorwin and Zander, Alvin (1968) Group Dynamics: Research and Theory. New York: Harper & Row.

Chai, Ling (2011) *A Heart for Freedom: The Remarkable Journey of a Young Dissident, her Daring Escape, and her Request to Free China's Daughters*. Carol Stream: Tyndale House Publishers.

Chan, Anita (1985) *Children of Mao: Personality Development and Political Activism in the Red Guard Generation*. London: Macmillan Press.

Chan, Che-po (1999) 'The Political Pragmatism of Chinese University Students: 10 Years after the 1989 Movement,' *Journal of Contemporary China* 8(22): 381–403.

Chan, Henry (2005) 'Chinese in Australia,' in Melvin Ember et al. (eds.) *Encyclopaedia of Diasporas: Immigrant and Refugee Cultures around the World. Vol. II*. New York: Springer, pp. 634–645.

Chant, Sylvia and Sarah A. Radcliffe (1992) 'Migration and Development: The Importance of Gender,' in Sylvia Chant (ed.), *Gender and Migration in Developing Countries*. London, Belhaven, pp. 1–29.

Cheek, Timothy (2006) *Living With Reform: China since 1989*. London: Zed Books.

Chen, Bangzhi (1987) 'Chinese Overseas Students and their Problems,' *People's Voice* (10): 38–39.

Chen, Fong-Ching and Jin, Guantao (1997) *From Youthful Manuscripts to River Elegy: The Chinese Popular Cultural Movement to Political Transformation 1979–1989*. Hong Kong: Chinese University of Hong Kong Press.

Chen, Li, and Lu, Wei (1994) 'Brief History of Chinese Alliance Democracy,' *Beijing Spring* 1994: 1–6. http://bjzc.org/bjs/mljs/index.htm (Accessed in May 2012).

Chen, Minglu (2008) 'The PRC Government's Policies towards the Private Economy and Private Entrepreneurs. A Historical Review: 1949–2007,' *Mexico y La Cuenca del Pacifico*, 11(33): 39–56.

Cheng, Xi (2002) 'Non-Remaining and Non-Returning: The Mainland Chinese Students in Japan and Europe since the 1970s,' in Pal Nyiri and Igor Saveliev (eds.), *Globalizing Chinese Migration: Trends in Europe and Asia*. Aldershot: Ashgate, pp. 158–172.

Cherrington, Ruth (1991) *China's Students: The Struggle for Democracy*. London: Routledge.

—— (1997a) *Deng's Generation: Young Intellectuals in 1980s China*. New York: St. Martin's Press.

—— (1997b) 'Generational Issues in China: A Case Study of the 1980s Generation of Young Intellectuals,' *British Journal of Sociology* 48(2): 302–320.

Chin, Ko-Lin (1999) *Smuggled Chinese: Clandestine Immigration to the United States*. Philadelphia: Temple University Press.

Ching, Frank (2008) *China: The Truth about its Human Rights Record*. London: Ebury Press.

Chong, Woei Lien (1989) 'The Chicago Congress: Recent Activities of the Front for Democratic China,' *China Information* 4(2): 1–27.

Chow, Gregory C. (1994) *Understanding China's Economy*. Singapore: World Scientific.

Chu, Yiu Kong (2000) *The Triads as Business*. London: Routledge.

Clark, Manning (1969) *A Short History of Australia*. London: William Heinemann.

Clennell, Walter James (1917) *The Historical Development of Religion in China*. London: Fisher Unwin.

Clyne, Michael and Kipp, Sandra (1999) *Pluricentric Languages in an Immigrant Context: Spanish, Arabic and Chinese*. Berlin: Mouton de Gruyter.

Cockerham, Geoffrey and William Cockerham (2010) *Health and Globalization*. Cambridge: Polity Press.

Cooney, Sean (1995) *The Transformation of Migration Law*. Canberra: AGPS.

Copper, John and Ta-Ling Lee (1997) *Coping With a Bad Global Image: Human Rights in the People's Republic of China, 1993–1994*. Lanham: University Press of America.

Corballis, Michael (2011) *The Recursive Mind: The Origins of Human Language, Thought, and Civilization*. Princeton: Princeton University Press.

COSHG (Collective of Self Help Groups) (1991) *Directory of Self Help Groups, 6th Edition*. Melbourne: COSHG.

Coughlan, James (2001) 'A profile of the Vietnamese in Australia,' in James Jupp (ed.) *The Australian people*. Melbourne: Cambridge University Press, pp. 728–731.

Cragg, Claudia (1995) *The New Taipans: A Vital Source Book on the People and Business of the Pacific Rim*. London: Century.

Crock, Mary (1996) 'Judicial Review and Part 8 of the Migration Act: Necessary Reform or Overkill?,' *Sydney Law Review* 18: 267–303.

—— (1998a) 'Apart from Us or a Part of Us: Immigrants' Rights, Public Opinion and the Rule of Law,' *International Journal of Refugee Law* 10(1–2): 49–76.

—— (1998b) *Immigration and Refugee Law in Australia*. Sydney: The Federation Press.

—— (2004) 'Judging Refugees: The Clash of Power and Institutions in the Development of Australian Refugee Law,' *Sydney Law Review* 26: 51–73.

—— (2006) 'Durable Solutions or Politics of Misery? Refugee Protection in Australia after Tampa,' in Natalie Bolzan, Michael Darcy and Jan Mason (eds.), *Fenced In Fenced Out: Border Protection, Asylum and Detention in Australia*. Melbourne: Common Ground Publishing, pp. 23–51.

Crock, Mary, Ben Saul and Azadeh Dastyari (2006) *Future Seekers II: Refugee and Irregular Migration in Australia*. Sydney: The Federation Press.

Cronin, Kathryn (1982) *Colonial casualties: Chinese in early Victoria*. Melbourne: Melbourne University Press.

—— (1993) 'A Culture of Control: An Overview of Immigration Policy-Making,' in James Jupp and Marie Kabala (eds.), *The Politics of Australian Immigration*. Canberra: AGPS, pp. 83–104.

Cunningham, Philip (2009) *Tiananmen Moon: Inside the Chinese Student Uprising of 1989*. New York: Rowman & Littlefield.

Dale, Gareth (2006) *The East German Revolution of 1989*. Manchester: Manchester University Press.

Davis, Deborah (2006) 'Urban Chinese Homeowners as Citizen-Consumers,' in Sheldon Garon and Patricia Maclachlan (eds.) *The Ambivalent Consumer: Questioning Consumption in East Asia And the West*. Ithaca: Cornell University, pp. 281–299.

Davis, Stephen and Buskist, William (2008) *21st Century Psychology: A Reference Handbook*. Thousands Oaks: Sage.

DIAC (Department of Immigration and Citizenship) (2010) *Fact Sheet 4: More than 60 Years of Post-war Migration*. http://www.immi.gov.au/media/fact-sheets/04fifty.htm (Accessed in January 2012).

DIEA (Department of Immigration and Ethnic Affairs) (1994) *Annual Report 1993–94*. Canberra: AGPS.

—— (1995) *Annual Report 1994–95*. Canberra: AGPS.

DILGEA (Department of Immigration, Local Government and Ethnic Affairs) (1989) *News Release, 6 June 1989*. Canberra: AGPS.

—— (1990) *Annual Report's 90*. Canberra: AGPS.

—— (1991) *Annual Report's 91*. Canberra: AGPS.

—— (1992) *Annual Report's 92*. Canberra: AGPS.

Dillon, Michael (2012) *China: A Modern History*. New York: Palgrave Macmillan.

DIMA (Department of Immigration and Multicultural Affairs) (1998) *Fact Sheet 35: The 13 June 1997 Visa Decisions*. Canberra: AGPS.

DIMIA (Department of Immigration and Multicultural and Indigenous Affairs) (2001) *Fact Sheet 60*. Canberra: AGPS.

Ding, Xueliang (2006) *The Decline of Communism in China: Legitimacy Crisis, 1977–1989*. Cambridge: Cambridge University Press.

Dodkin, Marilyn (2003) *Bob Carr: The reluctant Leader*. Sydney: University of New South Wales Press.

Domes, Jürgen and James Myers (1995) 'General Introduction,' in James Myers, Jürgen Domes and Milton Yeh (eds.) *Chinese Politics: Documents and Analysis*. Columbia: University of South Caroline Press.

Douglas, Roger (2006) *Douglas and Jones's Administrative Law, Fifth Edition*. Sydney: The Federation Press.

East Asia Analytical Unit (1995) *Overseas Chinese Business Networks in Asia*, Department of Foreign Affairs and Trade. Canberra: AGPS.

Easterbrook, Margaret (1992) 'Influx of Chinese Possible, Says Hand,' *The Age*, 13 May 1992, p. 5.

—— (1993) 'Student Debacle Poses Dilemma.' *The Age*, 25 September 1993.

Ebrey, Patricia Buckley (1996) *Cambridge Illustrated History, China*. Cambridge: Cambridge University Press.

—— (2010) *Cambridge Illustrated History, China*. Cambridge: Cambridge University Press.

Ellis, Donald and Fisher, Aubrey (1994) *Small Group Decision Making: Communication and the Group Process*. New York: McGraw-Hill.

Ember, Melvin, Carol Ember, and Ian Skoggard (2005) *Encyclopaedia of Diasporas: Immigrant and Refugee Cultures around the World*. New York: Springer.

Engel, Jeffrey (2009) '1989: An Introduction to an International History,' in Jeffrey Engel (ed.) *The Fall of the Berlin Wall: The Revolutionary Legacy of 1989*. New York: Oxford University Press.

Errington, Wayne and Narelle Miragliotta (2007) *Media & Politics: An Introduction*. Melbourne: Oxford University Press.

Fallers, Lloyd (1967) 'Introduction' in Lloyd Fallers (ed.), *Immigrants and Associations*. The Hague: Mouton, pp. 1–13.

Fan, Sidong (2007) 'Minlian Minzhen nao Huafu, haiwai Minyun daneihong' (The CAD and the FDC stir up trouble in Washington, a big internal strife in overseas democratic movement), http://blog.roodo.com/chinahero/archives/4224977.html (Accessed in June 2012).

Fararo, Thomas (2001) *Social Action Systems: Foundation and Synthesis in Sociological Theory*. Westport: Praeger.

Fawcett, James (1989) 'Networks, Linkages, and Migration Systems,' *International Migration Review* 23(3): 671–680.

Feng, Jicai (1996) *Ten Years of Madness: Oral Histories of China's Cultural Revolution*. San Francisco: China Books.

Fewsmith, Joseph (2001) *Elite Politics in Contemporary China*. New York: M.E. Sharpe.

Fielding, Anthony (1992) 'Migration and Culture,' in Anthony Champion and Anthony Fielding (eds.), *Migration Processes and Patterns, Vol. 1. Research Progress and Prospects*. London: Belhaven, pp. 201–214.

Findlay, Allan and Graham, Elspeth (1991) 'The Challenge facing Population Geography,' *Progress in Human Geography* 15(1): 149–162.

Firth, Stewart (2011) *Australia in International Politics: An Introduction to Australian Foreign Policy*. Sydney: Allen & Unwin.

Fitzgerald, John (2007) *Big White Lie: Chinese Australians in White Australia*. Sydney: University of New South Wales Press.

Fitzgerald, Stephen (1972) *China and Overseas Chinese: A Study of Peking's Changing Policy 1949–1970*. London: Cambridge University Press.

Fonteyne, Jean-Pierre (1994) 'Refugee Determination in Australia: An Overview,' *International Journal of Refugee Law* 6(2): 252–264.

Foot, Rosemary (2005) 'China's Regional Activism: Leadership, Leverage, and Protection,' *Global Change, Peace & Security*, 17(2): 141–153.

Forth, Gordon (1994) '"Golden Dreams and Grey Realities": Chinese Students' Perceptions of Australia and Australians,' in Don Grant and Graham Seal (eds.), *Australia in the World: Perceptions and Possibilities*. Perth: Black Swan Press, pp. 310–16.

Freedman, Maurice (1960) 'Immigrants and Associations: Chinese in Nineteenth-Century Singapore,' *Comparative Studies in Society and History* 3(1): 25–48.

—— (1962) 'Chinese Kinship and Marriage in Early Singapore,' *Journal of Southeast Asian History* 3(2): 65–73.

—— (1979) 'The Chinese in Southeast Asia: A Longer View' in George William Skinner (ed.), *The Study of Chinese Society: Essays by Maurice Freedman*. Stanford: Stanford University Press, pp. 235–239.

Friedkin, Noah and Johnson, Eugene (2011) Social Influence, Network Theory: A Sociological Examination of Small Group Dynamics. Cambridge: Cambridge University Press.

Frolic, Michael (1980) *Mao's People: Sixteen Portraits of Life in Revolutionary China*. Cambridge: Harvard University Press.

Fu, Poshek (1993) *Passivity, Resistance, and Collaboration: Intellectual Choices in Occupied Shanghai, 1937–1945*. Stanford: Stanford University Press.

Fung, Edmund (1996) 'Education, Science and Culture' in Colin Mackerras (ed.), *Australia and China: Partners in Asia*. Melbourne: Macmillan Education, pp. 121–140.

Fung, Edmund and Chen, Jie (1996) *Changing Perceptions: The Attitudes of the PRC towards Australia and China, 1989–1996*, Australia–Asia Paper No. 78. Brisbane: Griffith University.

Fung, Edmund, and Colin Mackerras (1985) *From Fear to Friendship: Australia's Policies towards the People's Republic of China 1966–1982*. St. Lucia: University of Queensland Press.

Fung, Yu-lan (1966) *A Short History of Chinese Philosophy*. New York: Free Press.

Gao, Bai (2009) 'The Rubik's Cube State: A Reconceptualization of Political Change in Contemporary China,' in Lisa Keister (ed.), *Work and Organizations in China After Thirty Years of Transition*. Bingley: Emerald, pp. 409–438.

Gao, Ge and Stella Ting-Toomey (1998) *Communicating Effectively with the Chinese*. California: Sage.

Gao, Jia (2001) 'Chinese Students in Australia,' in James Jupp (ed.), *The Australian People*. Melbourne: Cambridge University Press, pp. 222–225.

—— (2002) 'The Role of Primary Social Groups in Migration Decision-Making: A Case Study of Chinese Students,' *Asian and Pacific Migration Journal* 11(3): 375–398.

—— (2006a) 'Organized International Asylum Seeker Networks: Formation and Utilization by the Chinese Students,' *International Migration Review* 40(2): 294–317.

—— (2006b) 'Migrant Transnationality and its Evolving Nature: A Case Study of Mainland Chinese Migrants in Australia,' *Journal of Chinese Overseas* 2(2): 193–219.

—— (2006c) 'Radio-Activated Business and Power: A Case Study of 3CW Melbourne Chinese Radio,' in Sun, Wanning (ed.), *Media and the Chinese Diaspora: Community, Communications and Commerce*. London: Routledge, pp. 150–177.

—— (2009) 'Lobbying to Stay: The Chinese Students' Campaign to Stay in Australia,' *International Migration* 47(2): 127–154.

—— (2010) 'Negotiating State Logic: How Chinese Students Obtained Residency in Australia,' *Omnes: The Journal of Migration & Society*, 1(1): 35–66.

—— (2011) 'Seeking Residency from the Courts: The Chinese Experience in the Post-White Australia Era,' *Journal of Chinese Overseas*, 7(2011): 187–210.

Gao, Jia and Pookong Kee (2013) 'Striving for Relevance to Australia: A Political Economic Analysis of the Chinese Migrant Experience,' in Loretta Baldassar and Pookong Kee (eds.), *China in the World: Migration, Settlement, Diaspora Formations and Transnational Linkages*. Montreal: McGill Queen's University Press.

Gardner, Katy (1995) *Global Migrants, Local Lives: Travel and Transformation in Rural Bangladesh*. Oxford: Oxford University Press.

Geddes, Andrew (2003) *The Politics of Migration and Immigration in Europe*. London: Sage.

Gerdes, Peter (1982) 'China: People or Leaders' Television,' *Media Information Australia* 24: 33–41.

Germov, Roz and Francesco Motta (2003) *Refugee Law in Australia*. Melbourne: Oxford University Press.

Gittings, John (2006) *The Changing Face of China: From Mao to Market*. London: Oxford University Press.

Glover, Jonathan (2001) *Humanity: A Moral History of the Twentieth Century*. London: Jonathan Cape.

Gold, Steven (1992) *Refugee Communities: A Comparative Field Study*. California: Sage.

Goldman, Merle (1981) *China's Intellectuals: Advise and Dissent*. Cambridge: Harvard University Press.

—— (1994) *Sowing the Seeds of Democracy in China: Political Reform in the Deng Xiaoping Era*. Cambridge: Harvard University Press.

—— (2005) *From Comrade to Citizen: The Struggle for Political Rights in China*. Cambridge: Harvard University Press.

Goldsmith, Oliver (1850) *The Miscellaneous Works of Oliver Goldsmith: Including a Variety of Pieces*. New York: Putnam.

Gordon, Ian (1992) 'Modelling Approaches to Migration and the Labour Market,' in Tony Champion and Anthony Fielding (eds.), *Migration Processes and Patterns, Vol. 1. Research Progress and Prospects*. London: Belhaven, pp. 119–134.

Gordon, Michael (1993) *A Question of Leadership: Paul Keating*. St. Lucia: University of Queensland Press.

Gore, Lance (2011) *The Chinese Communist Party and China's Capitalist Revolution: The Political Impact of Market*. Abingdon: Routledge.

Granqvist, Hans (1967) *The Red Guard: A Report on Mao's Revolution*. Sydney: Thomas Nelson.

Grier, David Alan (1998) 'Politics. Control and Computer Networks: The Chinese Students Lobby of 1989,' *Communications of the ACM* 41(5es): 137–145.

Grier, David and Mary Campbell (2000) 'A Social History of Bitnet and Listserv, 1985–1991,' *IEEE Annals of the History of Computing* 22(2): 32–41.

Griffin, James (2008) *On Human Rights*. London: Oxford University Press.

Gu, Edward (2000) 'Plural Institutionalism and the Emergence of Intellectual Public Spaces in China: A Case Study of Four Intellectual Groups,' in Zhao, Suisheng (ed.), *China and Democracy: Reconsidering the Prospects for a Democratic China*. New York: Routledge, pp. 141–172.

Guo, Ting (2008) 'Translation and Activism: Translators in the Chinese Communist Movement in the 1920s–30s,' in Pieter Boulogne (ed.) *Translation and Its Other*. CETRA Research Seminar in Translation Studies 2007. http://www.kuleuven.be/cetra/papers/papers.html 1894665 (Accessed in January 2012).

Guo, Xiumei (2005) *Immigrating to and Aging in Australia: Chinese Experiences*, PhD thesis, Murdock University, http://researchrepository.murdoch.edu.au/89/4/02Whole.pdf (Accessed in May 2011).

Guo, Yingjie (2004) *Cultural Nationalism in Contemporary China: The Search for National Identity under Reform*. London: Routledge.

Halfacree, Keith and Boyle, Paul (1993) 'The Challenge facing Migration Research: The Case for a Biographical Approach,' *Progress in Human Geography* 17(3): 333–348.

Hall, David and Roger Ames (1998) *Thinking from the Han: Self, Truth, and Transcendence in Chinese and Western Cultures*. New York: State University of New York Press.

Han, Minzhu, and Sheng Hua (1990) *Cries for Democracy: Writings and Speeches from the 1989 Democracy Movement*. Princeton: Princeton University Press.

Harbison, Sarah (1981) 'Family Structure and Family Strategy in Migration Decision Making,' in Gordon De Jong and Robert Gardner (eds.), *Migration Decision Making:*

Multidisciplinary Approaches to Microlevel Studies in Developed and Developing Countries. New York: Pergamon, pp. 225–251.
Hardie, Edward (1994) 'Recruitment and Release: Migration Advisers and the Creation of Exile,' in Ronald Skeldon (ed.), *Reluctant Exiles? Migration from Hong Kong and the New Overseas Chinese*. New York: M.E. Sharpe, pp. 52–67.
Harding, Harry (1992) *A Fragile Relationship: The United States and China since 1972*. Washington: Brooking Institution.
Harris, Karen L. and Jan Ryan (1998) 'Chinese Immigration to Australia and South Africa: A Comparative Analysis of Legislative Control' in Elizabeth Sinn (ed.), *The Last Half Century of Chinese Overseas*. Hong Kong: Hong Kong University Press, pp. 373–89.
Hatton, Timothy (2011) *Seeking Asylum: Trends and Polices in the OECD*. London: Centre for Economic Policy Research.
He, Baogang (1996) 'Chinese Political Opposition in Exile,' in Gary Rodan (ed.), *Political Oppositions in Industrializing Asia*. London: Routledge, pp. 153–173.
—— (1997) *The Democratic Implications of Civil Society in China*. London: Macmillan Press.
He, Baogang and Guo Yingjie (2000) *Nationalism, National identity and Democratization in China*. New York: Ashgate.
He, Henry Yuhuai (2001) *Dictionary of the Political Thought of the People's Republic of China*. New York: M.E. Sharpe.
Healy, Ernest (1994) 'The management of the immigration portfolio under Senator Bolkus,' *People and Place*, 2 (4), 37–45.
—— (1997) *The Political Economy of Immigration and Multicultural Policies under Labor 1983–1996*, PhD Thesis, Monash University Library.
Heberer, Thomas and Christine Gobel (2011) *The Politics of Community Building in Urban China*. Abingdon: Routledge.
Herzog, Peter (1993) *Japan's Pseudo-Democracy*. Kent: Japan Library.
Ho, Peter and Richard Edmonds (2007) *China's Embedded Activism: Opportunities and Constraints of a Social Movement*. London: Routledge.
Hodge, Brian and Allen Whitehurst (1967) *Nation and People; An Introduction to Australia in a Changing World*. Sydney: Hicks Smith.
Holenbergh, Rosita (2004) 'Educational Links between Australia and China: The Learning Connection,' in Nicholas Thomas (ed.), *Re-orienting Australia-China Relations: 1972 to the Present*. London: Ashgate.
Homans, George (1951) *The Human Group*. London: Routledge and Kegan.
Hooper, Beverley (2000) 'Consumer Voices: Asserting Rights in Maoist China,' *China Information* 14(2): 92–128.
Hu, Ping (1988) 'The Tide of Going Abroad,' *Guangming Daily*, 22 to 28 February 1988.
Huan, Xiang (1985) 'China's Economic Reforms and Foreign Economic Relations,' in Hugh A. Dunn and Edmond Fung (eds.) *Sino-Australian Relations: The Records, 1972 1985*. Nathan: Centre for the Study of Australian-Asian Relations, pp. 119–1127.
Huang, Jianyi (1997) *Chinese Students and Scholars in American Higher Education*. Westport: Praeger.
Huang, Quanyu, Joseph W. Leonard, Chen Tong (1997) *Business Decision Making in China*. New York: International Business Press.
Hugo, Graeme (1981) 'Village-Community Ties, Village Norms, and Ethnic and Social Networks: A Review of Evidence from the Third World,' in Gordon De Jong and Robert Gardner (eds.), *Migration Decision Making: Multidisciplinary Approaches to Microlevel Studies in Developed and Developing Countries*. New York: Pergamon, pp. 186–224.
—— (1992) 'Women on the Move: Changing Patterns of Population Movement of Women in Indonesia,' in Sylvia Chant (ed.), *Gender and Migration in Developing Countries*. London: Belhaven, pp. 194–196.
—— (1995) 'International Labor Migration and the Family: Some Observations from Indonesia,' *Asian and Pacific Migration Journal* 4(2–3): 273–302.

Humphreys, James Charles (1985) 'Economic Relations in the Broad,' in Hugh A. Dunn and Edmond Fung (eds.) *Sino-Australian Relations: The Records, 1972 1985*. Nathan: Centre for the Study of Australian-Asian Relations, pp. 128–134.

Hunter, Alfred (1983) 'On Method,' in Michael Rosenberg et al. (eds.), *An Introduction to Sociology*. Agincourt: Methuen Publications, pp. 71–113.

Hunter, Albert and John Brewer (2003) 'Multimethod Research in Sociology' in Abbas Tashakkori, and Charles Teddlie (eds.) *Handbook of Mixed Methods in Social & Behavioral Research*. London: Sage, pp. 577–593.

Hurst, William (2004) 'Understanding Contentious Collective Action by Chinese Laid-off Workers: The Importance of Regional Political Economy,' *Studies in Comparative International Development* 39(2): 94–120.

Huters, Theodore (2005) *Bringing the World Home: Appropriating the West in Late Qing and Early Republican China*. Honolulu: University of Hawai'i Press.

Hyndman, Patricia (1989) 'The Australian Migration Legislation Amendment Act in 1989,' *International Journal of Refugee Law* 1(4): 546–549.

IFCSS (the Independent Federation of Chinese Students and Scholars in the United States) (1989) http://ifcss.org/home/ (Accessed in June 2010).

Ip, Manying (2003) *Unfolding History, Evolving Identity: The Chinese in New Zealand*. Auckland: Auckland University Press.

Iredale, Robyn (1994) 'Patterns of Spouse/Fiancé Sponsorship to Australia,' *Asian and Pacific Migration Journal* 3(4): 547–566.

—— (1997) *Skills Transfer: International Migration and Accreditation Issues*. Wollongong: The University of Wollongong Press.

Israel, John (1966) *Student Nationalism in China, 1927–37*. Stanford: Stanford University Press.

—— (1998) *Lianda: A Chinese University in War and Revolution*. Stanford: Stanford University Press.

Jacobs, Jane and Ruth Fincher (1998) 'Introduction,' in Ruth Fincher and Jane Jacobs (eds.), *Cities of Differences*. New York: The Guilford Press, pp. 1–11.

Johnson, Debra and Colin Turner (2003) *International Business: Themes and Issues in the Modern Global Economy*. Abingdon: Routledge.

Joint Standing Committee on Migration Regulations, Australia Parliament (1990) *Illegal Entrants in Australia: Balancing Control and Compassion*. Canberra: AGPS.

—— (1992) *Australia's Refugee and Humanitarian System: Achieving a Balance between Refuge and Control*. Canberra: AGPS.

Jones, Huw (1995) 'The Continuing Ethnic-Origins Dimension of Australian Immigration Policy,' *Applied Geography* 15(3): 233–244.

Joppke, Christian (1995) *East German Dissidents and the Revolution of 1989: Social Movement in a Leninist Regime*. Basingstoke: Macmillan.

Jordens, Ann-Mari (2001) 'Post-war non-British migration,' in James Jupp (ed.) *The Australian people*. Melbourne: Cambridge University Press, pp. 65–70.

Jose, Nicholas (1995) *Chinese Whispers: Cultural Essays*. Adelaide: Wakefield Press.

Joseph, William (2010) 'Ideology and Chinese Politics' in William Joseph (ed.) *Politics in China: An Introduction*. New York: Oxford University Press, pp. 129–163.

Jupp, James (1991) *Immigration*. Sydney: Sydney University Press.

—— (1993) 'The Ethnic Lobby and Immigration Policy,' in James Jupp and Marie Kabala (eds.), *The Politics of Australian Immigration*. Canberra: AGPS, pp. 204–221.

—— (1995) 'From "White Australia" to "Part of Asia": Recent Shifts in Australian Immigration Policy towards the Region,' *International Migration Review* 29(1): 207–228.

—— (2001) 'Introduction' in James Jupp (ed.) *The Australian People*. Melbourne: Cambridge University Press.

—— (2003) *From White Australia to Woomera: The Story of Australian Immigration*. Melbourne: Cambridge University Press.

Kabala, Marie (1993) 'Immigration as Public Policy,' in James Jupp and Marie Kabala (eds.), *The Politics of Australian Immigration*. Canberra: AGPS, pp. 3–9.

Keating, Paul (2000) *Engagement: Australia Faces the Asia-Pacific*. Sydney: Macmillan.

Kee, Pookong (1992) 'The Chinese in Australia: A Brief Historical Overview and Contemporary Assessment,' in the Chinese Association of Victoria (ed.), *Chinese Association of Victoria: 1982–1992 The First Ten Years*. Melbourne: The Chinese Association of Victoria, pp. 3–11.

—— (1995) 'The New Nanyang: Contemporary Chinese Populations in Australia,' in Ong Jin Hui, Chan Bun Kwok and Chew Soon Beng (eds.), *Cross Borders: Asian Transmigration*. Singapore: Prentice-Hall, pp. 290–316.

Keister, Lisa (2009) *Work and Organizations in China after Thirty Years of Transition*. Bingley: Emerald Group Publishing.

Kelliher, Daniel (1993) 'Keeping Democracy Safe from the Masses: Intellectuals and Elitism in the Chinese Protest Movement,' *Comparative Politics* 25(4): 379–396.

Kelly, Paul (2010) *The March of Patriots: The Struggle for Modern Australia*. Melbourne: Melbourne University Press.

Kennedy, Scott (1997) 'The Stone Group: State Client or Market Pathbreaker?,' *The China Quarterly* 52(Dec): 746–777.

Kirkpatrick, Samuel, Dwight Davis and Roby Robertson (1976) 'The Process of Political Decision-making in Groups: Search Behavior and Choice Shifts,' *American Behavioral Scientist* 20: 33–64.

Kornblum, William (2008) *Sociology in a Changing World*. Belmont: Thomson Wadsworth.

Knapp, Ronald (1999) *China's Living Houses: Folk Beliefs, Symbols, and Household Ornamentation*. Hawai'i: University of Hawai'i Press.

Kong, Fan (1999) 'Tanhuameng: Minyun Shuijingcheng Naoju' (A Flash in the Pan: A Farce made by Democratic Activists in Crystal City), in Lin Mohan and Wei Wei (eds.), *Women Tuoqi Neizhong Zhongguoren: Donglun 'Jingying' zai Haowai* (We Cast aside that Type of Chinese: Trouble-making Elites Overseas). Lanzhou: Gansu People's Press.

Kraus, Paul (1994) *A New Australian*. Sydney: Federation Press.

Kupperman, Joel (2006) *Classic Asian Philosophy: A Guide to the Essential Texts*. New York: Oxford University Press.

Lai, Him Mark (2004) 'The Chinese-Marxist Left, Chinese Students and Scholars in America, and the New China: Mid-1940s to Mid-1950s,' *Chinese America: History and Perspective*, 2004: 7–27.

Lake, Marilyn and Reynolds, Henry (2008) *Drawing the Global Colour Line: White Men's Countries and the International Challenge of Racial Equality*. London: Cambridge University Press.

Lampton, David (1994) 'China Policy in Clinton's First Year' in James Lilly and Wendell Willkie (eds.) *Beyond MFN: Trade with China and American Interests*. Washington: The AEI Press, pp. 9–35.

Landale, Nancy (1997) 'Immigration and the Family: An Overview,' in Alan Booth, Ann Crouter, and Nancy Landale (eds.), *Immigration and the Family: Research and Policy on U.S. Immigrants*. New York: Lawrence Erlbaum, pp. 281–292.

Langley, Andrew (2008) *The Cultural Revolution: Years of Chaos in China*. Minneapolis: Compass Point Books.

Lanza, Fabio (2009) 'Politics and the City: Student Activism and Urban Space, Beijing 1919,' *Contemporanea* 1: 5–28.

Lary, Diana (1998) 'Political Participation amongst Chinese Canadians: The Road to the 1993 Election,' in Elizabeth Sinn (ed.), *The Last Half Century of Chinese Overseas*. Hong Kong: Hong Kong University Press, pp. 217–227.

Laughland, John (2008) *A History of Political Trials: From Charles I to Saddam Hussein*. London: Peter Lang.

Le, Marion (2001) 'Migrants, Refugees and Multiculturalism: The Curious Ambivalence of Australia's Immigration Policy,' *Building the Nation, Embracing the World: The Alfred Deakin Lectures 2001*. http://www.abc.net.au/rn/deakin/stories/s295948.htm (Accessed in June 2010).

Lee, Ching Kwan (2010) 'Pathways of Labor Activism' in Elizabeth Perry and Mark Selden (eds.), *Chinese Society: Change, Conflict and Resistance*. Abingdon: Routledge, pp. 57–79.

Lee, Ching Kwan and You-Tien Hsing (2010) 'Social Activism in China: Agency and Possibility' in You-Tien Hsing and Ching Kwan Lee (eds.), *Reclaiming Chinese Society: The New Social Activism*. Abingdon: Routledge.

Levenson, Joseph (1986) *Liang Ch'i-ch'ao and the Mind of Modern China*. Berkeley: University of California Press.

Lévesque, Jacques (1997) *The Enigma of 1989: The USSR and the Liberation of Eastern Europe*. Berkeley: University of California Press.

Levine, Marilyn (1993) The Found Generation: Chinese Communists in Europe during the Twenties, Seattle: University of Washington Press.

Levine, Marilyn and Chen San-Ching (1996) 'Communist-Leftist Control of the European Branch of the Guomindang, 1923–1927,' *Modern China* 22(1): 62–92.

Lewin, Kurt (1973) *Resolving Social Conflicts: Selected papers on Group Dynamics*. London: Souvenir.

Li, He (2004) *From Revolution to Reform: A Comparative Study of China and Mexico*. Lanham: University Press of America.

Li, Lu (1990) *Moving the Mountain: My Life in China from the Cultural Revolution to Tiananmen Square*. London: Macmillan.

Li, Minghuan (1998) 'Transnational Links among the Chinese in Europe: A Study on European-Wide Chinese Voluntary Associations,' in Gregor Benton and Frank N. Pieke (eds.), *The Chinese in Europe*. London: Macmillan, pp. 21–41.

Li, Tiger (1990) 'Computer-Mediated Communications and the Chinese Students in the US,' *The Information Society* 7: 125–137.

Li, Xiaobing (2010) *Civil Liberties in China*. Santa Barbara: Greenwood.

Lin, Jing (2006) 'Education Stratification and the New Middle Class,' in Gerard Postiglione (ed.), *Education and Social Change in China: Inequality in a Market Economy*. New York: M.E. Sharpe, pp. 179–197.

Ling, Huping (1998) *Surviving on the Gold Mountain: A History of Chinese American Women and Their Lives*. New York: State University of New York Press.

Liu, Guande (1995) 'My Fortune in Australia' in Bruce Jacobs and Ouyang Yu (trans. and eds.), *Bitter Peaches and Plums: Two Chinese Novellas on the Recent Chinese Student Experience in Australia*. Melbourne: Monash Asia Institute.

Liu, Weiping (1989) (translated by Yichuan Sang and John Fitzgerald) 'Chinese Newspapers in Australia from the Turn of the Century,' http://www.chaf.lib.latrobe.edu.au/chinese_newspapers.htm (Accessed in May 2011).

Liu, Xiao-Feng and Glen Norcliffe (1996) 'Closed Windows, Open Doors: Geopolitics and Post-1949 Mainland Chinese Immigration to Canada,' *Canadian Geographer* 40(4): 306–320.

Lopes, Mark (2000) 'The Politics of the Origins of Multiculturalism: Lobbying and the Power of Influence,' *People and Place* 8(1): 22–28.

Lu, Diana (2006) Daughter of the Yellow River: An Inspirational Journey from Deprived Child during China's Cultural Revolution to Successful Global Entrepreneur. San Francisco: Image Global Impact.

Lu, Hongyan (2003) 'Bamboo Sprouts After the Rain: The History of University Student Environmental Associations in China,' *China Environment Series* 6: 55–66.

Lü, Xiaobo and Elizabeth Perry (1997) *Danwei: The Changing Chinese Workplace in Historical and Comparative Perspective*. New York: M.E. Sharpe.

Lubman, Stanley (1999) *Bird in a Cage: Legal Reform in China after Mao*. Stanford: Stanford University Press.

Lucassen, Jan, Leo Lucassen and Patrick Manning (2010) 'Migration Theory: Multidisciplinary Approaches,' in Jan Lucassen, Leo Lucassen and Patrick Manning (eds.) *Migration History in World History: Multidisciplinary Approaches*. Leiden: Brill, pp. 3–38.

Luo, Chenxi (1988) 'China's Economic Reforms Face Major Constraints,' *Far Eastern Economic Review* 139(January 28): 72.

Ma, Shu-Yun (1993) 'The Exile, Voice and Struggle to Return of Chinese Political Exiles.' *Pacific Affairs* 66(3): 369–389.

Ma, Yiyang (1989) 'Liuxuesheng Jiti Shangliangshan' (The Students were Forced to Take Action Collectively), *China Spring* 76, September 1989.

Mackie, Jamie (2003) 'Five Southeast Asian Chinese Empire-Builders: Commonalities and Differences,' in Michael Charney, Brenda Yeoh, and Tong Chee Kiong (eds.), *Chinese Migrants Abroad: Cultural, Educational, and Social Dimensions of the Chinese Diaspora*. Singapore: Singapore University Press, pp. 3–21.

Magno, Francisco (1999) 'Enviromental Movements in the Philippines' in Yok-shiu Lee and Alvin So (eds.) *Asia's Environmental Movements: Comparative Perspectives*, New York: M.E. Sharpe, pp. 143–176.

Mann, James (1999) *About Face: A History of America's Curious Relationship with China, from Nixon to Clinton*. New York: Alfred A. Knopf.

Marginson, Simon (1997) *Educating Australia: Government, Economy and Citizen since 1960*. Melbourne: Cambridge University Press.

Martin, Philip (1994) 'The United States: Benign Neglect towards Immigration,' in Wayne Cornelius, Philip Martin, and James Hollifield (eds.), *Controlling Immigration: A Global Perspective*. California: Stanford University Press, pp. 51–85.

Martin, Philip, Susan Martin and Patrick Weil (2006) *Managing Migration: The Promise of Cooperation*. Lanham: Lexington Books.

Massey, Douglas, Joaqiun Arango, Graeme Hugo, Ali Kouaouci, Adela Pellegrino and Edward J. Taylor (1993) 'Theories of International Migration: A Review and Appraisal,' *Population and Development Review* 19(3): 431–466.

Matloff, Norman (1997) 'The Internet and American Culture: Political networking,' *National Review* 28 July 1997.

—— (1998) 'A Fax on both your Houses: An Immigration Bill as a Case Study of Congressional Lobbying and our Failing Democracy,' *National Review* 7 September 1998.

McKeown, Adam (2001) *Chinese Migrant Networks and Cultural Change: Peru, Chicago, Hawaii, 1900–1936*. Chicago: University of Chicago Press.

Mackerras, Colin (1996) 'Australia-China relations: An agenda' in Colin Mackerras (ed.), *Australia and China: Partners in Asia*. Melbourne: Macmillan Education, pp. 1–6.

McMaster, Don (2001) *Asylum Seekers: Australia's Response to Refugees*. Melbourne: Melbourne University Press.

McMillan, John (2002a) 'Judicial Restraint and Activism in Administrative Law,' *Federal Law Review* 30(2): 335–371.

—— (2002b) 'Controlling Immigration Litigation: A Legislative Challenge,' *People and Place* 10(2): 16–29.

Meagher, Arnold (2008) *Coolie Trade: The Traffic in Chinese Laborers to Latin America, 1847–1874*. Dartford: Xlibris Corporation.

Menges, Constantine (2005) *China: The Gathering Threat*. Nashville: Thomas Nelson.

Melleuish, Gregory (1998) *The Packaging of Australia: Politics & Culture Wars*. Sydney: University of New South Wales Press.

Meredith, David and Barrie Dyster (1999) Australia in the Global Economy: Continuity and Change. New York: Cambridge University Press.

Metzger, Thomas (1980) 'Selfhood and Authority in Neo-Confucian Political Culture,' in Arthur Kleinman and Tsung-Yi Lin (eds.), *Normal and Abnormal Behaviour in Chinese Culture*. Boston: Kluwer, pp. 7–27.

—— (2005) *A Cloud across the Pacific: Essays on the Clash between Chinese and Western Political Theories Today*. Hong Kong: The Chinese University Press.

Meyer, Milton Walter (1994) *China: A Concise History*. Lanham: Rowan & Littlefield.

Miall, Hugh and McKinlay, Robert (2002) 'European Order, Global Governance and the Liberal Peace' in Hilary Ingham and Mike Ingham (eds.) *RU Expansion to the East: Prospects and Problems*. Cheltenham: Edward Elgar, pp. 245–263.

Miles, James (1996) *The Legacy of Tiananmen: China in Disarray*. Ann Arbor: University of Michigan Press.

Milner, David (2004) 'Exemption from Cessation of Refugee Status in the Second Sentence of Article 1C(5)/(6) of the 1951 Refugee Convention,' *International Journal of Refugee Law* 16(1): 91–107.

Moody, Peter, Jr. (1988) 'The Political Culture of Chinese Students and Intellectuals: A Historical Examination,' *Asian Survey* 11 (Nov.): 1140–1160.

—— (1994) 'Trends in the Study of Chinese Political Culture,' *China Quarterly* 139: 731–740.

Moon, Bruce (1995) 'Paradigms in Migration Research: Exploring 'Moorings' as a Schema,' *Progress in Human Geographer* 19(4): 504–524.

Moore, Marketa (2006) 'From "Loose Sand" to "Cloakroom Community": Chinese Associations in the Czech Republic,' in Khun Eng Kuah-Pearce and Evelyn Hu-DeHart (eds.), *Voluntary Organisations in the Chinese Diaspora*. Hong Kong: Hong Kong University Press: pp. 269–289.

Mosher, Steven (1998) 'Are the Chinese Ready for Liberty and Self-Government?,' *The American Enterprise* 9(4): 50–53.

Mulkay, Michael (1971) *Functionalism, Exchange and Theoretical Strategy*. London: Routledge and Kegan.

Munro, Robin (1190) *Punishment Season: Human Rights in China after Martial Law*. New York: Asia Watch.

Nakatsuji, Keiji (1999) 'Nancy Pelosi and Human rights in China,' *Ritsumeikan Journal of International Studies* 12(2): 103–117.

Nathan, Andrew (1989) 'Chinese Democracy in 1989: Continuity and Change,' *Problems of Communism* September–October 1989: 1–7.

—— (1992) 'Historical Perspective on Chinese Democracy: The Overseas Democracy Movement Today,' in Roger Jeans (ed.), *Roads Not Taken: the Struggle of Opposition Parties in Twentieth Century China*. Boulder: Westview Press, pp. 313–327.

Nathan, Andrew and Shi, Tianjian (1992) 'Cultural Requisites for Democracy in China: Findings from a Survey,' *Daedalus* 122: 95–124.

Neumann, Klaus (2004) *Refuge Australia: Australia's Humanitarian Record*. Sydney: University of New South Wales Press.

Newman, Sheila (2002) 'The Growth Lobby and its Absence: The Relationship between the Property Development and Housing Industries and Immigration Policy in Australia and France.' http://candobetter.net/sheila/populationspeculation.htm#_edn748 (Accessed in May 2011).

Ninnes, Peter (2005) 'Higher Education Engaging with the "Developing" World: The Case of the Virtual Colombo Plan,' in Peter Ninnes and Meeri Hellsten (eds.), *Internationalizing Higher Education: Critical Exploration of Pedagogy and Policy*. Dordrecht: Springer.

Oakman, Daniel (2004) *Facing Asia: A History of the Colombo Plan*. Canberra: Pandanus Books.

O'Neil, Angela (2003) 'Justiciability: The Role of Courts in Reviewing Electoral Administration,' in Graeme Orr et al. (eds.), *Realising Democracy: Electoral Law in Australia*. Sydney: Federation Press, pp. 193–203.

Opperman, Hubert (1966) *Australia's Immigration Policy*. Canberra: AGPS.

Opoku-Dopaah, Edward (2006) 'African Immigrants in Canada: Trends, Socio-demographic and spatial Aspects,' in Kwadwo Konadu-Agyemang et al. (eds.), *The New African Diaspora in North America: Trends, Community Building, and Adaption*. Lanham: Lexington Books, pp. 69–93.

Orleans, Leo (1988) *Chinese Students in America: Policies, Issues, and Numbers*. Washington: National Academic Press.

Ozdowski, Sev A. (1985) 'The Law, Immigration and Human Rights: Changing the Australian Immigration Control System,' *International Migration Review* 19(3): 535–554.
Palfreeman, Anthony (1967) *The Administration of the White Australia Policy*. Melbourne: Melbourne University Press.
Pan, Yihong (2003) *Tempered in the Revolutionary Furnace: China's Youth in the Rustication Movement*. New York: Lexington Books.
Papastergiadis, Nikos (2000) *The Turbulence of Migration: Globalization, Deterritorialization and Hybridity*. Malden: Polity Press.
Parekh, Bhikhu (2006) 'Finding a proper Place for Human Rights,' in Kate E. Tunstall (ed.), *Displacement, Asylum, Migration*. London: Oxford University Press, pp. 17–44.
Parnwell, Mike (1993) *Population Movements and the Third World*. London: Routledge.
Parsons, Paul and Xu Xiaoge (2001) 'News Framing of the Chinese Embassy Bombing by the *People's Daily* and the *New York Times*,' *Asian Journal of Communication* 11(1): 51–67.
Pepper, Suzanne (2000) *Radicalism and Education Reform in Twentieth-Century China: The Search for an Ideal Development Model*. Cambridge: Cambridge University Press.
Perry Elizabeth (1997) 'From Native Place to Workplace: Labor Origins and Outcomes of China's Danwei System,' in Xiaobo Lu and Elizabeth Perry (eds.), *Danwei: The Changing Chinese Workplace in Historical and Comparative Perspective*. New York: M.E. Sharpe, pp. 42–58.
—— (2001) 'Challenging the Mandate of Heaven: Popular Protest in Modern China,' *Critical Asian Studies* 33(2): 163–180.
Pieke, Frank (1996) *The Ordinary and the Extraordinary: An Anthropological Study Of Chinese Reform and the 1989 People Movement in Beijing*. London: Kegan Paul International.
—— (1998) 'Introduction,' in Gregor Benton and Frank N. Pieke (eds.), *The Chinese in Europe*. London: Macmillan, pp. 1–13.
Pong, David and Edmund Fung (1985) *Ideal and Reality: Social and Political Change in Modern China, 1860–1949*. Lanham: University Press of America.
Portes, Alejandro and Josh DeWind (2007) 'A Cross-Atlantic Dialogue: The Progress of Research and Theory in the Study of International Migration,' in Alejandro Portes and Josh DeWind (eds.), *Rethinking Migration: New Theoretical and Empirical Perspectives*. New York: Berghahn Books, pp. 1–27.
Price, Charles (1975) *Australian Immigration: A Review of the Demographic Effects of Post-War Immigration on the Australian Population*. Canberra: AGPS.
—— (1991) *Australian National Identity*. Canberra: Academy of the Social Sciences in Australia.
Pritchard, Duncan (2010) *What Is This Thing Called Knowledge?* Abingdon: Routledge.
Pulliam, Susan (2010) 'From Tiananmen Square to Possible Buffett Successor,' *The Wall Street Journal*, 30 July 2010.
Pye, Lucian (1968) *The Spirit of Chinese Politics: A Psychological Study of the Authority Crisis in Political Development*. Boston: MIT Press.
—— (1981) *The Dynamics of Chinese Politics*. Cambridge: Oelgeschlager, Gunn & Hain.
—— (1990) 'Tiananmen and Chinese Political Culture: The Escalation of Confrontation from Moralizing to Rage,' *Asian Survey* 30(4): 331–347.
Qian, Ning (2003) *Chinese Students Encounter America*. Seattle: University of Washington Press.
Qin Jin (2012) *Qiusuo yu Shouwang: Zhongguo Minyun Jianhu Huiyilu* (*Pursuit and Insistence: Memoirs of the Chinese Democratic Movement*). Taipei: ShowWe.
Qiu, Hong (2003) 'Communication among Knowledge Diasporas: Online Magazines of Expatriate Chinese Student,' in Karim Haiderali Karim (ed.), *The Media of Diaspora*. London: Routledge, pp. 148–161.
Raby, Geoff (2012) 'Australia and China Forty Years on,' *Meanjin*, 11 August 2012, http://meanjin.com.au/articles/post/australia-and-china-forty-years-on/ (Accessed in May 2011).

RACS (Refugee Advice and Casework Service) (1990) *History of Government Policy on PRC Nationals*. Melbourne: RACS.

Rankin, Mary B. (1971) *Early Chinese Revolutionaries: Radical Intellectuals in Shanghai and Chekiang, 1902–1911*. Cambridge: Harvard University Press.

—— (1986) *Elite Activism and Political Transformation in China: Zhejiang Province, 1865–1911*. Stanford: Stanford University Press.

Reese, Stephen and Dai, Jia (2009) 'Citizen Journalism in the Global News Arena: Chinese's New Media Critics,' in Sturt Allan and Einar Thorsen (eds.) *Citizen journalism: Global perspectives*. New York: Peter Lang.

Reilly, James (2006) 'China's History Activism and Sino-Japanese Relations,' *China: An International Journal* 4(2): 189–216.

—— (2010) 'China's Online Nationalism toward Japan' in Simon Shen and Shaun Breslin (eds.) *Online Chinese Nationalism and China's Bilateral Relations*. Lanham: Lexington, pp. 45–71.

Reynolds, Larry and Littlefield, Alice (2005) 'Homans on Social Exchange' in Berberoglu, Berch (ed.) *An Introduction to Classical and Contemporary Social Theory: A Critical Perspective, Third Edition*. Lanham: Rowman & Littlefield, pp. 115–120.

Rivett, Kenneth (1975) *Australia and the Non-White Migrant*. Melbourne: Melbourne University Press.

Robertson, Roby (1980) 'Small Group Decision Making: The Uncertain Role of Information in reducing Uncertainty,' *Political Behavior* 2(2): 163–188.

Robinson, Vaughan (1993) 'Retrospect and Prospect: Where Next for Geography and Refugee Studies,' in Robert Black, and Vaughan Robinson (eds.), *Geography and Refugees: Pattern and Progresses of Change*. London: Belhaven, pp. 211–217.

Rolls, Eric Charles (1992) *Sojourners: The Epic Story of China's Centuries-old Relationship with Australia: Flowers and the Wide Sea*. St Lucia: University of Queensland Press.

Rosen, Stanley (1982) *Red Guard Factionalism and the Cultural Revolution in Guangzhou (Canton)*. Boulder: Westview Press.

—— (1989) 'China,' in Philip Altbach (ed.), *Student Political Activism: An International Reference Handbook*. New York: Greenwood Press, pp. 75–87.

Ruddock, Philip (2002) 'Immigration Policy and the Separation of Powers,' *The 14th Conference of the Samuel Griffith Society*. http://www.samuelgriffith.org.au/papers/html/volume14/v14contents.htm (Accessed in June 2010).

Saxon, Mike (2006) *An American's Guide to Doing Business in China*. Avon: Adams Media.

Sausmikat, Nora (2003) 'Generations, Legitimacy, and Political Ideas in China: The End of Polarization or the End of Ideology?' *Asian Survey* 43(2): 352–384.

Schoenhals, Michael (1996) *China's Cultural Revolution, 1966–1969: Not a Dinner Party*. New York: M.E. Sharpe.

Schloenhardt, Andreas (2003) *Migrant Smuggling: Illegal Migration and Organised Crime in Australia and the Asia-Pacific Region*. Leiden: Brill.

Schrift, Melissa (2001) *Biography of a Chairman Mao Badge: The Creation and Mass Consumption of a Personality Cult*. New York: Rutgers University Press.

Schwarcz, Vera (1986) *The Chinese Enlightenment: Intellectuals and Legacy of the May Fourth Movement of 1919*. Berkeley: University of California Press.

Schwartz, Benjamin I. (1985) *The World of Thought in Ancient China*. Cambridge: Harvard University Press.

Schwartman, Roy and Carlone, David (2008) 'A Rhetorical Reconsideration of Knowledge Management: Discursive Dynamics of Nanotechnology Risks' in Alex Koohang, Keith Harman and Johannes Britz (eds.) *Knowledge management: Theoretical Foundations*. Santa Rosa: Informing Science Press, pp. 1–41.

Scott, David (2008) China and the International System, 1840–1949: Power, Presence, and Perceptions in a Century of Humiliation. Albany: State University of New York Press.

Seal, Graham (2001) *Encyclopedia of Folk Heroes*. Santa Barbara: ABC-CLIO.

Senate Hansard (The Senate of Australian Federal Parliament) (1996) http://www.aph.gov.au/Parliamentary_Business/Hansard/Hanssen261110 (Accessed in June 2012).

Shaw, Victor (1996) *Social Control in China: A Study of Chinese Work Units*. Westport: Praeger Publishers.

Sheehan, Paul (2002) 'Theophanous Falls: How Times Have Changed for ALP.' *The Sydney Morning Herald* 27 May 2002. http://www.smh.com.au/articles/2002/05/26/1022243291129.html (Accessed in June 2010).

Shen, Simon and Shaun Breslin (2010) 'When China Plugged in: Structural Origins of Online Chinese Nationalism,' in Simon Shen and Shaun Breslin (eds.), *Online Chinese Nationalism and China's Bilateral Relations*. Lanham: Lexington Books.

Shi, Jinling (2007) 'Aozhou Huaren Shehui Qianzhan (Australia's Chinese Community Prospects), http://ayzx.xznu.edu.cn/onews.asp?id=111 (Accessed in May 2011).

Shi, Yu (2005) 'Identity Construction of the Chinese Diaspora, Ethnic Media Use, Community Formation, and the Possibility of Social Activism,' *Continuum: Journal of Media & Cultural Studies* 19(1): 55–72.

Siani-Davies, Peter (2005) *The Romanian Revolution of December 1989*. Ithaca: Cornell University Press.

Simmel, Georg (2012) 'Group Expansion and the development of Individuality [1908]' in Craig Calhoun et al. (eds.) *Classical Sociological Theory, Third Edition*. Oxford: Wiley-Blackwell, pp. 366–408.

Sinclair, John, Audrey Yue, Gay Hawkins, Kee Pookong and Josephine Fox (2000) 'Chinese Cosmopolitanism and Media Use,' in Stuart Cunningham and John Sinclair (eds.), *Floating Lives: The Media and Asian Diasporas*. Brisbane: University of Queensland Press, pp. 35–90.

Sinha, Jai (2009) *Culture and Organizational Behaviour*. New Delhi: Sage.

Siu, Paul Chan Pang (1987) *The Chinese Laundryman: A Study of Social Isolation*. New York: New York University Press.

Skeldon, Ronald (1995) 'The Challenge facing Migration Research: A Case for Greater Awareness,' *Progress in Human Geography* 19(1): 91–96.

Skinner, George William (1958) *Leadership and Power in the Chinese Community of Thailand*. Ithaca: Cornell University Press.

Slattery, Luke (1991) 'Government Acts on Malpractice in Private Colleges,' *The Age*, 9 March 1991.

Smith, Christopher (1991) *China: People and Places in the Land of One Billion*. Boulder: Westview Press.

Smith, Paul (1997) 'Chinese Migrant Trafficking: A Global Challenge' in Paul J. Smith (ed.) *Human Smuggling: Chinese Migrant Trafficking and the Challenge to America's Immigration Tradition*. Washington: Centre for Strategic & International Studies.

Snow, David and Robert Benford (1999) 'Alternative Types of Cross-National Diffusion in the Social Movement Arena,' in Donatella Porta et al. (ed.), *Social Movements in Globalising World*. London: Macmillan, pp. 23–39.

Spurr, David (1993) *The Rhetoric of Empire: Colonial Discourse in Journalism, Travel Writing and Imperial Administration*. Durham: Duke University Press.

Stacker, Julie and Steward Peri (2004) *Chinese Immigration and Chinese-Australians in New South Wales*. Canberra: National Archives of Australia.

Stillwell, John and Congdon, Peter (1991) 'Migration Modelling: Concepts and Contents,' in John Stillwell and Peter Congdon (eds.), *Migration Models: Macro and Micro Approaches*. London: Belhaven, pp. 1–16.

Su, Fubing and Yang, Dali (2005) 'Elections, Governance, and Accountability in Rural China,' *Asian Perspective* 29(4): 125–157.

Su, Xiaokang and Wang, Luxiang (1991) *Death Song of the River: A Reader's Guide to the Chinese TV Series Heshang*, translated by Richard Bodman and Wan, Pin P. New York: Cornell University Press.

Suettinger, Robert L. (2003) *Beyond Tiananmen: The Politics of U.S.-China Relations, 1989–2000*. Washington: Brookings Institution Press.

Sun, Chang Li (1987) 'Some Considerable Problems to Study Abroad,' *Editorial References*, Beijing: June (2): 57–59.

Sun, Wanning (2002) *Leaving China: Media, Migration, and Transnational Imagination*. Lanham: Rowman & Littlefield.

Sun, Wanning, Jia Gao, Audrey Yue and John Sinclair (2011) 'The Chinese-language press in Australia: A preliminary scoping study,' *Media International Australia*, 138: 137–148.

Suryadinata, Leo (1978) *Overseas Chinese in Southeast Asia and China's Foreign Policy: An Interpretative Essay*. Singapore: Institute of Southeast Asian Studies.

—— (2005) *China and the ASEAN States: The Ethnic Chinese Dimension*. Singapore: Marshall Cavendish Academic.

Taft, Jessica (2011) *Rebel Girls: Youth Activism and Social Change across the Americas*. New York: New York University Press.

Tai, Zixue (2006) *The Internet in China: Cyberspace and Civil Society*. New York: Routledge.

Thompson, Richard (1980) 'From Kinship to Class: A New Model of Urban Overseas Chinese Social Organization,' *Urban Anthropology* 9(3): 265–293.

Tian, Guang (1999) *Chinese-Canadians, Canadian-Chinese: Coping and Adapting in North America*. New York: Edwin Mellen Press.

Tismăneanu, Vladimir (1999) 'Introduction' in Vladimir Tismaneanu (ed.) *The Revolutions of 1989*. London: Routledge, pp. 1–17.

Tok, Sow Keat (2010) 'Nationalism-on-Demand? When Chinese Sovereignty Goes Online' in Simon Shen and Shaun Breslin (eds.) *Online Chinese Nationalism and China's Bilateral Relations*. Lanham: Lexington, pp. 13–43.

Topley, Marjorie (1961) 'The Emergence and Social Functions of Chinese Religious Associations in Singapore,' *Comparative Studies in Society and History* 3(3): 289–314.

Tsai, Shih-shan Henry (1983) *China and the Overseas Chinese in the United States, 1868–1911*. Fayetteville: University of Arkansas Press.

—— (1986) *The Chinese Experience in America*. Bloomington: Indiana University Press.

Turner, Christopher (1969) *Family and Kinship in Modern Britain*. London: Routledge and Kegan.

UNHCR (the United Nations High Commissioner for Refugees) (1988) *Handbook on Procedure and Criteria for Determining Refugee Status of the UNHCR*, Geneva: Office of the UNHCR.

Videbeck, Sheila (2010) *Psychiatric-Mental Health Nursing*. Philadelphia: Wolters Kluwer/ Lippincott Williams & Wilkins.

Viviani, Nancy (1996) *The Indochinese in Australia, 1975–1995: From Burnt Boats to Barbecues*. Melbourne: Oxford University Press.

Vrachnas, John, Boyd, Kim, Bagaric, Mirko, and Dimopoulos, Penny (2005) *Migration and Refugee Law: Principles and Practice in Australia*. Melbourne: Cambridge University Press.

Wagner, Rudolph (1991) 'Political Institutions, Discourse and Imagination in China at Tiananmen,' in James Manor (ed.), *Rethinking Third World Politics*. Harlow: Longman, pp. 121–144.

Waldron, Arthur (1993) 'Representing China: The Great Wall and Cultural Nationalism in the Twentieth Century,' in Harumi Befu (ed.), *Cultural Nationalism in East Asia: Representation and Identity*. Berkeley: Institute of East Asian Studies, pp. 36–60.

Walsh, Jim (1999) *In the Net: An Internet Guide for Activists*. London: Zed Books.

Wang, Anyun (1987) 'The Fever of Going Abroad among the Shanghai Youth,' *Xinjiang Youth* 10: 9–11.

Wang, Fenghua (1999) 'Subscribing to Democracy through the Internet.' *Journal of the Association for History and Computing* II (3): 1–16.

Wang, Gungwu (1970) 'Chinese Politics in Malaya,' *China Quarterly* 45: 1–30.

—— (1981) *Community and Nation: Essays on Southeast Asia and the Chinese*. Sydney: Heinemann Educational Books.
Wang, Jing (1996) *High Culture Fever: Politics, Aesthetics, and Ideology in Deng's China*. Berkeley: University of California Press.
—— (2008) *Brand New China: Advertising, Media, and Commercial Culture*. New York: Harvard University Press.
Wang, John (1980) *Contemporary Chinese Politics: An Introduction*. Englewood Cliffs: Prentice-Hall.
Wang, Sing-wu (1978) *The Organization of Chinese Emigration, 1848–1888: with Special Reference to Chinese Emigration to Australia*. San Francisco: Chinese Material Centre.
Wang, Zhixiong and Lai, Lili (1987) 'A Survey about Guangzhou Young People Studying in Australia at their own Expense,' *The Youth Studies* 9: 23–29.
Warhurst, John (2008) 'The Catholic Lobby: Structures, Policy Styles and Religious Networks,' *Australian Journal of Public Administration* 67(2): 213–230.
Wasserstrom, Jeffrey (2005) 'Chinese Students and Anti-Japanese Protests, Past and Present,' *World Policy Journal* 22(2): 59–65.
Weidlick, Wolfgang and Haag, Gunter (1983) *Concepts and Models of a Quantitative Sociology: The Dynamics of Interacting Populations*. Berlin: Springer-Verlag.
Westcott, Brooke (1895) *The Gospel of Life: Thoughts Introductory to the Study of Christian Doctrine*. London: Macmillan.
Wheelan, Susan (2005) *The Handbook of Group Research and Practice*. London: Sage.
White, Lynn T. (1999) *Unstately Power: Local Causes of China's Intellectual, Legal and Governmental Reforms Volume II*. New York: M.E. Sharpe.
White, Stephen (1980) 'A Philosophical Dichotomy in Migration Research,' *Professional Geographer*, 32: 6–13.
Wickberg, Edgar (1982) *From China to Canada: A History of the Chinese Communities in Canada*. Toronto: McClelland and Stewart.
—— (1994) 'Overseas Chinese Adaptive Organizations, Past and Present,' in Ronald Skeldon (ed.), *Reluctant Exiles: Migration from Hong Kong and the New Overseas Chinese*. New York: M.E. Sharpe, pp. 68–85.
—— (1998) 'Chinese Organizations in Philippine Cities since the Second World War: The Case of Manila,' in Wang, Ling-Chi and Wang Gungwu (eds.), *The Chinese Diaspora: Selected Essays Volume 1*. Singapore: Times Academic Press, pp. 174–194.
Willard, Myra (1967) *History of the White Australia Policy to 1920*. Melbourne: Melbourne University Press.
Wong, Koon-Kwai (2005) 'Greening of the Chinese mind: Environmentalism with Chinese Characteristics,' Asia-Pacific Review, 12(2): 39–57.
Woodard, Garry (1997) 'Australia and China,' in Mark McGillivray and Gary Smith (eds.) *Australia and Asia*. New York: Oxford University Press, pp. 136–155.
Working Group for the Basic Human Rights of PRC Citizens in Australia (1990) Human Rights Abuses in China: A Survey of Chinese Citizens in Australia. Melbourne.
Wright, Teresa (1999) 'State Repression and Student Protest in Contemporary China' *The China Quarterly* 157: 142–172.
Wu, Fengshi (2009) Environmental Activism in China: Fifteen Years in Review, 1994–2008, Harvard-Yenching Institute Working Paper Series. Boston: Harvard-Yenching Institute.
Wu, Wei (1999) 'Cyberspace and Cultural Identity: A Case Study of cybercommunity of Chinese Students in the United States,' in Michael Prosser and K.S. Sitaram (eds.), *Civic Discourse: Intercultural, International, and Global Media*. Stanford: Ablex Publishing, pp. 75–90.
Xiao, Qin and Zeng, Ni (2005) 'Chen Yonglin and Hao Fengjun Appear at Australian Chinese Union,' *The Epoch Times*, 2 August 2005. http://www.theepochtimes.com/news/5-8-3/30907.html (Accessed in June 2010).
Xie, Lei (2009) *Environmental Activism in China*. Abingdon: Routledge.
Xie, Tao (2009) *US-China Relations: China Policy on Capital Hill*. Abingdon: Routledge.

Xu, Ben (1999) *Disenchanted Democracy: Chinese Criticism after 1989*. Ann Arbor: University of Michigan Press.

Yan, Jiaqi (1992) *The Third Republic: Political Path of China*. New York: Global Publishing.

Yang, Benjamin (1993) 'The Making of a Pragmatic Communist: The Early Life of Deng Xiaoping, 1904–49,' *The China Quarterly* 135: 444–456.

Yang, Dali (1996) *Calamity and Reform in China: State, Rural Society, and Institutional Change since the Great Leap Famine*. Stanford: Stanford University Press.

Yang, Guobin (2000) 'The Liminal Effects of Social Movements: Red Guards and the Transformation of Identity,' Sociological Forum 15(3): 379–406.

—— (2000) 'Achieving Emotions in Collective Action: Emotional Processes and Movement Mobilization in the 1989 Chinese Student Movement,' *The Sociological Quarterly* 41(4): 593–614.

—— (2003) 'Weaving a Green Web: The Internet and Environmental Activism in China,' China Environment Series 6: 89–98.

—— (2003) 'China's *Zhiqing* Generation: Nostalgia, Identity, and Cultural Resistance in the 1990s,' *Modern China* 29(3): 267–97.

—— (2005) 'Environmental NGOs and Institutional Dynamics in China,' *The China Quarterly* 181: 46–66.

—— (2009) *The Power of the Internet in China: Citizen Activism Online*. New York: Columbia University Press.

—— (2011) 'The Routinization of Liminality: The Persistence of Activism among China's Red Guard Generation.' in Jeffrey Broadbent and Vicky Brockman (eds.), *East Asian Social Movements: Power, Protest, and Change in a Dynamic Region*. New York: Springer, pp. 437–455.

Yang, Jiechi (2001) 'China-US Relations in the New Century,' *China Daily*, 25 July 2001.

Yang, Tingrong (1988) 'Problems about Studying in Australia as the Language Students,' *World Outlook* 22: 20–21.

Yen, Ching Hwang (1976) *The Overseas Chinese and the 1911 Revolution: With Special Reference to Singapore and Malaya*. London: Oxford University Press.

—— (2006) 'Overseas Chinese Nationalism in Singapore and Malaya 1877–1912,' in Liu Hong (ed.), *The Chinese Overseas*. London: Routledge, pp. 137–161.

Yong, Ching Fatt (1977) *Chinese Community Structure and Leadership in Pre-War Singapore*. Singapore: South Seas Society.

York, Barry (2003) *Australia and Refugees, 19012002: An Annotated Chronology Based on Official Sources*. http://www.aph.gov.au/library/pubs/online/refugees_s3.htm (Accessed in May 2011).

Yu, Zhiyuan and Dingxin Zhao (2006) 'Differential Participation and the Nature of a Movement: A Study of the 1999 Anti-U.S. Beijing Student Demonstrations,' *Social Forces* 84(3): 1755–1777.

Yuan, Chung-Ming (2001) 'Chinese in White Australia 1901–1950,' in James Jupp (ed.), *The Australian People*. Melbourne: Cambridge University Press, pp. 204–206.

Zanasi, Margherita (2006) *Saving the Nation: Economic Modernity in Republican China*. Chicago: University of Chicago Press.

Zappala, Gianni (1999) 'The Phases of the Political Participation of Ethnic Minorities in Australian Politics,' *Journal of Intercultural Studies* 20(1): 65–79.

Zhang, Hong and Marsha Smith (2009) 'Navigating a Space for Labor Activism: Labor NGOs in the Pearl River Delta of South China,' in Jonathan Schwartz and Shawn Shieh (eds.), *State and Society Responses to Social Welfare Needs in China: Serving the People*. London: Routledge, pp. 66–87.

Zhang, Sheldon (2207) *Smuggling and Trafficking in Human Beings: All Roads lead to America*. Westport: Greenwood Publishing.

—— (2008) *Chinese Human Smuggling Organizations: Families, Social Networks, and Cultural Imperatives*. New York: Stanford University Press.

Zhao, Dingxin (2000) 'State-Society Relations and the Discourses and Activities of the 1989 Beijing Student Movement,' *American Journal of Sociology* 105(6): 1592–1632.

—— (2009) 'Organization and Place in the Anti-U.S. Chinese Student Protests after the 1999 Belgrade Embassy Bombing,' *Mobilization: An International Quarterly* 14(1): 107–129.

Zhao, Suisheng (1993) 'Deng Xiaoping's Southern Tour: Elite Politics in Post-Tiananmen China,' *Asian Survey* 33(8): 739–756.

Zhao, Yuezhi (1998) *Media, Market, and Democracy in China: Between the Party Line and the Bottom Line*. Urbana: University of Illinois Press.

Zhou, Kate Xiao (2009) *China's Long March to Freedom: Grassroots Modernization*. New Brunswick: Transaction Publishes.

Zhou, Yongming (2006) *Historicizing Online Politics: Telegraphy, the Internet, and Political Participation in China*. Stanford: Stanford University Press.

Zhu, Minshen (2003) 'Aodaliya Xinyiminde Chengzhang he Huawen Baoyede Fazhan' (The Increase in New Migrants in Australia and the Development of the Chinese Newspaper Industry), http://tech.sina.com.cn/other/2003-08-08/1412218758.shtml (Accessed in May 2011).

Zlotnik, Hania (1995) 'Migration and the Family: The Female Perspectives,' *Asian and Pacific Migration Journal* 4(2–3): 253–271.

INDEX

www.ingramcontent.com/pod-product-compliance
Lightning Source LLC
Chambersburg PA
CBHW071435230926
51846CB00001B/235
* 9 7 8 9 0 0 4 2 5 8 6 1 7 *